THE NEW

BOOK OF

WHOLE GRAINS

Also by Marlene Anne Bumgarner

Organic Cooking for (Not-So-Organic) Mothers

Working with School-Age Children

MARLENE ANNE BUMGARNER, ED. D.

Illustrations by Johanna Roy

THE NEW
BOOK OF
WHOLE GRAINS

More Than 200 Recipes Featuring Whole
Grains, Including Amaranth, Quinoa, Wheat,
Spelt, Oats, Rye, Barley, and Millet

 St. Martin's Griffin ❧ New York

Library of Congress Cataloging-in-Publication Data

Bumgarner, Marlene Anne.
    The new book of whole grains : more than 200 recipes featuring whole grains, including amaranth, quinoa, wheat, spelt, oats, rye, barley, and millet / Marlene Anne Bumgarner.—1st St. Martin's Griffin ed.
      p. cm.
    Includes bibliographical references and index.
    ISBN 0-312-15601-4
    1. Cookery (Cereals) 2. Cereals as food. I. Title.
TX808.B85   1997
641.6'31—DC21   97-5727
                                        CIP

10 9 8 7 6 5 4 3 2

For Doña, John, Jamie, and Deborah

Many thanks to Boyd Foster, Al Guisto,

---

and all the recipe testers

CONTENTS

INTRODUCTION

TO THE

1997 EDITION

When I began writing the first edition of *The Book of Whole Grains* I was raising my family in a rural setting; tending goats, rabbits, chickens, and ducks; harvesting vegetables from an extensive kitchen garden; and baking bread daily. We had no electricity or running water. I cooked on a woodburning stove, and typed the manuscript on a manual typewriter. When we could forget the Vietnam War, the early seventies were a romantic time for those of us who chose to move back to the land. Many young parents learned, as I did, the challenges and rewards of cooking whole and natural foods for their families.

Following the publication of the book in 1976, however, our family's life began to change. First, I was asked to write a column for the local newspaper.

Then, responding to demands for a local source of whole grains, I opened a natural foods store. A second book followed, in which I tried to answer the questions asked by readers of the column and my customers. Soon, I was teaching cooking classes at the local community college.

One thing leads to another, if you allow it, and two decades later I am a tenured college instructor, teaching not only cooking, but also child development and psychology. A single parent, I no longer live on a farm, but in a centrally located townhouse. College tuitions are a very real part of my life, as are high school dances and junior high soccer games. Time to spend cooking is far more scarce than it was twenty years ago. My manuscripts are now typed on a computer, and my grown-up children send e-mail when they want to communicate.

These changes are not necessarily bad, but they have required some adjustments in the way in which I nourish my family and myself. I still enjoy baking bread, but I do it less often, and sometimes use a bread machine. Soups and stews take precious time, so they are usually accomplished on early Sunday mornings, when it is quiet and I can linger over the newspaper between stirs and sniffs. I use the freezer more, and our microwave oven has become my friend. Times change, but our body's need for healthful food does not. The time each of us spends preparing food for others is a gift, and I share that gift with my children by encouraging them to participate.

In *The New Book of Whole Grains* I have tried to be conscious of the changes in the lives of modern families, and of the scarcity of time and energy people have to prepare food, or to do anything for that matter. But I have also tried to keep in the front of my mind the undeniable reality that our loved ones, and their health, are still our responsibility.

In the last twenty years we have learned much about the relationship between what we eat and how we feel, and the updated and new recipes in this book reflect that knowledge. Less fat, less salt, less meat, but no fewer whole grains; in fact, the USDA Food Guide Pyramid introduced in 1992 simply repackages the wisdom of ancient civilizations. Long before the Four Food Groups—now discredited as encouraging a meat- and dairy-based diet leading to heart disease and cancer—millions of people thrived on diets in which grains, nuts, seeds, legumes, and vegetables provided their major sources of protein as well as carbohydrates. And, contrary to the nutritional dogma of the 1970s, it now appears that as long as adequate calories are eaten from a wide variety of nutritious foods, we can ignore amino acid charts and still obtain adequate protein from plant foods.

So, as I did with my readers in 1976, I invite you to explore the world of whole foods . . . to find the particular recipes and ways of serving them that you and your family enjoy the most, and to incorporate them into your lives permanently. Not only will you be improving your family's health and helping to reduce world food shortages, you may also find, as I have, that working in the kitchen is very satisfying, especially when it results in pleasant fragrances, flavors, and mealtimes.

Marlene Anne Bumgarner

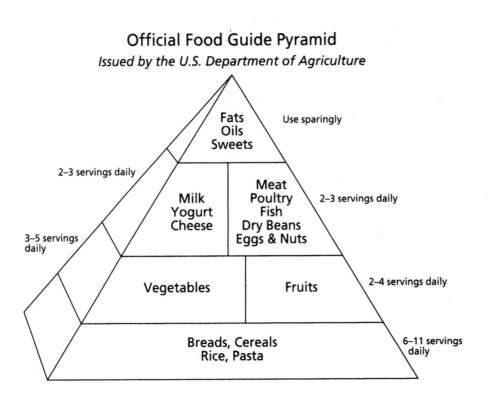

Official Food Guide Pyramid
Issued by the U.S. Department of Agriculture

Fats
Oils
Sweets

Use sparingly

2–3 servings daily

Milk
Yogurt
Cheese

Meat
Poultry
Fish
Dry Beans
Eggs & Nuts

2–3 servings daily

3–5 servings
daily

Vegetables

Fruits

2–4 servings daily

Breads, Cereals
Rice, Pasta

6–11 servings
daily

INTRODUCTION (1976)

WHY USE

WHOLE GRAINS?

This book is about cereals. Not cereals the way television commercials present them—precooked, prepackaged products which in no way resemble their natural forms—but cereals as the peoples of ancient times knew them: tall grasses rippling across the fields, golden ears of corn adorning graceful green stalks, heads of millet or sorghum drying on rooftops, paddies of rice planted carefully by hand.

A history of cereal grains is the story of our transition from a nomadic life to one of settlement and agriculture. Wild grasses, nuts, and seeds were once gathered by primitive groups of people in all parts of the world, then pounded into flour or roasted and eaten whole. Perhaps, returning to the same fields year after year, someone noticed that grasses badly thinned out would not reseed themselves. Or perhaps some seeds, accidentally scattered, had caused grain to grow where formerly it had not. However it began, eventually men and women who had always wandered in search of food started to plant it instead, and to remain in one place at least long enough to harvest their crop. It is no exaggeration to say that the beginning of agriculture marked the beginning of civilization, for once freed from constant foraging, our ancestors could devote their strength to building cities and the systems necessary for their survival.

Agriculture began at different times in different parts of the world, and which cereal grains were domesticated depended upon soil and climate. Food patterns that developed centuries ago have remained to this day: in Mexico, beans, corn, and rice are the staples, while in Europe, rye bread and cheese predominate. In Africa, grain sorghum and peanuts make up many meals, but Chinese and Indian people usually mix soybeans and rice.

These patterns of eating developed independently in all parts of the world, but displayed a common characteristic: the custom of combining cooked grains with beans or peas, nuts, and dairy products to form complete meals. Researchers are only now learning why these combinations worked so well, and why they endured.

Basically, the reason for such combinations is that each of the major groups of non-meat foods is missing some of the essential amino acids, ingredients necessary for our bodies to be able to make use of the protein contained in any food. If these essential amino acids are not all present simultaneously, the protein in food cannot be converted into usable form by the body, and is wasted. Grains and legumes, for example, are each deficient in some of these amino acids, but in different ones. When grains and legumes are combined in the same meal, the amount of protein which can be used by the body is considerably higher than it would have been if the grains and legumes were eaten separately. The different food groups which can be combined, and the best combinations and proportions, are discussed in Frances Moore Lappé's *Diet for a Small Planet*. Her book is a valuable text for anyone interested in cooking whole grains.

But who wants to cook whole grains? While I was preparing this book some of my closest friends advised me, "But no one really cares about using whole grains! Most people are so used to convenience foods that they simply won't bother to try your ideas." I don't believe that. While teaching in a small elementary school near my home, I taught a children's cooking class on whole grains. Before we had completed our study, requests began coming in from mothers and fathers for recipes that we had used in our class. Conversations with these parents over the months have encouraged me in this venture. More and more, they and people like them want to learn about nutritious and economical ways to change their families' diets.

What makes a whole grain different from a "refined" one? Modern milling machinery scrapes off the outer layers of the grain and removes the embryo, or germ. Only the residue is ground into flour. The resulting product is lighter-colored than flour ground from the entire grain kernel, and will keep longer without spoiling. Flour ground from grain milled according to modern techniques is very fine, and produces lighter, puffier breads and pastries. But the food value of these baked goods is considerably lower than it would have been had the flour been ground from the entire kernel.

Whole grains in some form are a traditional part of every culture's eating habits. Yet the trends toward white sugar, white rice, and white flour are strong, and many Americans eat virtually no unrefined grains. Some religious sects discourage the consumption of unrefined corn and other grains, but most nutritional experts now feel that is unwise. In addition to the vitamins and minerals in the oil-rich germ (embryo) of the grain, the fiber contained in the outside layers is thought to be important in the prevention of cancer of the colon, gallbladder ailments, and perhaps even heart disease. In areas of the world where fiber-rich whole grains are a major part of the diet, the incidence of intestinal and bowel complaints is remarkably low.

Cereal grains cost less to grow than meat, less than eggs, less even than fish. The money that is spent to feed animals, and the land on which they graze, could provide many more meals if devoted instead to planting, harvesting, and marketing wheat, rye, oats, and other grains. This is not intended to be a bid for entirely vegetarian eating habits. However, North America stands out as the world's highest consumer of meat, and I'm not so sure that is a statistic of which we should be proud. If we were each to eat a little less meat, more land would be available for growing grain for consumption by humans instead of by animals, and the food grown on that land would feed more hungry people.

To bring the economic argument closer to home—consider the cost of meat! Whole grains entered our life as a means of living within an impossibly tiny graduate-school budget, and they have remained an integral part of our diet for the same reason, as well as for the simple reason that we enjoy the variety in tastes and textures that whole grains can provide.

So I urge you to experiment. Buy a box of bulgur, or a package of brown rice. Next time you run out of flour, try whole wheat instead of white. There's no need to become a health-food faddist, to stop eating meat, or to join a food cooperative. Simply add some whole grains to what you are presently eating. A family which has eaten only refined sugars and flours may find pastries made with whole wheat flour too heavy, or sorghum too foreign, but very few people will turn down fresh whole wheat bread, or cornbread made from whole grain cornmeal, or long grain and wild rice stuffing in their Thanksgiving turkey.

When you have found the grains your family prefers, make it a practice to always keep two or three pounds of each on hand. Grain can be stored for over a year in coffee tins or large jars (the kind institutions get their mayonnaise or mustard in work well). If you invest in a blender, food processor, or grain mill, your flexibility increases. You can prepare flour as you need it—a quarter cup or six cups—without having to worry about storing bags of flour or meal which may spoil. Or instead of grinding whole grains very finely, to make flour, you can break them into small pieces, called grits or cracked grain, for faster cooking. Most grains can also be sprouted and added to breads, soups, and salads.

If your experience follows ours and that of many of our friends, you will soon find that you prefer whole grains to refined ones, and occasionally or often will prepare entire meals without meat and without missing it. If you discover yourself doing that at some time in the future, take a moment to feel just a little bit pleased with yourself. Not only are you improving your family's health and saving money on food, you are really helping to solve the world food problem.

GLOSSARY OF TERMS

Cereal grains have been used in numerous ways, but the staples of each major geographical area have much in common. Typically a grain is cracked or ground coarsely, cooked in some liquid, and served as a porridge or mush. Such dishes are *kasha, bulgur, pilaf,* and *congee.* But which is which? As ethnic traditions have spread from one continent to another, the distinctions between one cereal dish and another have blurred. To help the reader sort out some of these terms, the following list is provided. Also included in this glossary are some parts of the cereal grain (husk, germ, endosperm, and bran) and one or two versions of the word porridge (gruel, pottage), kernel (berries, groats), and flour (meal, farina, semolina).

Berries—hulled wheat kernels

Bolt—to sift through a cloth or sieve

Bran—the partly ground husk of wheat or other grain, separated from flour by bolting

Bulgur—parched cracked wheat (Middle East)

Cracked—broken into several pieces

Congee—rice or millet gruel (Chinese)

Couscous—steamed semolina or millet (North African)

Endosperm—nutritive outside material of cereal grain

Farina—flour or meal made from degerminated cereal grains, usually wheat

Flour—finely ground meal of grain, sometimes bolted

Germ—embryo of a plant in its early stages, contained within the cereal grain

Grits—grain hulled and very coarsely ground

Groats—hulled, whole kernels of grain, usually oats, buckwheat, rye, or barley

Ground—reduced to a fine powder by grinding

Gruel—liquid food made by boiling a cereal, especially oats, in water or milk to make a thin porridge

Hominy—whole, hulled corn, from which the bran and germ have been removed by processing the whole kernel in a lye bath

Hull—same as husk

Husk—the dry outside covering of a seed or (as in corn) group of seeds

Kasha/Kaska—much made from whole or coarse cracked grain, especially buckwheat, but also barley, millet, rye, wheat, or rice (Eastern European)

Kernel—(1) a whole seed grain

        (2) the softer, usually edible part inside the shell of a nut

Meal—the edible part of any grain or pulse ground to a coarse powder, usually unbolted

Mush—meal boiled in water until it forms a thick soft mass substantial enough to mold into a loaf for slicing and frying

Porridge—a soft food made by boiling meal of grains or legumes in milk or water (variation of pottage)

Pottage—a thick soup made of vegetables, with or without meat

Pilaf/Pilau—rice, usually combined with meat and vegetables, fried in oil, steamed in stock, and seasoned (often with saffron or curry) (Middle Eastern)

Semolina—a granular, milled product of durum wheat, consisting almost entirely of endosperm particles. Used chiefly in the making of macaroni

SOME

THOUGHTS ON

BREAD BAKING

After the first edition of this book was on its way to the publisher, the months of research and recipe testing rapidly fading in my memory, I met a woman who had been trying to bake bread and was unhappy with the results. She asked me for advice, and after one or two more tries she succeeded in producing the kind of bread she wanted.

This incident reminded me of my own earliest bread-baking experiences. It's so easy to forget the first difficulties encountered in the loneliness of one's kitchen, with only the printed page of a cookbook to help you. I didn't know anyone who baked their own bread; I was far from home, and in any case my own mother had not kneaded dough for many years. When breads were produced primarily in the home, most girls learned the techniques of kneading and rising dough over a period of years, under the watchful eyes of relatives who had perfected their methods over a lifetime of daily baking. Most of us did not have that opportunity, although for those of you who have yet to learn this art, I urge you to ask around and try to arrange that at least your first session take place with the help of a friend.

If that isn't possible, be patient. If your first batch seems a bit heavy, or a bit crumbly, or didn't rise at all, throw it out and try again. Don't despair until you have ruined at least ten batches—and I'll be very surprised if you don't have the knack already by number two or three.

There are four crucial things to remember in bread baking—only four. All others are refinements, and serve to simply improve the product you are preparing.

(1) Don't scald the yeast. I usually use dry granulated yeast, which is available (in grocery stores) in packages of one tablespoonful each, in jars of several ounces, or (in bakeries) in cans of a pound. I find dry yeast more dependable than cake yeast. Dissolve either kind in lukewarm water (90°–110°F.). Your elbow is probably more reliable for testing than your fingers, which are less sensitive, and it is a good idea to use a thermometer for the first few batches, until you develop a feel for the right temperature. If the water is too cold, it will take longer for the yeast to begin working; if it is too hot, you'll kill the yeast.

Dissolving the yeast separately from the rest of the ingredients gives you a chance to watch the bubbling action, and saves you the heartbreak of completing the batch and discovering too late (when after an hour your dough is still sitting in the bowl like a lump) that the yeast was dead. If the yeast and water mixture does not bubble and foam in two or three minutes, throw it out and try again, testing the temperature again carefully. I usually use the measuring cup, which I previously used for the honey or molasses that will be mixed with the dough; the sugar provides food for the yeast and speeds its action.

(2) Develop the gluten. The gluten in wheat must be developed if it is to result in a light, moist loaf of bread. To do this, combine about half the flour with all of the liquid in the recipe and beat it vigorously (300 strokes by hand; 10 minutes at low speed if you use an electric mixer), then add the remaining flour and knead the dough until it is smooth, elastic, and no longer sticky. Kneading dough is one of those things we learn to do by doing. Place the lump of moist dough on a well-floured surface (I use a cloth; some people prefer a board or table top), and with well-floured hands grasp a piece of the edge of the dough and push it into the center. Revolve the dough 45°; repeat.

Continue doing this for as long as you can (one nineteenth-century book says 30 minutes "by the clock," although generally five or ten minutes will suffice). If you are combining wheat with other flours, or with sprouts, cracked grain, raisins, etc., add the wheat flour to the liquid first and beat thoroughly, then add other ingredients and any remaining wheat flour and knead well. This way the gluten in the wheat is thoroughly developed first, and can carry the load of the other constituents.

(3) Do not accidentally chill the rising dough. I have never learned the physical reason for beautifully rising dough to suddenly fall, but I do know that a draft from an open door or window will make it happen. Since I always seem to have drafty kitchens, my cure for the problem is to place the rising dough inside my oven with the heat turned off (this will work whether your oven is gas or electric, but gas ovens have the additional benefit of a pilot light which provides a warm environment for the rising dough; 85°F. is an ideal temperature for the yeast action). One woman I know puts her dough inside a large plastic bowl with a tight-fitting cover; another places the mixing bowl inside a Dutch oven with the top on. Drafts present more of a problem when the dough is rising in bread tins, although you can also place them inside the oven for most of the time, transferring them carefully to a warm shielded corner while you preheat the oven. Covering the loaves with a towel while they rise helps too.

There is one time when you *can* chill the dough. If you have difficulty finding three or four hours in a row when you can bake bread from start to finish, mix the dough the night before you want to bake it, and refrigerate it overnight. The cool temperature will inhibit the growth of the yeast without killing it, and the next morning you can punch it down, knead it until it is evenly warmed, and place straight into bread tins. Let the dough risefor half an hour or so, until just above the edge of the tin, and bake.

(4) Don't let the dough over-rise. If your bread rises too high, it will fall back into the pans, a doughy mess. If this happens you can usually recoup by kneading the dough lightly and allowing it to rise again. Prevention, however, is preferable. A good rule to remember is to let the bread rise only ⅔ as high as you expect it to be when baked (remember that whole wheat bread will never rise as high as bread made with all white flour). Place a towel over the bread pan when the dough is set aside to do its last rising, and when the towel is lifted just slightly in the middle, bake your bread; it should continue to rise in the oven. (This will only work for baking temperatures of 375°F. or under. If you will be baking at a higher temperature, allow slightly more rising time.)

Removing bread from its bread pan is another one of those mysterious processes which some women learned from their mothers. I never did. My earliest batches were taken out in chunks, salted with frustrated tears, and there is still an occasional one which refuses to plop out like it should. Butter seems to work better than oil to grease the pans, and I like to cool the loaves for a couple of minutes before removing them. Hit the side of a pan sharply against the edge of a counter or table, then invert it. If luck is with you, it should drop out quite nicely. Occasionally a knife blade slipped around the edge of the loaf inside the pan is necessary. Occasionally it just doesn't come. That's one secret I don't have.

Bread baked with coarsely ground whole wheat flour sometimes turns out crumbly, because the large bran particles do not absorb sufficient moisture. If you have this problem, try grinding your flour more finely, and/or allowing the bread dough to sit overnight in order to soak the bran. This can be done by either omitting the yeast and a third of the flour, adding them the next day, or by refrigerating the fully mixed dough as mentioned above.

Although bread machines were available when the first edition of this book went to press, they were expensive and unreliable. No longer!

Many excellent machines that will accommodate whole-grain bakers are now on the market. They produce a 1-to-2-pound loaf. If freshly baked bread sounds good to you, but making it from scratch doesn't, I encourage you to research the bread machines available in your area, and refer to the following section: *How to Adapt Your Favorite Recipes for the Bread Machine.*

I hope that this long discussion hasn't discouraged you. Bread baking has been one of the most satisfying achievements of my adult life, and I feel that everyone, man, woman, or child, should have a chance to create their own daily bread. Happy baking.

HOW TO ADAPT YOUR FAVORITE RECIPES FOR THE BREAD MACHINE

The following is adapted from *The Bread Machine Magic Book of Helpful Hints*, by Linda Rehberg and Lois Conway. It provides dozens of problem-solving hints and troubleshooting techniques for getting the most out of your bread machine, and is available from St. Martin's Press.

1. Reduce volume of original recipe to the flour and liquid capacities of your bread machine. Most recipes will have to be reduced by half or two-thirds.

2. Adjust quantities of essential ingredients to fall within the following parameters:

½-POUND LOAF
1⅛–1¼ cups liquid
1–4 tablespoons oil or fat
1–4 tablespoons sweetening
3–4 cups flour
½–1 teaspoons salt
1 tablespoon vital gluten per cup of whole grain flour*
1 teaspoon active dry yeast per cup of whole grain flour*

1-POUND LOAF
⅞–1 cup liquid
2 teaspoons–3 tablespoons oil or fat
2 teaspoons–3 tablespoons sweetening
2–2⅔ cups flour
¼–¾ teaspoon salt
1 tablespoon vital gluten per cup of whole grain flour*
1 teaspoon active dry yeast per cup of whole grain flour*

3. Odd measurements of incidental ingredients can be rounded up or down; it is the liquid, flour, yeast, and salt that are the crucial ingredients. Be sure to measure them accurately.

4. When a recipe calling for 1 egg results in a bread machine recipe calling for a fraction of an egg, either use 1 egg and reduce the total liquid by 2 tablespoons, or use 2 tablespoons of egg substitute instead of the egg and leave the liquid as it is.

5. Monitor your machine's activity closely the first few times you try to adjust a recipe, and be sure to write down any adjustments you make during the knead cycle.

*reduce slightly if white flour is added

KITCHEN

EQUIPMENT

This whole book was born when we bought a flour mill and didn't know how to use it. We've come a long way since then, but there still isn't an awful lot of information available to people who want to grind their own flour. If you decide to grow your own grain or buy it in bulk, you will probably want to get a mill, and there are a few other pieces of equipment you might want to accumulate gradually to help cut food preparation time down. No one wants to spend all day in the kitchen—at least no one I know—and the point of some of these aids is to allow you to cook whole grains without feeling like a martyr. We've been grinding our own flour for many years now, and have collected suggestions from a number of other folks who grind their own and like to cook from scratch. Don't let this section limit your experimentation and don't take it as the gospel—nothing in this book is infallible. But if it saves you from making some of the mistakes we made, its purpose will have been served.

Bread Machines

Automatic bread makers maintain a warm, draft-free environment for bread mixing, raising, and baking. Many people who would never have considered making their own bread now do so daily (my father, for instance). Many excellent brands exist, and new ones show up every year. I suggest you request a demonstration, if you can, and ask your friends about their machines. Be sure that you can make both 1- and 1½- pound loaves, and that the machine has a whole grain cycle.

Coffee Grinder

A coffee grinder is useful when you need to grind or crack only small amounts of grain or seeds. They're relatively inexpensive, and if you're a coffee addict I suggest buying two. Use one for your beans, and one for your grains.

Flour Mill

This may be the most powerful tool in my kitchen. A grain of uncooked wheat appears unpalatable, yet when passed through a closely adjusted grain mill it emerges as the finest of flour, from which tender pastry can be made. Adjusted to a less fine grind, the mill will turn out meal that can be used to texture baked goods, or cracked wheat ready to cook into bulgur or breakfast cereal.

There are two major types of flour mill (I use "grain mill" and "flour mill" interchangeably): the kind with stone grinding faces, or *buhrs*, and the kind which uses steel blades. Naturally, both have their advantages and disadvantages. A stone wheel grinds more finely; that is, you can get fine flour in only one grinding. However, by making two or three passes through a steel blade, you can obtain flour just as fine. A stone wheel cannot be used to grind nuts or seeds which contain a large amount of oil, because the oil is squeezed out in the grinding process, and it will soak into the wheel and glaze it, gradually making it smooth and useless. If you want to use your mill to grind nuts and seeds into butter, buy a metal-bladed mill. Soybeans have a tendency to clog the stone wheel, and you can't make peanut butter in it. But the cornmeal ground in a stone mill is so fine and even and the cornbread made from it so tender and moist that I would not even consider using steel blades for my corn (though my husband would).

At least one manufacturer makes a convertible grain mill; you can attach either stone or metal buhrs to it. Reports from people who have purchased this type indicate that the wheels may need a little work to make them line up evenly when mounted to the dual-use chassis, but otherwise this may be a good buy. Prices of hand-powered grain mills range from about $35 to $100.

You can buy electrically powered grain mills, although the cost is steep. Think $200 to $300 for a really good one. Lower cost electric mills are available, but you usually can expect much less for your money. Be certain that the speed of your mill is fairly slow, or you'll lose vitamins and flavor. It is difficult to get an electric mill with a speed less than 1,725 rpm, which is awfully fast, but some are adjustable. If you succumb to the ease of an electric mill, be sure to use your flour immediately after milling, which saves as many vitamins as possible. Be sure you can take the mill apart for cleaning, or at least reach all parts with a brush, and check to see if there is a coarseness adjustment. Hand-powered mills are infinitely adjustable; paying all that money to get just one or two grades of fineness in flour (and no cracked wheat) seems like a poor bargain. The best way to decide which model is for you is to contact several sources, and preferably to try out the leading contenders. Some health food stores and home brew shops carry flour mills, so don't neglect the trusty Yellow Pages. The Sources section lists several manufacturers and distributors of both hand-powered and electric grain mills. Or, check the Internet for suppliers.

If they are to work to their fullest capacity, hand-powered grain mills must be firmly attached to a very sturdy table or workbench. Mine was clamped to a wobbly kitchen table for several months, and you should see the marks on the floor made by the feet dancing about the linoleum as we ground our grain each week. Choose a better place than we did, if you can. If there is a vertical lip on an otherwise appropriate table which makes attachment difficult, cut a keyhole-shaped hole in the lip and insert the clamp through. Some models have notches or holes in the chassis through which you can pass a couple of bolts. We've found that the extra time it takes to secure the mill is well worth the energy we would otherwise spend in stopping to tighten the mill (it tends to work loose as you grind). It also helps to prevent scars on the counter top made by the mill's movement.

After each use, completely dismantle the wheel and handle from the chassis, brushing all flour particles from the surfaces with a stiff brush (I use a vegetable brush). Any broken grain or flour left in the mill will turn rancid, and may affect the flavor of your next batch. If you wash any parts of your mill, dry them completely or leave them to dry in a warm place (such as the inside of a gas oven with the pilot light on) to prevent the metal from rusting. It's best to avoid washing grinding stones; if you accidentally grind something too oily, such as soybeans or peanuts, clean the grinding surfaces by grinding rice or wheat, and brush well. Metal grinding blades may be washed, but be sure they are dried thoroughly, or they may rust.

FOOD MILL

Once the standby of every kitchen, the old-fashioned meat grinder or universal food mill is an amazingly versatile piece of equipment. Most of us know about grinding leftover meat into hamburger in one of these jewels, but you can also make peanut butter from whole roasted peanuts, crack soybeans into grits and flour, grind soaked whole or sprouted grains for addition to breads, and more.

Once you have a food grinder in your home, many more uses will occur to you. There are several different types, ranging from the old cast metal clamp-type variety to the vacuum-clamp-type, and varying in cost. There are also electric models available. Food mills can be found in most department stores in the housewares section. If you have difficulty locating one, try Goodwill and Salvation Army stores or check the Sources section for suppliers.

The clamp-type meat chopper/food grinder can be safely attached to your kitchen table, if it has a mar-proof finish, by slipping a piece of cardboard between the clamp and the tabletop. I wouldn't advise fastening it to a wooden table, because the clamp exerts enough pressure to mar anything that soft. You don't exert much sideways tug on the chassis when using one of these mills, compared to what you do with a flour mill, so you could clamp it to a pull-out cutting board if marring the board somewhat doesn't bother you. The vacuum-type clamp was designed to protect table and counter tops, but often doesn't hold tightly enough. Try one out in the store.

Use the blades with the largest teeth if you want to chop meat (or make chunky peanut butter), and the smallest if you're after a purée (or smooth peanut butter). Place a bread tin or pie plate below the blades to catch the food as it comes from the blades. If you're doing something juicy, expect some leakage at the handle attachment, and wipe it off occasionally to avoid getting it on your floor. Run some bread through after you're done with meat, vegetables, beans, or other juicy stuff to clean out the blades. Completely dismantle the grinder after each use and wash thoroughly with hot soapy water, leaving to drain in a warm place to prevent rust.

NUT/SEED GRINDER

When a nut is crushed, the oil within it is released, resulting in a sticky, creamy substance which we generally refer to as nut butter. For some purposes, however, notably meringues, marzipan, and some cakes, it is desirable to grate nuts rather than chop or crush them. A blender or food processor can be used for this task, but a finer result can be obtained by using a special purpose nut and seed grinder. From one of these, the nuts and seeds emerge as a dryish powder. The best one I have ever seen is made in Austria, and resembles a universal food grinder, being made out of cast metal and clamped to a table top. A more readily available nut grinder is made by Moulinex and can be purchased from gourmet food shops and restaurant supply houses. If you are unable to locate one or have one ordered, a hand-cranked cheese and vegetable grater, commonly available in housewares departments or gourmet food shops, will do the job, although rather slowly.

MORTAR AND PESTLE

One of the oldest pieces of kitchen equipment in existence, the mortar and pestle is still very useful to the person who cooks with whole grains. Sesame and poppy seeds frequently must be crushed, and many herbs and spices can be ground this way before adding to recipes. The mortar is the name of the bowl in which the pestle is placed and worked in a circular motion, pressing the seeds to be ground against the sides of the mortar in a squishing sort of action. They come in all shapes and sizes (I have one which is three to four inches high and made of wood, and a stone set which I once used for grinding corn, which is several feet high). They are also available in ceramic.

Mortars and pestles are available in gourmet food shops and the houseware section of many department stores. If you get into collecting them as you travel around, you'll have quite an interesting selection.

Their care is quite simple: wash or brush out after each use and replace on the shelf.

PURÉE CONE

I never owned a purée cone until one summer when my husband came home from work with a pickup full of tomatoes. After discovering the mysteries of tomato paste and catsup, we pressed many gallons of applesauce, grape juice, and soup through our $2.95 investment.

A purée cone looks a lot like a mortar with holes, and is used to crush things that are rather wet. Any residue (such as skins of fruit, strings of celery) is left in the cone while the puréed food is pressed through.

A good cone will be made out of stainless steel or aluminum, and have a sturdy frame with legs set far enough apart so that you can place the cone over a medium-sized bowl or saucepan. Place the items you wish to purée (all should be cooked first) into the cone, and work the pestle around within it until all but the skins and strings have been pressed through. Empty the residue into your compost container, put another batch of food into the cone, and so on.

A wooden pestle has a tendency to pick up odors and tastes. After washing thoroughly in soapy water, an application of cooking oil will help to prevent this. Some purée cones now come with plastic or aluminum molded pestles, which may absorb less but probably are less durable. The frame and cone should be washed and dried thoroughly before being returned to the cupboard. Although inexpensive, this piece of equipment should last for many years.

FOOD PROCESSORS

I don't, in fact, own a food processor. I realize, though, that in recent years, many people have added them to their kitchens and found them valuable. In many cases where I use a blender or grain mill, you can substitute a food processor. I've tried to note these places, but, in general, reliable sources tell me that with a food processor you can do the following with no problem: chop meat, make nut butter or nut flour, and blend porridges to make them smoother. You can't crack wheat in a food processor, nor can you make flour from the harder grains such as corn. Also, be careful when making nut flour, and pulse the nuts briefly and frequently. Otherwise, the nuts will release their oil and become closer to nut butter than to flour, not to mention be difficult to clean off your blades. In any case, feel free to experiment, and if you come up with any fabulous uses for your food processor and grains, let me know!

WHEAT

Let us gather up the sunbeams
Lying all around our path;
Let us keep the wheat and roses,
Casting out the thorns and chaff.
—From "If We Knew St. 6 1867"
   by May Riley Smith

Wheat is definitely the universal bread grain; it is grown in nearly every country in the world, and has replaced corn, rye, barley, and millet as the grain staple in most cultures. There are two major reasons for the predominance of wheat. First, it is a hardy and forgiving plant which grows in just about every temperature zone as long as the ground is fertile and there is adequate water. Second, wheat contains gluten-forming proteins which, when leavened with yeast, cause dough made from wheat flour to rise and become light, definitely desirable for baking bread.

Wheat vies with barley for the honor of being the oldest cultivated cereal grain, but its wild origins are relatively obscure. The Greeks considered all cereals gifts of Demeter, the goddess of agriculture, and the Romans gave credit to Ceres, their equivalent deity. Isis was the provider in Egypt: she was believed to have discovered wheat growing in Phoenicia (Lebanon) and gathered some to take home to her worshippers.

Ancient beliefs notwithstanding, authorities generally agree that wheat was first cultivated in Western Asia. Charred pieces of wheat similar to the modern variety *einkorn* have been found in the 8,700-year-old village of Jarmo, in Iraq, and archaeological excavations there indicate that this village may have been one of the earliest known sites of agriculture. Wheat was undoubtedly one of the cereal grains that permitted the nomadic tribes of the Near East to change their way of life to a more sedentary, agriculturally based one. Wheat has also been cultivated in China for centuries, and a ceremony which dates back at least to 2800 B.C. honored wheat along with five other cereals planted in the spring.

The Egyptians were milling wheat along with their barley by about 4000 B.C. They used large, heavy grinding stones to break down the hard outside layers of the grain, added water to make a dough, shaped the dough into large flat cakes something like pancakes, and baked them in clay ovens. This first bread was very heavy, but edible, and became the mainstay of these early settled people.

The early Hebrews soured their dough in order to leaven it; the Egyptians deduced that the leavening agent was yeast, and they isolated this agent and grew it separately. They were the first people to introduce live yeast into fresh dough and make bread with the resulting product. Although we think of bread as being made into round or rectangular loaves, the early bakers were more imaginative. Sumerian and Egyptian breads came in varied geometrical shapes— circles, cones, triangles, spirals. In Eastern Europe even today some of these shapes have persisted, and braided or twisted bread is quite common there.

Egypt provided the wheat for most of the Roman Empire, and so became the source of the grain which eventually spread to Europe, Britain, and the Orient. Bread was so basic to the everyday diet by this time that the writers of the Old Testament used the word as a synonym for food ("Man does not live by bread alone," Deuteronomy 8:4), and the prayer in Matthew, which was later incorporated into the Lord's Prayer, "Give us this day our daily bread" used it the same way. My English father has called bread the "staff of life" ever since I can remember, and the loaves that come out of his bread machine are truly life-giving.

The cultivation of wheat spread widely. The wheat which grew in the Nile River valley had descendants on the Spanish ships making their way to the New World in the sixteenth century. Wheat apparently did not grow wild in the western hemisphere, but Columbus carried seeds with him to the West Indies in 1493, Cortez took some to Mexico in 1519, and missionaries traveled along the Pacific coast with the grain as they spread their faith. English colonists grew wheat beginning in 1618, and although it did not grow as well in coastal areas as did corn, some varieties were found which succeeded, and as settlers moved west the wheat fields sprang up along their paths. By the 1800s wheat was being cultivated in every major nation. At present, world production centers are China, the United States, India, Russia, and France.

Almost all the wheat produced today for human consumption is used for making bread, but the very earliest farmers didn't use their wheat that way. The evidence from Jarmo seems to indicate that they parched the grains, perhaps to make it easier to remove the husks and chew the grain within. The next step was probably to soak or cook the kernels into a porridge or gruel. Perhaps some grinding took place to break the kernels into smaller pieces that would cook faster. If this porridge was left in a warm place for a few days, it fermented from the action of wild yeast, and it is likely that in this way the secret of making leavened bread was eventually discovered—and also the secret of making alcoholic beverages. This is probably why brewing and baking were always linked in ancient times. It is known, for example, that the Egyptians were making a beerlike drink at least five thousand years ago by fermenting half-baked bread.

Parching the grain before threshing paradoxically slowed down the development of successful bread-baking techniques, though it sped up the process of threshing. Parching changed the protein structures in the grain, rendering them less elastic, and any rising due to the introduction of yeast became minimal. For bread to be light, the carbon dioxide bubbles produced by yeast under favorable conditions have to stretch the dough into millions of spongy, cell-like structures that then harden during baking. Heating the protein before the yeast can do its work prevents the dough from rising adequately. Eventually, however, different varieties of wheat and more refined threshing techniques led to the development of satisfactory leavened bread.

The earliest yeasts came from various sources. Since wild yeast often produced unpredictable results, peasants learned to use yeasts from fermented wine and freshly brewed beer. Porridge was sometimes mixed with wine, and the soured combination added to dough. Sliced new potatoes, scalded and set out overnight, could also be used to grow a yeast. The liquid extracted from the potatoes was added to bread dough. Once a fermented dough was obtained, bakers would keep part of it out each day to use as a "starter" for the next batch, a practice which is maintained even today in the preparation of renowned San Francisco Sourdough.

A grain of wheat is, first of all, a seed. The heart of the grain, so to speak, is the germ, or embryo. This is the part which, if the seed is planted, will develop into a new plant, and it is logically where most of the vitamins and minerals are stored. The major portion of the seed, the endosperm, contains the gluten-forming proteins glutenin and gliaden, and starch, food for the developing embryo. Surrounding the endosperm is a layer of aleurone cells (another protein) and several layers of bran, covered by a thin husk.

Milling techniques have changed drastically since the first wheat kernels were ground into flour. The earliest mills pulverized the germ right along with the endosperm, releasing the vitamin-rich wheat germ oil into the flour, coloring and flavoring it slightly. Although this seems desirable to those of us seeking to improve the vitamin and mineral content of our foods, it was not convenient to the grocer or baker, since wheat germ oil soon becomes rancid, and bags of flour left long on the shelf will spoil. The invention in the mid-nineteenth century of roller mills which separated the germ from the wheat kernel and allowed the germ to be sifted out was considered a great technological advance.

Later developments in milling have included screening out most of the bran along with the germ, blowing off any remaining bran or aleurone layers, and bleaching the remaining fine powder. Since the flour resulting from these "refinements" is depleted of most of its nutrients, not to mention fiber, modern nutritionists have had to be called upon to "enrich" flour by putting a few vitamins and minerals back into their product.

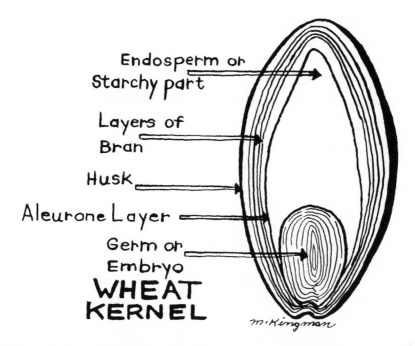

Endosperm or
Starchy part

Layers of
Bran

Husk

Aleurone Layer

Germ or
Embryo

**WHEAT
KERNEL**

m. Kingman

With such "improvements" in milling techniques, how is one to obtain wheat flour and still get the nutrition that this grain so naturally provides? Actually, most large grocery outlets now carry a wide variety of flours, and with some facts in mind the vitamin-seeking consumer can do fairly well.

There are five main types of wheat flour. Enriched, bleached, all-purpose flour is the finest, highest quality result of modern milling techniques, and the flour which most American bakers use. It is consistently fine, soft, and pure white, blends well with other ingredients, and keeps indefinitely on the shelf. It also contains practically none of its original vitamins, minerals, or fiber. Buy all-purpose flour only if you are making angel food cake or something you are preparing for its beauty alone. (I've never seen *un*enriched bleached all-purpose flour, but avoid it if you see it.)

Next on the shelf you will probably find self-rising flour, often called cake flour. This is all-purpose flour with salt and baking powder added, and is more expensive. Don't buy it unless your recipe specifically calls for it.

If your friendly grocer is following modern trends, you will probably next see a few bags of unbleached white flour. Since this flour is probably unenriched (check the label), and is almost sure to be more expensive (since it was put there specifically for health food faddists), and because it is slightly yellow and will color your light, fluffy white cake, there's really no reason to buy this either, unless you're vehemently opposed to the bleaching agents used in all purpose flour.

Now we move on to whole wheat flour. Once upon a time this label could be put on any flour that was made wholly of wheat. Now, thanks to the U.S. Food and Drug Administration standards, it can only be used to label flour made from the whole grain. But don't grab it too fast. Does it say "stone ground" whole wheat flour, or just whole wheat flour? Grinding the whole wheat kernel into flour is great, but if it is done with a high-speed roller mill, hammer mill, or steel plate mill, the oil released from the germ is not distributed evenly through the flour, and is heated in the process, forming masses of rancid oil which flavor the flour and spoil it. Whole wheat flour which has been milled in a high-speed process is usually cheaper than that which is stone ground—check the price tag. Stone ground whole wheat flour may not be available at your local grocery store, but your grocer can get it. So can you, from natural food stores or from the companies listed in the Sources section. Make loud noises if you want your local grocers to supply you with superior products. They'll listen.

Perhaps you don't want to buy commercially ground whole wheat flour, but would rather grind your own. Or, you buy flour at a health food store, but you'd like to have some cracked wheat to cook for breakfast. The whole wheat grain, when sold for food, is called a berry. Wheat berries can be purchased at most natural foods stores, and from the companies listed in the Sources section. You can buy cracked wheat from these places, too, and often at ordinary grocery stores as well, but if you want any control over the size of the pieces, you'll need to grind your own. Cracked wheat is simply wheat berries that have been crushed into several pieces with a flour mill. The smaller the pieces, the faster they cook, and the smoother the consistency of the resulting product.

If you get into baking all the bread for your family and want to cut down the cost, think about buying wheat in bulk. There are two major ways to do this.

Storing foods in bulk has become an increasingly popular activity in our high-pressure times, and a number of businesses now exist primarily to supply families with packaged bulk foods for long-term storage. Wheat is one of the items carried by these suppliers. If you cannot locate a bulk storage outlet in your area, call one of the numbers listed in your telephone directory for the Church of Jesus Christ of Latter Day Saints and ask them for help in locating one. One of the programs of the Mormon Church is food storage, and members are usually knowledgeable and helpful in this regard.

The other way to buy bulk wheat is from a feed store. A 100-pound sack of uncleaned wheat (that means it has bits and pieces of straw and other grains mixed in with it) will cost as little as a quarter of the price of 100 pounds of wheat purchased through commercial outlets.

If you buy wheat in bulk or plan to grow your own, you will need to know the types available.

Hard Red Spring Wheat is a bread wheat, used for making high quality flour. The kernels are short, thick, asymmetrical, and hard, and are rich in protein.

Hard Red Winter Wheat is similar to hard red spring wheat in its uses. It has longer, narrower kernels.

Soft Red Winter Wheat is higher in starch and lower in protein than the hard wheats, and is primarily used for pastry products and for livestock feed. The kernels are long and wide.

Durum Wheat. When varieties of wheat were given Latin names, the most durable and hard-kerneled was named *durus*. One of the ancient grains (the earliest evidence of durum's existence has been dated by scientists at 3,000 B.C.), modern durum is known for its glass-like and lustrous amber kernels. From durum roots have developed a number of common derivatives: semolina, pasta, couscous, bulgur, and certain kinds of breads. One variety of durum wheat, Kamut®, which is noted for its extra-long kernels and nutty flavor, was cultivated in Montana from seeds reported to have come from King Tut's tomb.

Spelt Wheat (*triticum spelta*) is an ancient wheat that originated in the Middle East and later moved through western Europe. In Italy it is known as *farro*. Nearly forgotten after the nineteenth century due to its low yield and the need to dehull the grain mechanically before milling, spelt has recently emerged into the commercial food market. Higher in protein than other wheats, spelt also contains more B vitamins, and minerals. Many people who are allergic to wheat seem to tolerate spelt well, and it is popular with kosher bakers. In addition to traditional breads, spelt seems well suited for baked goods such as pancakes, biscuits, and cakes, and the result is often lighter than such products made with other whole grain wheat flours. The unbroken grains take over an hour to cook when boiled, but have a rich flavor and chewy texture.

Flour made from hard wheat is generally considered to be better for baking bread, mostly because it absorbs more water and rises to a larger degree. Bread made from soft wheat is much denser, but it tastes just as good, and the kind you choose is really more a matter of what is grown in your area and your personal preference. Pastry flour is made from soft wheat.

Spring wheat is planted, naturally enough, in the spring. It requires at least a 90-day growing season, and is usually planted as early as the ground can be worked, for harvest in the autumn. Spring wheat is grown in the colder areas, such as the northern wheat belt in the United States, and in Canada and Russia.

Winter wheat is planted in the fall, and grows best where autumnal rains are good and the winter temperatures not too severe. It grows a few inches before the frost, then matures when warm weather comes. Seeding is usually done in the middle of September, but planting times vary with individual farmers, based on moisture content of the soil, weather, and varieties being planted. Find out what grows best where you live by listening in at feed stores, talking with farmers, or calling your local Agricultural Extension Agent. Try to purchase seed which has been certified to be free of weed seeds and tested for germination.

Wheat was originally planted by hand broadcasting, sown thickly enough to discourage weed growth, trampled in with cattle, and left to grow without cultivation or irrigation. This way still works, but you'll get more grain if you prepare your land, try to eliminate weeds, and provide adequate water. Dig compost and fertilizer into your field if it is light or clay-filled; a rich loam produces the best grain. Plow just before planting, and sow seed at a rate of three to four bushels an acre.

If you plant clover or alfalfa along with your wheat, you'll get fewer weeds and a double crop. Harvest the wheat first, then cut the slower-growing crop in late summer or fall. Irrigation is a must for spring wheat, or for winter wheat if the rains let you down. Watch the farmers, and water when they do.

Harvesting a field of grain is quite an adventure. It's also a big job, so invite your friends to help and search junk shops for sickles, scythes, and grain cradles. Grain is still harvested by hand in most of the world, so don't feel too lonely out there, but remember that it is going to be hard work.

Wheat is usually harvested when it is dead ripe, which means the stalks are entirely golden and the grains hard and brittle. If you harvest by machine, this is when you should get to work. Most of us don't have friends who own a combine, however, so chances are you'll be harvesting by hand. The methods have been tested by centuries of farmers, and the key to success is to cut the wheat before the grain is fully ripe, so you don't lose grains in the field. Try to squish a kernel between two fingernails; it should be soft enough to dent, but not so soft that it smashes flat.

The wheat can be cut with a sickle, but a large scythe is much better, and if you can find or make a grain cradle to attach to it, you'll really appreciate the difference. A grain cradle consists of three or four curved tines and a frame to hold them, and is attached just above the blade of the scythe, so that the tines and the blade are parallel. When you swing the scythe, the cradle catches the cut stalks and makes them fall in a neat pile which can then be tied into bundles called *sheaves*, and stood up in *shocks* to dry. The secret of making a shock is to take two sheaves and rub their ends together, weaving the grain heads into each other. Use these two standing together with their heads pointing upward to support several more sheaves, which can lean on them to form a stable bunch. You can tie a piece of twine around the shock if you want, but if it's done right, only a storm will blow it over, and you hope to get all your grain under cover before then anyway.

Leave your wheat in the field for from ten days to three weeks, assuming you can count on dry weather during this period. If you can't, move the bundles into a barn to finish drying, but be sure you have either a mouse-proof barn or a cat, or you'll come back to find half your crop gone.

The next job is threshing, removing the heads of grain from the stalks. This task has been done for centuries by beating the straw with sticks and flails, by walking horses over it, or by banging sheaves over the edge of a "threshing horse" or chair (or barrel, but don't count on catching much of the grain in the barrel; most of it will go on the floor). Any of these methods work, so just try one, then another, until you find one which makes you happiest. Winnow the grain, or remove leftover pieces of straw (called *chaff*) from it, by pouring it slowly from a bucket into a pile on a clean tarp, or into another bucket, on a windy day. If it doesn't happen to be a windy day, an electric fan works well. The chaff that blows out can be swept up and fed to your animals or used as bedding for the chickens, who will enjoy picking out the light grains of wheat that escaped your notice.

Your wheat is now ready for storage until you want to cook it or crack it or grind it into flour. Keep it in a cool, dry place, and protect it from bugs and rodents. Wheat is best ground, in my opinion, in a stone mill. Somehow a metal blade just doesn't seem to get it fine enough to make good bread or pastry unless you run it through two or three times. Experiment, though, and you may reach a different conclusion. Grind only as much flour as you need in a week, because, remember, you have the whole grain there, wheat germ oil and all, and your flour will begin to taste stale if left too long.

WHEAT BERRY BREAKFAST

Some folks are partial to the chewy texture of cooked wheat berries. They take a long time to cook, though, so think about your breakfast the night before.

METHOD I

2 cups whole wheat berries	4 cups water
	1 teaspoon salt

Cook wheat in salted water, tightly covered, for 40–50 minutes (see Note), until berries are tender and water is completely absorbed. The kernels should burst as they cook, permitting the starchy insides to take in the water. Add more liquid if necessary. Let stand for 15 to 20 minutes.

METHOD II

Soak 1 cup of wheat 8–10 hours in 2 cups of water. Drain the water into a measuring cup and add enough to total 2 cups liquid. Add 1 teaspoon salt and the wheat and bring to a boil. Pour into preheated 1-quart stainless-steel thermos bottle. Cap tightly and lay on its side. Leave overnight.

Serve wheat berries like porridge, with milk and sugar or honey.

NOTE: Kamut® may take as long as 1½ hours.

CRACKED WHEAT

Cracked wheat can be cooked for breakfast as a cereal, or for an accompaniment to a meat dish instead of rice. Mixed with vegetables and stock, it becomes a main dish all by itself. If you have whole wheat berries, and a flour mill (or a blender if you sift out the flour afterwards), you can create cracked wheat in textures varying from very fine to super coarse and crunchy. Cooking time for any cracked grain varies with the size of the pieces, so experiment with the methods below until you have a feel for the correct length of time. You can also buy cracked wheat in some large grocery stores. Use the package directions as a guide to cooking time.

METHOD I

This method of cooking is ideal for breakfast cereal, or for those of you who like your grains all stuck together. The consistency tends to be creamier than the result of Method II.

2 cups water	½ teaspoon salt
1 cup cracked wheat or other grain	

Place grain in salted water and bring to a boil over medium flame. Stir once, cover, and reduce heat to very low. Simmer for 10–20 minutes, until grain is tender and water is absorbed.*

METHOD II

This basic recipe is the one I use for most cracked grains. Sautéing the kernels first separates the broken pieces and helps to keep them from sticking together.

1 tablespoon light cooking oil	2 cups water or stock
1 cup cracked wheat or other grain	1 teaspoon salt

Sauté grain in oil until slightly brown, 3–5 minutes. Lower heat, add stock and salt, cover, and simmer until grain is tender and liquid is absorbed, 10–20 minutes.* Stir lightly with a fork and serve.

*To check cooking progress when a grain is steaming, remove lid for only the briefest moment. Escaping steam may cause the grain to dry out and burn, so add liquid as necessary.

BULGUR

Bulgur is the name given to wheat which is cooked and parched before grinding. It is a staple grain in many southern areas of Eastern Europe and in the Middle East. Bulgur has a subtle, nutty flavor which makes it a fine accompaniment to meat and poultry, and because it is partially cooked before grinding, it can be prepared more quickly than ordinary cracked wheat of an equivalent coarseness. Bulgur can be purchased commercially, but it is quite easy to make at home.

Boil whole wheat berries in twice their volume of water for 45 minutes, or until the kernels are just tender. Drain, saving any liquid for soup stock. Spread kernels on baking sheets and toast at 250°F., stirring occasionally, for 45–60 minutes, until completely dry. Grind coarsely and store in tight containers.

NOTE: bulgur or cracked wheat can be used interchangeably in the following recipes. Remember that cooking time varies with the coarseness of the broken pieces of grain, and that bulgur will cook faster than cracked wheat of the same size.

ARMENIAN PILAF

Pilaf (or *pilau*) is usually made with rice. This wheat version was served at an international cuisine banquet I attended, and I find it to be a good basic recipe for many occasions.

1 tablespoon olive oil	2½–3 cups vegetable or meat stock
1 medium onion, chopped	2 tomatoes, peeled and chopped (or
1 clove garlic, minced	use canned stewed tomatoes)
1 cup medium cracked wheat or	1 teaspoon ground cumin
bulgur (see Note above)	¼ teaspoon salt or to taste

Heat oil in a heavy skillet; sauté onion and garlic until tender. Add cracked wheat and cook, stirring constantly, until wheat begins to brown. Add stock, tomatoes, seasonings, and stir well. Bring to boil, lower heat, and simmer, covered, until wheat is tender, about 30 minutes. Add more liquid if necessary. Makes 4 ½-cup servings.

KAMUT® AND SPELT PILAF

This is a chewy pilaf with an attractive texture. To prepare the grain, boil 1 cup whole kamut® grain and 1 cup whole spelt grain with 4 cups lightly salted water until tender, about 1 hour. The cooked grain can be frozen or refrigerated until needed.

1 tablespoon olive oil
1 small onion, chopped
1–2 cloves garlic, sliced
1 inch fresh ginger root, slivered
½ bell pepper, sliced
2–3 cups cooked spelt and kamut®
    grain

salt to taste
pepper to taste
¼–½ teaspoon cumin to taste
1–2 teaspoons chili powder to taste
1 large tomato, chopped

Heat olive oil in large skillet. Add onion, garlic, and ginger root and sauté until onion is translucent. Add bell pepper and grain and cook, stirring occasionally, until pepper is tender. Add salt, pepper, cumin, and chili powder. Just before serving, stir in tomato. This is also good topped with a spoonful of fruit chutney or yoghurt.

BULGUR SLAW

1 small head of cabbage
1 small green bell pepper
1 small onion
1 carrot
½ cup bulgur or cracked wheat,
  soaked overnight

1 cup sour cream or yoghurt
1 teaspoon onion, finely minced
1 teaspoon salt
¼ teaspoon pepper
½ teaspoon caraway or celery seeds

Shred cabbage; finely chop pepper, onion, and carrot. Rinse, drain, and refrigerate until ready to serve. Meanwhile, stir together sour cream, minced onion, and seasonings. Chill. Just before serving, toss vegetables with drained bulgur and stir in dressing.

The toasted taste of bulgur is best for this, but cracked wheat or triticale may be substituted with satisfactory results.

PARSLEY SALAD

2 bunches of parsley, chopped (3–4
  cups)
1 small cucumber, diced
1 small tomato, chopped
½ cup cooked cracked wheat or
  triticale

juice of 1 lemon
1 tablespoon olive oil
1 teaspoon salt

Wash parsley thoroughly and remove stems before chopping. Mix together parsley, cucumber, tomato, and wheat. Press with the back of a spoon to release the flavor of the parsley. Add lemon juice, olive oil, and salt and mix well. Refrigerate at least one hour before serving.

VEGETABLE PILAF

1 tablespoon vegetable oil
1 onion, chopped
1 celery stalk, chopped
1 carrot, chopped
¼ pound mushrooms, sliced
1 cup bulgur or cracked wheat (see
  note on p. 30)

¼ cup pumpkin, sunflower, or sesame
  seeds
1 tablespoon fresh parsley or 1
  teaspoon dried
1 teaspoon salt
2 cups vegetable or meat stock

Sauté onion, celery, carrot, and mushrooms in oil until tender. Add bulgur and seeds, stirring until grain is slightly browned. Sprinkle with parsley and salt and add stock, stirring until combined. Cover and simmer over low heat until all moisture is absorbed, about 15 minutes.

STUFFED PEPPERS

4 bell peppers
1 tablespoon vegetable oil
¼ pound sliced mushrooms
¼ cup chopped celery
2 cups cooked cracked wheat or
  bulgur (see note on p. 30)

½ cup cooked meat or beans,
  chopped fine
1 cup beef or vegetable stock
1 teaspoon salt
½ teaspoon basil
¼ teaspoon pepper

Preheat oven to 375°F. Cut tops off peppers; cut out veins and remove seeds. Rinse and drain. Sauté mushrooms and celery in oil until tender. Remove from heat. Add cracked wheat and meat. Stir in stock and seasonings, and fill peppers with mixture. Place in deep casserole and bake for 30 minutes covered and 30 minutes uncovered.

CORNISH PASTY

The fine people of Sennen Cove, Cornwall, would probably not think that these pasties (the "a" is pronounced like the "a" in "apple") much resemble the gems they served me. The Cornish pasties there were scrumptious, but I really do prefer this whole wheat version.

FILLING

1 cup finely chopped beef (preferably top round)
1 cup chopped onions
1 cup finely diced potatoes
1 teaspoon salt
½ teaspoon sage
½ teaspoon pepper

CRUST

3 cups whole wheat pastry flour
½ teaspoon salt
½ cup butter
2 eggs

Combine filling ingredients in a bowl. Preheat oven to 400°F.

To make the crust, stir together flour and salt; cut in butter. Beat eggs slightly and stir into mixture with a fork. Mixture will be slightly sticky, but since egg sizes differ you may need to add more flour to get the right consistency. Turn dough onto a well-floured surface and with floured hands and floured rolling pin, press and roll into a flat piece about ¼ inch thick. Cut circles about 6 inches in diameter (a cereal bowl makes a good guide), gathering scraps together and rolling them out as necessary. Place ¼ cup filling on one side of each circle, wet edges with water, fold in half and seal, crimping with fingers or fork. Slash pasty lengthwise to permit steam to escape. Place on greased baking sheet, brush with egg or milk, and bake 30–35 minutes.

THREE-GRAIN PATTIES

1 cup coarsely cracked cornmeal
1 cup medium cracked wheat
½ cup sorghum or millet
4 cups water or vegetable stock

2 medium onions, finely chopped
2 eggs
2 tablespoons whole wheat flour
½ teaspoon salt

Cook grains in boiling water until tender, about 30 minutes. Drain and pulse in a food processor or put through food mill or meat grinder. Combine other ingredients with grain mixture and mix well. Form into pancake-like patties on greased griddle by dropping large spoonfuls and flattening with a spatula. Fry until crisp; turn and cook other side.

CARDAMOM DELIGHTS (PANCAKES)

1 cup whole wheat flour
1½ teaspoons baking soda
1 teaspoon crushed cardamom seeds
½ teaspoon salt
2 eggs

¼ cup vegetable oil
¼ cup honey
1 cup yoghurt or sour cream
1 cup buttermilk

Stir together flour, baking soda, and seasonings. Beat eggs and add oil, honey, yoghurt, and buttermilk, blending well. Combine with dry ingredients, stirring only until mixed. Drop by large spoonfuls onto a lightly greased griddle. Serve dusted with powdered sugar and topped with fruit preserves.

RICH WHOLE WHEAT PIE CRUST

Believe me, this crust is worth the butter!

1 ½ cups whole wheat flour
½ teaspoon salt

½ cup butter
¼ cup ice water

Stir together flour and salt. Cut in butter. Add ice water by tablespoonfuls until dough can be pressed together in a ball. Roll out on floured board. Makes 1 pie shell.

FLAKY PASTRY

3 cups whole wheat flour
1 teaspoon salt
½ cup vegetable oil

1 egg
6 tablespoons ice water

Stir together flour and salt. Beat together oil and egg; add to dry ingredients. Add water, 1 tablespoonful at a time, until dough can be pressed together into a ball. Divide in two and roll out pieces with floured rolling pin on a floured cloth or board. Makes 1 2-crust pie shell.

ONION-PARSLEY QUICHE

Here is a suggestion for filling one of those pie shells.

1 onion, finely chopped
2 slices bacon or 1 tablespoon bacon
    bits
1 tablespoon vegetable oil
¼ cup fresh parsley (or 1 tablespoon
    dried parsley)
2 cups grated mild cheese (Swiss,
    Port Salut, Gouda, etc.)

1½ cups milk
½ cup powdered milk
3 eggs
1 teaspoon salt
½ teaspoon thyme
½ teaspoon marjoram

Preheat oven to 350°F. Sauté onion and bacon in 1 tablespoon oil. Sprinkle crumbled bacon with onion and parsley over prepared pie crust. Cover with cheese. Combine milk, powdered milk, eggs, and seasonings. Pour over cheese. Bake for 25–30 minutes, or until firm. Serves 6.

YORKSHIRE PUDDING

My mother would shoot me if she knew that I made my Yorkshire Puds with whole wheat flour, but we've grown to prefer them that way. They are a little heavier than when made with all-purpose white flour, but they rise quite well and taste delicious.

Have all ingredients at room temperature:

2 eggs
1 cup milk
½ teaspoon salt

1 cup whole wheat pastry flour
2 tablespoons beef drippings or
    vegetable oil

Beat eggs, milk, and salt together until foamy; stir in flour just until blended. Preheat oven to 425°F. Let batter sit at room temperature until oven is preheated and baking pan or muffin tin, greased with drippings or oil, has been heated to oven temperature. Beat pudding mixture once more and pour into hot pan, placing immediately in oven. Bake for 15 minutes, then, without opening oven door, lower temperature to 375°F and bake for 20 additional minutes. Serve puddings immediately. If you baked them in a large pan, slice into serving pieces. This dish is traditionally served with roast beef and gravy. Makes 1 large pudding or 12 individual ones.

YORKSHIRE STEAK

This recipe has been adapted from a wartime recipe book put out by a small-town newspaper in Yorkshire. It makes a pound of ground meat go a long way.

1 pound ground meat	2 eggs
1 medium onion, finely chopped	1 cup milk
Vegetable oil for browning	½ teaspoon baking powder
1 teaspoon salt	½ teaspoon salt
½ teaspoon sage	1 cup whole wheat flour
¼ teaspoon marjoram	

Preheat oven to 450°F. Brown meat and onion in oil or other fat in large heavy skillet; drain and stir in seasonings. Grease 8-inch square baking pan, spread meat mixture in it, and brown in oven for 10 minutes. Meanwhile, beat eggs and milk together; mix together baking powder, salt, and flour and add to liquid ingredients, stirring only until blended. When meat is removed from oven, stir batter once and pour over hot meat, returning to oven for 30–35 minutes, or until brown and puffy. Cut into squares and serve immediately with gravy and vegetables. Serves 6.

WHOLE WHEAT NOODLES

These can also be made with barley flour, rye flour, etc.

3 eggs, well beaten
½ teaspoon salt

1 tablespoon milk
3–4 cups whole wheat flour

Beat eggs, salt, and milk together. Stir in flour until mixture is too stiff to stir. Then turn out onto a well-floured board and knead in enough additional flour so that the dough can be rolled out. Roll very thin. Cut into strips and hang on chairs to dry, or leave on board for 3–5 hours and cut with scissors. When noodles are thoroughly dry, cook in boiling water or keep in airtight container until ready for use.

CHAPATI

This unleavened whole wheat bread is one of the most popular breads of India. A similar bread is called *phulka*, and can be made using the same recipe if the dough is rolled out more thickly.

2½ cups whole wheat flour
¾ teaspoon salt

about 1 cup water

Mix flour and salt in a bowl. Add water slowly to make a soft dough. Knead on a well-floured board until smooth, about 5 minutes. Shape dough into balls about the size of golf balls, then roll out very thin. Cook on hot, lightly greased griddle until blistered, then turn and bake other side. Chapatis should be lightly brown and crisp. Serve hot with butter.

100% WHOLE WHEAT BREAD

This is our family's standard fare. A loaf will keep fairly well from one baking Sunday to the next if wrapped in a plastic bag and kept cool, but if it begins to crumble, lightly toast the slices before serving. If bread is to be used for sandwiches, be sure not to let it over-rise, or it will have holes in it and be less able to contain jelly or honey. If you start baking bread for your family, be forewarned: they may never accept store-bought bread again.

3 cups milk or water*	¼ cup molasses
3 tablespoons vegetable oil	2 tablespoons active dry yeast
1 tablespoon salt	¼ cup lukewarm water
½ cup honey	6½–7 cups whole wheat flour

Combine milk, oil, salt, honey, and molasses in a saucepan. Heat and stir until blended; remove from heat and cool until lukewarm. Dissolve yeast in ¼ cup lukewarm water (if you use the cup you used to measure the honey and molasses, the yeast will bubble faster). Pour cooled liquids from saucepan into a large bowl and add yeast. Stir in 3 cups of flour, beating well to develop gluten. Stir in remaining flour and turn onto a well-floured board. Knead thoroughly, until dough is smooth and elastic. Turn into oiled bowl, turning dough once to coat. Cover with damp cloth and let rise 1 hour. Punch down, form into 2 loaves, and place in 2 well-greased bread tins; let rise, covered, 45 minutes. Preheat oven to 375°F. Bake for 45 minutes, or until loaf sounds hollow when thumped.

50% WHOLE WHEAT BREAD

This recipe is for those of you who prefer a lighter loaf. It is still very nutritious and more substantial than most commercial breads.

---

*Water brings out the flavor of the wheat best, but milk makes a more nutritious loaf.

1 cup water	1 cup wheat germ
¼ cup honey	2 tablespoons yeast
1 tablespoon salt	¼ cup lukewarm water
⅓ cup vegetable oil	3 cups whole wheat flour
¾ cup milk	3 cups white flour

Combine water, honey, salt, and oil in a saucepan. Heat, stirring until blended. Cool to lukewarm and pour into large bowl. Combine milk and wheat germ; let soak while honey mixture is cooling. Dissolve yeast in ¼ cup lukewarm water. Add wheat germ mixture and yeast to liquids in bowl. Stir in flours, kneading when mixture gets too stiff to stir. Turn onto a floured board and knead well until dough is smooth and elastic. Cover with a damp cloth and let rise in warm place 1 hour, or until dough doubles in bulk. Punch down, shape into 2 loaves, and place in oiled bread tins. Let rise, covered, 45 minutes. Preheat oven to 375°F. Bake for 50 minutes. Let cool slightly before slicing.

HERB BREAD

This bread only rises once, and is excellent with soup. Start it when you put the soup pot on, and it will be ready when the soup is done.

2 tablespoons active dry yeast	1 tablespoon sage
½ cup lukewarm water	1 tablespoon freshly crushed dill
3 cups lukewarm water	seeds
1½ tablespoons salt	1 tablespoon crumbled dried dill
¼ cup vegetable oil	weed
¼ cup molasses	6 – 7 cups whole wheat flour
¼ cup yoghurt	

Dissolve yeast in ½ cup lukewarm water. Combine water, salt, oil, and molasses in saucepan and heat until combined. Pour into large bowl and cool until lukewarm. Stir in yeast mixture, yoghurt, and herbs. Stir in 3 cups flour and beat well to develop gluten. Add remaining flour, kneading if necessary. Turn out onto a floured board and knead thoroughly. Divide dough into 2 parts, form into loaves, and place in oiled bread tins. Let rise in warm place, covered with a cloth, for 40 minutes, or until bread is above the tops of the pans. Preheat oven to 375°F. Bake for 45 minutes. Run knife around edges of loaves before removing from pans. Serve hot with soup.

WHOLE WHEAT BAGELS

These have become a favorite among our friends. Join us one Sunday afternoon for bagels and cream cheese.

1¼ cups boiling water	2 tablespoons yeast
3 tablespoons honey	¼ cup lukewarm water
1 tablespoon salt	4 – 4½ cups whole wheat flour

Combine boiling water, honey, and salt in a large bowl. Cool to lukewarm. Dissolve yeast in ¼ cup lukewarm water (use the spoon you used to measure the honey to stir the yeast, and it will bubble a bit faster); add to honey mixture when it has cooled. Stir in 2 cups flour and beat well to develop gluten. Add remaining flour, kneading well until dough is smooth and elastic.

Shape dough into 12 balls. Poke a hole in the middle of each one, pulling gently to enlarge the whole and working each into a doughnut-like shape. Cover lightly with a dry cloth and let rise for 30 minutes.

Preheat oven to 375°F. In a large kettle of salted water, boil bagels, 4 or 5 at a time, for 7 minutes, turning once with a slotted spoon. Place on ungreased baking sheet and bake for 30–35 minutes. Enjoy.

BAGEL BREAD

One day I converted my bagel recipe into loaves and was quite pleased with the results. This rises quickly and results in delicious, chewy loaves.

3¾ cups boiling water	6 tablespoons yeast
¾ cup honey	¾ cup lukewarm water
3 tablespoons salt	12–13 cups whole wheat flour

Combine water, honey, and salt in large bowl. Stir and cool until lukewarm. Meanwhile, dissolve yeast in ¾ cup lukewarm water. Add to cooled honey mixture and stir in 6 cups flour, beating well. Incorporate rest of flour into dough, kneading when it becomes necessary on a floured board. Form into 3 medium or 4 small loaves and place in oiled bread tins.

Cover and let rise in warm place 30–45 minutes, or until above the tops of the bread pans. Preheat oven to 375°F. Bake for 45 minutes, or until nicely browned and hollow-sounding when rapped with the knuckles. Cool slightly and remove from pans. Allow to cool before slicing.

SPELT BREAD

Because spelt (see page 25) is tolerated well by many people who cannot eat other wheat products, it may be worth using spelt in wheat recipes. Adjust amounts until you arrive at a proportion of this gluten-containing flour to wheat flour that produces the best texture with the least allergic reaction. Here is a delicious 100% spelt bread for a start.

1½ cups water or milk	1 tablespoon active dry yeast
1 tablespoon vegetable oil	¼ cup lukewarm water
2 tablespoons honey or molasses	4–5 cups finely ground spelt flour
1 teaspoon salt	

Combine water, oil, sweetener, and salt in a pan and warm to a simmer. Set aside. Meanwhile, dissolve yeast in ¼ cup lukewarm water. After yeast bubbles, combine with water mixture and stir in about 2 cups of spelt flour. Beat with an electric beater for 3 to 5 minutes, until mixture begins to develop a stringy texture. Add remaining flour gradually, stirring with a wooden spoon until the dough is too stiff to stir. Turn out onto a board floured with spelt flour and knead for 5 to 10 minutes. Place in an oiled bowl, cover, and keep warm and free from drafts until doubled in size, about an hour. Punch down a second time and allow to double in size again, about 45 minutes in a warm place. Shape dough into a medium-sized loaf or several sandwich rolls. Place in oiled loaf pan or on baking sheet. Cover once more and keep warm until risen, about 1 hour. Preheat oven to 350°F. Bake for 40 minutes, or until loaf sounds hollow when thumped. Remove from pan and cool on wire rack. This bread slices best when cool.

VARIATIONS:
- add 1 cup oat or soy flour in place of 1 cup spelt flour
- add ¼ cup poppy seeds and ½ cup sunflower seeds to liquids before adding flour
- roll loaf in a mixture of rolled oats, poppy seeds, and sunflower seeds before last rising

SPELT BREAKFAST BISCUITS

2 cups spelt flour
1 teaspoon baking powder
¼ teaspoon salt

1 cup buttermilk, soy, or rice milk
2 teaspoons honey

Preheat oven to 425°F. Mix flour, baking powder, and salt. Stir in buttermilk and honey. Batter should be quite thick. Drop by heaping tablespoons onto baking sheet sprayed with vegetable oil. Bake for 12–15 minutes, or until lightly browned. Makes 12 biscuits.

SPELT PASTA

1¾ cups spelt flour   ¾ cup plus 2 tablespoons water
½ teaspoon salt

Mix flour and salt. Add water and press with a wooden spoon or use your hands until dough sticks together. Knead until smooth, then let rest 10–15 minutes. Roll dough on floured surface until ⅛ inch thick. *For noodles:* Cut into ¼-inch strips with pizza cutter. Cook in boiling water for 20 minutes, or hang to dry and store in airtight containers. *For ravioli:* Preheat oven to 350°F. Roll dough into long rope and divide into 20 pieces. Roll each piece into a ball and flatten into circle (do this on a floured surface with floured hands). Add cheese or chopped meat, fold in half, and pinch edges securely by dipping fingers into water before pinching edges. Bake in a covered casserole for 20 minutes. Boil for 3 to 4 minutes before serving. Makes 20 ravioli.

MALT BREAD

This is the "sticky brown bread" my grandmother used to make and that still makes my father's eyes sparkle. The malt syrup called for can be purchased in health food stores and some large chain supermarkets under the Blue Ribbon label in the U.S., or the Gold Medal label in Canada. Order from one of the Ingredient Sources in the back of this book if you cannot find it locally. Malt syrup is very sticky; be prepared for a mess the first few times you use it. A combination of dark and light molasses or corn syrup can be used in place of the malt syrup (in the U.K., Canada, and Australia black treacle and honey can be combined), although the final product tastes slightly different. This recipe is fat-free and makes 1 loaf.

2½ cups whole wheat flour   1 tablespoon hot water
1 cup raisins or sultanas   1 cup milk (nonfat for fat-free)
¼ cup brown sugar   ½ cup malt syrup
½ teaspoon salt   ¼ cup sweet molasses
1 teaspoon baking soda

Preheat oven to 325°F. Stir together flour and raisins in a large bowl; add brown sugar and salt and mix well. Dissolve baking soda in hot water; add milk. In a microwave or on the stove, heat malt syrup and molasses to melting; add to milk and then add foaming mixture to flour. Bake in a well-oiled 1-pound loaf pan for 1½ hours. Cool slightly before removing from pan. This bread slices best when completely cooled.

EASTER EGG BREAD

½ cup milk
½ cup honey
½ teaspoon salt
½ cup canola oil
grated peel of 2 lemons
2 tablespoons active dry yeast
¼ cup warm water
2 eggs, beaten

4½–5 cups whole wheat bread flour
12 hard-cooked eggs, colored with
    Easter egg dye
1 beaten egg
poppy or sesame seeds, slivered
    almonds, or colored candy
    sprinkles

Combine milk, honey, salt, oil, and lemon peel. Dissolve yeast in warm water. (If you use the same cup used to measure the warm water as you did to measure the honey, the yeast will proof faster.) Add to milk mixture after it bubbles up, about 5 minutes. Stir in the eggs and half the flour and beat until smooth.

Stir in remaining flour, a little at a time, until you form a dough you can handle with floured hands. Continue to add flour, kneading thoroughly until smooth and elastic. Place into a slightly greased bowl, cover with a cloth, and allow to rise in a warm place until double, about 1 hour.

Punch down dough and form into four ropes. Twist two ropes together to form loose loops on a baking sheet, bringing the ends together to form a ring. Nestle six eggs in the loops. Do the same with the other 2 ropes. Or, make 12 dough circles, with 1 egg in each.

Allow dough to rise again until doubled, covered with a cloth to keep out drafts and passing children. Preheat oven to 375°F. Brush dough with the beaten egg and sprinkle with poppy or sesame seeds, slivered almonds, or col ored candy sprinkles. Bake for 25 to 30 minutes (about 20 minutes for individual rings).

This bread can be personalized with the addition of raisins, currants, candied fruit, or nuts, and can also be made the night before and heated just before serving. You can also prepare the dough up to the first rising the night before and refrigerate overnight. Punch down and knead until warm; form into ropes and bake as above.

PENNSYLVANIA DUTCH SOFT PRETZELS

1 teaspoon active dry yeast
¾ cup warm water
2–2½ cups whole wheat bread flour
¼ teaspoon salt

¾ cup cool water
1 tablespoon baking soda
coarse salt

Dissolve yeast in warm water, and set aside. Mix salt and half the flour in a mixing bowl. Add yeast mixture and stir. Continue to add flour until dough is too stiff to stir. Knead well until dough feels elastic and smooth. Put into a warm place and let rise for 30 minutes. Meanwhile, spray a baking sheet with vegetable oil. Preheat oven to 400°F. Stir together baking soda and cool water in a shallow bowl. On lightly floured surface, punch down dough and divide into 8 pieces. Roll each piece into an 18-inch rope and twist into pretzel shapes. Dip into baking soda solution and place on baking sheet 2 inches apart. If desired, sprinkle with coarse salt. Bake 15–20 minutes, or until golden-brown. Remove from oven and cool slightly on wire rack. Serve warm.

SOURDOUGH STARTER

1 tablespoon active dry yeast
2 cups lukewarm water

2 cups whole grain flour (wheat or rye)

Dissolve yeast in water, add flour, and stir thoroughly. Place in a crock or jar, cover loosely, and keep at room temperature for 3 days. Return 1 cup to crock and store in a cool place; use the rest to prepare bread, pancakes, etc. When you need the starter again, add 2 cups water and 2 cups flour to the crock and leave at room temperature for 8 to 24 hours. If starter will not be used within a week, it must be "freshened" or renewed with 1 cup flour and 1 cup water to keep it alive.

NOTE: This starter can be used to make biscuits or pancakes.

SOURDOUGH WHOLE WHEAT BREAD

1 cup sourdough starter
1 cup milk
2 cups whole wheat flour
½ cup molasses

½ teaspoon baking soda
1½ teaspoons salt
¼ cup vegetable oil
2–3 cups whole wheat flour

Stir together sourdough starter, milk, and 2 cups flour in large bowl. Cover with cloth and leave overnight. The next day, stir in molasses, baking soda, salt, oil, and sufficient flour to make a stiff dough which can be kneaded. Knead thoroughly, form into 2 loaves, cover with cloth and leave in warm place until double in bulk, about 1½ hours. Preheat oven to 350°F. Bake for 1 hour.

HARVEST ROLLS

1 teaspoon salt

1 tablespoon yeast

2 tablespoons honey

1 cup lukewarm milk

¼ cup sunflower or canola oil

1 egg

1 cup currants

3–3½ cups whole wheat flour

Dissolve salt, yeast, and honey in milk. Add butter, oil, eggs, and currants. Stir in flour, kneading as necessary at end. Cover ball of dough with a cloth and let rise in warm place for 30 minutes. Shape into 24 slightly flattened balls, cover again and let rise 45–50 minutes. Preheat oven to 425°F. Bake for 10–15 minutes. These are delicious served hot, split in half with a fork, and spread with butter.

VARIATION: For soul cakes, add 1 teaspoon cinnamon.

PUMPKIN NUT BREAD

My mother clipped the original recipe for this sweet bread from a newspaper 25 or 30 years ago. It changed through the years, and underwent a metamorphosis when I left home and began preparing it with whole wheat flour. Probably quite different from the early version by now, this bread has become an expected part of our Thanksgiving and Christmas dinners.

2 cups fresh cooked pumpkin (or canned)

2 cups brown sugar

½ cup vegetable oil

2½ cups whole wheat flour

1 teaspoon cinnamon

2 teaspoons baking soda

2 teaspoons ground cloves

½ cup chopped nuts

Preheat oven to 350°F. Combine pumpkin, sugar, and oil in a saucepan. Heat but do not boil. Add flour, spices, baking soda, and nuts, stirring thoroughly. Pour batter into tin cans (#10 soup cans work well), filling each can ⅔ full. You can also use a small loaf pan. Bake for 45–60 minutes, or until a cake tester comes out clean. Cool slightly before removing from cans and slicing. This bread slices best when refrigerated overnight.

NUTLESS NUT BREAD

Why would anyone want to make a nut bread without nuts? Only if you're absolutely craving some nut bread and you don't have any nuts, right? Well, if that ever happens to you, add some cracked wheat to your favorite nut bread recipe (soak it for a while if your grind is very coarse), or try this one. This is also terrific if you are allergic to nuts.

4½ cups whole wheat flour	½ cup honey
4 teaspoons baking powder	4 eggs
½ teaspoon baking soda	3 cups mashed bananas
1 teaspoon salt	1 cup cracked wheat
¼ cup vegetable oil	

Preheat oven to 325°F. Stir together flour, baking powder, baking soda, and salt, pressing out any lumps. Cream oil and honey; add eggs and beat well. Stir in bananas, cracked wheat, and dry ingredients and beat thoroughly. Bake in 2 well-greased loaf pans for 1½ hours. Cool before removing from pans.

STEAMED BOSTON BROWN BREAD

1 cup stone-ground cornmeal	¾ teaspoon salt
1 cup whole wheat flour	¾ cup sweet molasses
1 cup rye meal	1¾ cups sour milk, buttermilk, or
1 cup raisins	kafir
1 teaspoon baking soda	

Stir together cornmeal, flour, rye meal, raisins, baking soda, and salt. Combine molasses and milk in a second bowl, then add to cornmeal mixture. Line the inside of several #10 cans with baking parchment or spray with vegetable oil. Fill each can no more than ⅔ full. Place cans on a rack in a large pan, adding warm water to half the height of the molds. Bring water to gentle boil, then cover pan and steam for 1 to 2 hours, or until a wooden skewer comes out clean. Add water to pan from time to time as necessary. Remove from cans while still hot. (It helps to take bottom of can off with can opener; then you can just push the loaves out.) Traditionally served hot with Boston Baked Beans (see page 269).

BRAN MUFFINS

These are the old standby—serve them steaming hot with butter.

⅓ cup sunflower oil	1 teaspoon baking soda
½ cup honey	½ teaspoon salt
1 egg	1 cup bran
2 cups whole wheat pastry flour	1 cup buttermilk or yoghurt
1½ teaspoons baking powder	

Preheat oven to 400°F. Cream oil and brown sugar; add egg and beat well. Stir together flour, baking powder, baking soda, salt, and cereal, breaking up any lumps. Stir dry ingredients into first mixture, alternating with buttermilk until well blended. Coat a muffin tin with nonstick cooking spray and fill each with batter. Bake for 20 minutes. Makes 1 dozen.

EGGLESS BANANA MUFFINS

Occasionally our chickens stop laying, or I go on an egg-eating binge and run out just when I want to bake. This recipe can save the day in such a situation.

2½ cups whole wheat flour
½ teaspoon salt
1 teaspoon baking soda
2 teaspoons baking powder
⅓ cup powdered milk

¼ cup honey
3 mashed ripe bananas
2 tablespoons vegetable oil
1½ cups water

Preheat oven to 400°F. Stir together flour, salt, baking soda, baking powder, and powdered milk, pressing out any lumps. Cream together honey and bananas, stirring in oil and water and beating well. Add dry ingredients, stirring only until blended. Bake for 25 minutes in well-greased muffin tins.

BAKING POWDER BISCUITS

2 cups whole wheat flour
2 teaspoons baking powder
½ teaspoon salt

¼ cup salt butter
¾ cup milk*

Preheat oven to 300°F. Stir together flour, baking powder, and salt. Cut in butter, blending in with a fork until dough has the consistency of cornmeal. Add milk and stir well. Turn onto a floured board and pat lightly with floured hands until dough is ½ inch thick. Cut into rounds with a floured glass or a biscuit cutter. Place on a slightly greased baking sheet, close together for soft sides, 1 inch apart for crusty sides.

   Bake for 15–20 minutes. Makes 20 2-inch biscuits or 12 2½-inch ones.

*Sour cream, yoghurt, sour milk, or buttermilk may be substituted for the milk or a portion of it.

BIZCOCHOS

These Mexican Christmas cookies were introduced to me when we lived in New Mexico, and for years I searched for a recipe for them. This one is adapted from a collection of local favorites published by the Junior League of El Paso, and features the distinctive anise flavor which I remembered so well. Bizcochos were originally made with lard, but I find that shortening works just fine.

1 cup vegetable shortening
1 cup honey
1 tablespoon cinnamon
1 tablespoon nutmeg
1 tablespoon anise seeds,
    crushed in a mortar and pestle

1 cup sweet wine or fruit juice
2 egg yolks
3 cups whole wheat pastry flour

Preheat oven to 350°F. Cream shortening and sugar; add spices. Stir in wine and egg yolks and beat until creamy. Add flour to make into a soft, pliable dough. Roll out ½ inch thick on a floured board. Cut into various shapes and bake for 15 minutes. Check often to prevent burning. Dredge warm cookies in a sugar/cinnamon mixture.

FLUFFY SPICE CAKE

That's right, folks, a whole wheat spice cake. This is especially light if made with spelt flour.

2½ cups whole wheat pastry flour or spelt flour
3 teaspoons baking powder
1 teaspoon baking soda
1 teaspoon salt
1 teaspoon cinnamon

½ teaspoon nutmeg
½ cup oil
½ cup molasses
1 cup yoghurt
4 eggs, beaten
2 egg whites, beaten until stiff

Preheat oven to 350°F. Stir together flour, baking powder, baking soda, salt, and spices, breaking up any lumps. Beat eggs; add oil, molasses, and yoghurt and beat well. Fold in beaten egg whites. Make a well in flour mixture; pour in liquid, mixing only until well blended. Pour into springform pan; bake for 45 minutes. Cool slightly before removing from pan. Top with vanilla butter icing.

VANILLA BUTTER ICING

3 tablespoons butter
2 cups powdered sugar

1 teaspoon vanilla
1–2 tablespoons boiling water

Cream butter and powdered sugar together, pressing out any lumps. Beat until smooth and shiny. Stir in boiling water until smooth. Add vanilla and spread on cooled cake.

WHOLE WHEAT COFFEE CAKE

2 cups whole wheat pastry flour or
   spelt flour

3 teaspoons baking powder

1 teaspoon baking soda

1 teaspoon salt

1 teaspoon cinnamon

½ teaspoon nutmeg

½ cup powdered milk

½ cup chopped nuts

1 cup brown sugar

4 eggs

¾ cup vegetable oil

1 cup yoghurt or buttermilk

TOPPING

¼ cup melted butter

½ cup brown sugar

1 teaspoon cinnamon

1 tablespoon whole wheat flour

1 teaspoon grated lemon rind

¼ cup chopped nuts

1 tablespoon water

Preheat oven to 350°F. Stir together dry ingredients, breaking up all lumps. Beat eggs; add to dry ingredients. Stir in oil and yoghurt. Mixture should be moist enough to pour, but not thin. Add milk if necessary. Set aside.

Stir sugar into melted butter; add remaining ingredients and stir until smooth. Spread on bottom of 9-inch round or square cake pan. Pour cake batter over topping. Bake for 45 minutes. Cool slightly before removing and inverting.

WHOLE WHEAT CHOCOLATE CHIP COOKIES

Here we have a genuine whole wheat recipe for America's favorite; make them thin and crunchy or thick and softer. If you substitute ¼ cup powdered milk for ¼ cup of the flour, you can stop feeling guilty about eating these goodies and know you're getting some protein at the same time.

1½ cups brown sugar
1 cup margarine, butter, or vegetable oil
1 teaspoon vanilla
2 eggs
1 tablespoon molasses

2½ cups whole wheat flour
1½ teaspoons baking soda
1 teaspoon salt
1 12-ounce package chocolate chips
1 cup raisins

Preheat oven to 375°F. Cream sugar and margarine; add vanilla, eggs, and molasses and beat well. Stir together flour, baking soda, and salt, pressing out lumps. Stir into sugar mixture; add chocolate chips and raisins and blend. Add milk if you want a thinner batter. Drop by tablespoonfuls onto a lightly greased baking sheet. Bake for 10 minutes.

GRANOLA COOKIES

½ cup margarine, butter, or vegetable oil
1½ cups brown sugar
1 egg
1 teaspoon vanilla

1¼ cups whole wheat flour
1 teaspoon salt
½ teaspoon baking soda
3 cups granola (see p. 64)
¼ cup water

Preheat oven to 375°F. Cream margarine and brown sugar; beat in egg and vanilla. Stir together flour, salt, and baking soda, pressing out any lumps. Add to creamed mixture, stirring well. Blend in granola and water. Bake for 10–12 minutes.

PALACINKE

Palacinkes were introduced to me by the original editor of this book; this version was worked up especially for him. A rich, sinfully delicious dessert. Wherever you are, Paul, here's to you!

2 eggs, separated	2 tablespoons brandy or rum
½ cup milk	1 cup whole wheat flour
½ cup water	rum sauce (see below)
1 tablespoon honey	chocolate sauce (see below)
¼ teaspoon salt	½ cup finely chopped nuts

Combine egg yolks with milk, water, honey, salt, and brandy. Stir in flour only until blended. Beat egg whites until stiff; fold in. Heat a lightly greased 7- to 8-inch skillet. Pour in ¼ cup batter; tilt pan to spread evenly. Cook over medium heat until golden; turn carefully and cook on other side. Keep warm until all are baked. Spread each one with fruit preserves and fold into quarters. Spoon rum sauce and chocolate sauce over each palacinke and sprinkle with chopped nuts. Serve immediately.

RUM SAUCE	½ cup plain yoghurt
1 egg yolk	2 tablespoons brandy essence
½ cup powdered sugar	

Beat egg yolk until light; stir in sugar until dissolved. Add yoghurt and brandy essence; stir until smooth.

CHOCOLATE SAUCE	1 tablespoon cocoa powder
1 egg yolk	1 tablespoon boiling water
½ cup powdered sugar	¼ cup whipping cream

Beat egg yolk until light; stir in sugar until dissolved. Dissolve cocoa powder in boiling water; add to egg mixture. Beat whipping cream until stiff; fold into sauce. Stir until smooth.

BRANDY SNAPS

These traditional English holiday goodies go very well with cold milk or eggnog.

¼ cup butter	¼ cup whole wheat flour
2 tablespoons molasses or sorghum syrup	1 teaspoon brandy
	1 teaspoon ground ginger
¼ cup brown sugar	¼ teaspoon grated lemon rind

Preheat oven to 350°F. Melt butter, syrup, and sugar. Remove from heat and add flour, brandy, ginger, and lemon rind. Mix well and drop by teaspoonfuls onto a greased baking sheet. Space about 3 inches apart, as they spread. Bake for about 7 minutes, or until they are light brown and set. Allow to cool on baking sheet for 2 minutes, then loosen with a metal spatula. Remove and roll each one quickly around the handle of a wooden spoon to shape into cylinders. Cool before serving.

OATS

Oats. *A grain, which in England is gen-erally given to horses, but in Scotland supports the people.*
Dictionary of the English
Language (1755),
by Samuel Johnson

Oats are probably best known in the United States as animal food. As a matter of fact, the whole or cracked grain, when rolled, does make fine horse feed, and the straw is one of the best for both feed and fertilizer. But oats are also a fine human food, as the Scots have known for centuries.

This grain doesn't have as long a history as the other cereals; it was not mentioned in the Bible, and even in early Roman times was apparently thought of as just a weed that grew among the other grasses. Oats are thought to have developed around 2500 B.C. in northern Africa, the Near East, and the temperate areas of Russia, where they were first found growing in fields of barley. When it was finally realized that oats could be used to supplement barley and wheat, the legions of the Roman Empire began to carry them. Thus the seeds found their way to Europe and Britain. Being particularly well suited to the cool, wet areas of the British Isles, oats became a dietary staple in Scotland, Ireland, and the north of England. By the thirteenth century oats, known then as *pilcorn*, were a part of every Scot's daily fare, and Scotland is still a leading user of this cereal.

A sea captain took oats with him to the New World in 1602 and planted them on the Elizabeth Isles, off the coast of Massachusetts. The colonists quickly discovered that oats grew well in their coastal towns, and oatmeal porridge became a common breakfast there too. In Ireland the gruel, served for breakfast, was called *stirabout*; it was originally made by cooking the whole grains, called *groats*, for an hour or more in milk. The modern Scottish porridge, even when made from steel-cut or rolled oats, is also cooked a long time until quite creamy, but usually in salted water.

If you examine wild oats growing in nooks and crannies near your home, you will see that each grain is enclosed within two tough husks. Oats are milled by first removing these husks, a task made easier by cleaning, drying, and toasting to make the hulls more brittle. Once hulled, the inner grain or groat is scoured to remove some of its outer skin.

Oats may be purchased hulled from feed stores which cater to bird fanciers, or sometimes at natural food stores. An oat groat (the whole, hulled grain) is much softer than a wheat berry, as you can see if you press one between two fingernails. It can be easily smashed by pounding with a wooden mallet or rolled on a flat with a rolling pin. By breaking down the hull in this manner and exposing more surface to the outside, you can cook the smashed groat more quickly than in its original form. Commercially rolled oats, however, are just as nutritious as those prepared at home, and are so readily available that this exercise is not worth much of your time. I keep both whole oats (groats) and rolled oats on hand so that either is readily available for cooking.

Steel-cut oats, oats sliced thinly lengthwise with sharp blades, were first packaged in glass jars for the American market in 1854. Later they were packed and shipped to the local grocers in bulk, so they could be weighed locally and sold by the pound. The original rolled oats were quite thick, and were made by rolling whole groats. This is still the method for making old-fashioned oats, but today new forms of the cereal are also marketed: quick-cooking flakes and instant oatmeal. Quick-cooking flakes are thinner; they are rolled from groats cut into about three pieces. Instant oatmeal is made by pre-cooking the cut groats and rolling them superthin. All three forms have the same food value, although the latter is nearly always packaged with flavorings and sugar. Steel-cut oats and old-fashioned oats may be used in recipes calling for rolled oats, but if quick-cooking oats are specified, use that type or pound rolled oats in a mortar and pestle to break them into smaller pieces before substituting them.

Oats can be grown under many different conditions, being very adaptive, so are a good bet for home farmers. There are both winter and spring varieties, as with wheat, although fall and winter plantings are limited to those areas where winters are mild. Spring oats should be sown as early as possible, as they require cool weather and lots of moisture to develop well. As with barley, a soil too rich in nitrogen produces weak-stemmed plants that lodge (fall over), and for that reason they should not follow legumes (peas, beans, peanuts) in rotation, as those plants tend to enrich the soil with nitrogen. Oats usually need no fertilizer if they are rotated with corn, wheat, and clover, but it would be a good idea to have a soil sample analyzed by your local agricultural agent to be sure.

The amount of seed you can sow depends on the anticipated rainfall in your area. The more rain, the more plants that can be supported. Since seeding varies from four to fifteen pecks per acre, it would be smart to contact local farmers and get their advice. The type of seed you plant should also be determined by asking around to see what has been successful in your locality.

Hull-less varieties of oats exist, although since they have never been successful commercially, they may be hard to find. Three such varieties are James, Liberty, and Nakota, although new research may have developed others with higher yields. Contact seed dealers and feed companies for up-to-date information.

Harvest and thresh your oat crop as you would wheat (see Wheat section), and store the winnowed groats in a cool dry place, free from bugs and rodents.

You can use whole groats in many ways. Sprinkle a quarter of a cup into a pot of soup, or soak some overnight and add them to bread dough. Cook oats slowly in soup stock to make kasha, or boil them in milk the night before and reheat the next morning for a delicious porridge.

Grinding the groats in a grain mill or food processor yields a substance generally called oat flour, but which might be better named oat flakes. The grain is so soft that in going through the mill it mushes and slips from between the stones as a soft substance more like instant mashed potatoes than the powder we usually think of as flour. This may be added to breads and other yeast doughs for added nutrition, flavor, and keeping quality, but because oats have very little gluten content, be sure to use sufficient wheat flour and develop the gluten by kneading the dough thoroughly to provide the cell walls that form the bread's structure. One cup of oat flour to four cups of whole wheat flour is about the right proportion.

Oat groats tend to clog a grinding stone, and two grindings with a steel blade will provide fine flour with less effort to the arm. If you must use a stone mill, take one reverse turn with the crank for every three to four forward turns. This provides a cleaning action in the grooves of the stones.

People who have difficulty digesting whole wheat products or who are allergic to wheat may discover that baked goods made entirely from oat flour (or barley flour, for that matter) are easier to digest and cause no allergic reactions. Babies who are beginning their exploration of solid foods will have little or no difficulty digesting instant oatmeal made by mixing warm milk with oat flour. Oats in any form sweeten a dough, so use honey and sugar cautiously in any oat mixture until you discover the right amount for your taste.

BASIC OAT GROATS

Cooked oat groats can be incorporated into many of your own recipes, or substituted for oatmeal in others. You can also serve cooked oats as a breakfast cereal or as a side dish, like rice.

    1 cup whole oat groats   1 teaspoon salt
    2 cups water, milk, or stock

Combine ingredients in a heavy pan with a tight cover and cook slowly, 45 minutes to 1 hour. If you use a double boiler, cooking takes somewhat longer, but you reduce to nearly zero the chance that your oats will stick and burn at the bottom. Stir occasionally, either way.

SPROUTED OATS

Any whole grain can be sprouted, but oats seem to be the easiest because they germinate quickly. After learning the technique, however, you might want to try wheat and rye also.

Wash thoroughly 2 tablespoons of oat groats. Place in a jar (a wide-mouth 1-quart canning jar works well) and cover with water; leave for 8–10 hours. Drain off liquid (it contains many valuable vitamins; drink it or add it to soup), rinse groats and drain. Placing a piece of clean window screen or unbleached muslin over the mouth of the jar and fastening it with the canning rim is my way of draining.

Put the jar where it will be dark and slightly cool; rinse groats 2 or 3 times a day. After about 2 days, when the main sprout is ¼-inch long, place the jar in sunlight for 3 or 4 hours so that the chlorophyll can develop, increasing the vitamin C content of your sprouts. Rinse sprouts thoroughly, drain, and place in a covered container in the refrigerator.

Sprouts should be used within a week. They are delicious in sandwiches and salads, may be chopped in a food mill or meat grinder and added to bread dough, and they add vitamins to soup and stir-fried vegetable combinations.

SCOTS OATMEAL

The oatmeal I have eaten in Scotland has a unique creamy texture which is obtained by soaking steel-cut oats overnight and then cooking them for several hours. This method is a bit faster, but just as good.

3 cups water
1 teaspoon salt

1 cup steel-cut oats

Place ingredients in the top of a double boiler; bring to a boil over direct heat. Remove from heat, cool, and place in refrigerator overnight. The next morning, bring water in saucepan to boil and cook oatmeal over it, covered, for 30 minutes, stirring occasionally. Serve with milk and honey.

NONSTICK OATMEAL

The secret is out, and for all of you who hate gummy porridge I predict many enjoyable bowls of this nicely textured oatmeal.

1½ cups water
1 teaspoon salt

½ cup raisins
1 cup old fashioned (rolled) oats

Bring water, salt, and raisins to a boil. Add oats. Stir once to moisten oats, cover tightly, and remove pan from heat. Allow to sit for 3–5 minutes. Serve with milk and honey.

GRANOLA

Homemade granola was popular among our college crowd long before commercial "natural" cereals became available. I still prefer it to the more expensive mass-produced ones. Use my recipe as a basis, then add or subtract ingredients until you find the combination you like best.

6 cups rolled oats	¼ cup vegetable oil
1 cup shredded coconut	½ cup honey
1 cup wheat germ	½ cup water
½ cup sunflower seeds	1½ teaspoons salt
¼ cup sesame seeds	1 teaspoon vanilla
¼ cup finely chopped nuts	1 cup raisins

Preheat oven to 350°F. Combine oats, coconut, wheat germ, seeds, and nuts in a large bowl. In another container, mix together oil, honey, water, salt, and vanilla. Pour over grains, stirring thoroughly. Spread mixture thinly on cookie sheets, and bake for 25–30 minutes, stirring frequently. Oats should be crisp and brown, but coconut should not be burned. Allow to cool thoroughly, then add raisins and place in an airtight container for storage.

Serve with milk for breakfast or snacks.

OAT FLOUR PANCAKES

1 cup oat flour	1 beaten egg
1 teaspoon baking powder	½ cup yoghurt or sour cream
½ teaspoon baking soda	½ cup milk
½ teaspoon salt	

Stir together dry ingredients, pressing out lumps. Blend egg, yoghurt, and milk together, beating well. Add to dry ingredients and mix well. Drop by tablespoonfuls onto a hot greased griddle. Turn once and serve hot with butter and honey or syrup.

VARIATIONS: Separating the egg and adding the beaten egg white last makes a fluffier, lighter pancake. Heating the flour, milk, and yoghurt together slowly before adding other ingredients makes a smoother, creamier pancake. Also try adding chopped nuts to the batter, or pieces of fresh fruit, especially berries.

OAT BLINTZES

3 cups milk
1 cup oat flour
½ teaspoon salt
1 tablespoon brown sugar

3 eggs
dash freshly ground nutmeg
ricotta or cottage cheese

Add milk to the oat flour in a saucepan. Heat slowly, stirring constantly, and cook until creamy and somewhat thickened. Cool. Separate eggs, combining yolks with salt, sugar, and a dash of freshly ground nutmeg. Add to cooled milk mixture. Beat egg whites until stiff but not dry and fold into batter. Fry by large spoonfuls on a hot greased griddle. Place 1 tablespoon ricotta or cottage cheese in center of each blintz and roll. Serve hot with fruit syrup.

OAT FLOUR MUFFINS

1 cup oat flour
1 teaspoon baking powder
½ teaspoon salt
1 teaspoon baking soda
1 tablespoon honey

½ cup raisins, chopped dates, or
   chopped nuts
1 tablespoon vegetable oil
⅓ cup yoghurt or buttermilk
1 egg, beaten

Preheat oven to 425°F. Stir together dry ingredients, pressing out any lumps. Mix liquids and fruit together and add to dry mixture, stirring lightly. Pour into 6 greased muffin tins and bake for 15–20 minutes.

BANANA OAT MUFFINS

2 cups rolled oats, ground into flour
   in a blender or food processor
2 teaspoons baking powder
½ teaspoon salt
1–2 very ripe bananas, mashed
1 egg

2 tablespoons dark molasses
2 tablespoons canola or sunflower oil
½–1 cup orange or apple juice
½ cup chopped dried fruit
¼ cup sesame meal, optional

Preheat oven to 375°F. Stir together oat flour, baking powder, and salt. Set aside. Combine bananas, egg, molasses, oil, and about ½ cup of juice. (I use my blender for this.) Stir into flour mixture; add fruit and blend. Add more juice, if necessary, to obtain a muffin batter that will spoon nicely into a tin. It should almost pour, but not quite. Bake for 20 minutes or until a tester comes out clean. Makes about 12 muffins.

COOKED OATMEAL MUFFINS

2 cups whole wheat flour
4 teaspoons baking powder
½ teaspoon salt
1 cup leftover oatmeal

½ cup milk
2 eggs
2 tablespoons honey
3 tablespoons vegetable oil

Preheat oven to 400°F. Stir together flour, baking powder, and salt, breaking up any lumps. Thin oatmeal with milk in large bowl. Beat eggs and add to oatmeal mixture; stir in honey and oil and beat well. Stir in dry ingredients, blending thoroughly. Pour into greased muffin tins and bake for 25 minutes. Makes 1 dozen.

SCOTTISH OATCAKES

Oatcakes are the scones of Scotland. Eaten at every meal, they are best still hot from the griddle, split with a fork and spread with fresh butter. Some versions are made with rolled oats, some with oat flour. Experiment until you find the texture you like best.

1¼ cups oat flour	1 egg, beaten
¼ teaspoon baking soda	1 tablespoon vegetable oil
¼ teaspoon salt	¼ cup water

Mix dry ingredients, then add liquids. Add water or flour as necessary to obtain a dough that can be rolled out on a floured board. Roll to a ¼-inch thickness, cut into rounds with a biscuit cutter or a floured glass rim, and fry on a well-greased griddle (called a *girdle* in Scotland), fairly hot, for 5 minutes. Turn and fry on the other side until brown.

YORKSHIRE OATCAKES

While Scotland is typically thought of as the land of the oats, south of the English border in Yorkshire oats have also been used as a staple for centuries. Here is an old recipe from my hometown of Bradford.

1 teaspoon honey	¼ cup oat flour
1 tablespoon active dry yeast	½ teaspoon salt
2 cups lukewarm milk or buttermilk	1 cup quick-cooking oats

Dissolve honey and yeast in lukewarm milk. Stir in flour, salt, and oats. Stir gently and leave to stand in a warm place for 30 minutes. Stir again and cook like a large pancake on a griddle or in a large heavy skillet. Eat while still warm.

VERMONT OATCAKES

Oatcakes were probably carried in ship stores when the colonists traveled across the Atlantic Ocean. In any case, they became a common sight in country kitchens all up and down the colonial coast. This version is sweeter than any I have eaten in Scotland.

½ cup soft butter
2 cups oat flour
⅓ cup cream or half-and-half

4 teaspoons maple syrup
½ teaspoon salt
About 2 teaspoons additional butter

Preheat oven to 325°F. Cut butter into flour with a fork or 2 knives. Mix cream, maple syrup, and salt together, then add gradually to flour and butter. Press into 2 well-greased 8-inch square cake pans and mark into 9 squares each. Dot each square with ¼ teaspoon butter. Bake for 25 minutes. Cool completely before cutting.

OATMEAL BREAD

This is a sweet bread, especially good toasted.

2 tablespoons yeast
3½ cups milk
½ cup honey
2 cups rolled oats
1 tablespoon salt

½ teaspoon cinnamon
¼ cup vegetable oil or butter
6 cups whole wheat flour
½ cup chopped nuts
1 cup raisins

Soften yeast in ½ cup milk to which 1 teaspoon of the honey has been added. Add remaining 3 cups milk to oats, mix well, and blend in salt, the rest of the honey, and oil. Combine with yeast mixture and stir in half the flour and the nuts and raisins.

Add remaining flour gradually, working in with your hands when the dough becomes too stiff to stir. Knead thoroughly, until dough becomes smooth and elastic. Cover with damp cloth and let rise 1 hour in an oiled bowl. Punch down and put into 2 bread pans. Let rise until dough is slightly above the top of the pans. Preheat oven to 325°F. Bake for 1 hour. Remove from pans and let cool before slicing.

OAT FLOUR BREAD

2 tablespoons yeast	¼ cup butter
3 cups lukewarm water	1 egg, slightly beaten
½ cup honey	2 cups oat flour
1 tablespoon salt	6 cups whole wheat flour

Dissolve yeast in ½ cup water in which 1 teaspoon of the honey has been dissolved. Combine the rest of the water and honey with salt, butter, and beaten egg; add yeast mixture and 4 cups whole wheat flour. Beat vigorously 300–400 strokes to develop the gluten, then add oat flour and remaining wheat flour, kneading when dough becomes too stiff to stir.

Knead thoroughly, place dough in an oiled bowl, cover with a damp cloth, and let rise for about 1 hour. Punch down and let rise again, 30–45 minutes. Shape into 3 small loaves or 2 large ones and let rise until the dough is slightly above the tops of the bread pans, or has nearly doubled in bulk. Preheat oven to 325°F. Bake for 1 hour. Remove from pans while still hot, but cool before slicing.

RAISIN OATMEAL BREAD

4 tablespoons vegetable oil

2 cups milk

2 tablespoons honey

2 teaspoons salt

2 tablespoons active dry yeast

¼ cup warm water

5½–6 cups whole wheat flour

2 cups rolled oats

1 cup raisins

Combine oil, milk, honey, and salt in saucepan. Heat to lukewarm. Dissolve yeast in warm water; add to cooled liquid. Stir in 3 cups flour and beat well to develop gluten. Stir in oatmeal and raisins and as much flour as can be incorporated in the bowl, then turn out on board and knead in enough flour to make a workable dough. Knead thoroughly, until dough is smooth and elastic. Place in oiled bowl, cover with a cloth, and allow to rise in warm place about 1 hour. Punch down; form 2 loaves. Allow to rise another hour, or until dough has doubled. Preheat oven to 375°F. Bake for 45 minutes. Remove from pans and allow to cool before slicing.

OAT KASHA

Kasha is a mush made from whole or coarsely ground grains and is served as an accompaniment to meat meals in East European countries. Buckwheat groats and cracked rye are most popular, but oats make a very nice kasha, too.

1 cup whole oat groats

1 tablespoon vegetable oil

2 cups hot water or stock

½ teaspoon salt

Sauté oats in oil over medium heat until separated and slightly dry. Add water to pan, cover tightly, and cook over low heat for 20–30 minutes, or until tender. (Or bring to a boil, remove from heat, and leave for several hours, reheating just before serving and cooking for 10–15 minutes.)

Kasha can be used as the basis for a complete meal with the addition of nuts, cheese, and a variety of vegetables—onions, mushrooms, green peppers, chopped celery, sliced carrots—look in your larder and see what you have. One of my favorite additions to oat kasha is diced celery root. Leftover oat groats can be sautéed in butter, or added to other dishes.

CHEESE BANNOCKS

These are a favorite teatime snack in Scotland and the north of England. Serve them hot with a cup of tea if you want to be authentic.

1 cup quick-cooking oats	¼ cup butter, softened
1 cup oat flour	1 cup grated sharp cheddar cheese
¼ teaspoon salt	½ cup warm water

Preheat oven to 400°F. Stir together oatmeal, flour, and salt. Cut in butter with a fork, then stir in cheese. Add water and mix, kneading when dough becomes too stiff to stir. Divide dough into 2 parts and roll into circles, ¼ inch thick. Cut each circle into 4 wedges (or farls) and bake on a lightly greased baking sheet for 20 minutes. Makes 8 bannocks.

OAT GROAT STUFFING

vegetable oil for frying	¼ teaspoon thyme
6 cups cooked oat groats	1 teaspoon salt
2 cups finely chopped celery tops	¼ teaspoon pepper
1 medium onion, finely chopped	½ cup melted butter
2 tablespoons finely chopped parsley	

Sauté oats in oil until browned. Combine in a bowl with celery tops, onion, parsley, and seasonings. Mix thoroughly. Stir in melted butter and blended. Makes about 8 cups stuffing.

GOURMET MEAT LOAF

1 cup cooked oat groats

1 medium onion, coarsely chopped

1 tablespoon vegetable oil

½ cup chopped celery

1 egg

1 pound ground beef or turkey

1 tablespoon chopped parsley

1 teaspoon thyme

1 teaspoon basil

1 teaspoon salt

Preheat oven to 325°F. Sauté oats and onion 5 minutes in 1 tablespoon oil. Add celery and cook until tender. Beat egg; combine with other ingredients. Form into a loaf and place on baking sheet. Bake for 1 hour. Cool slightly before slicing to serve.

OAT SOUFFLÉ

½ cup oat flour

1 cup milk

½ cup grated cheddar cheese

1 cup water or stock

¼ teaspoon ground cloves

3 eggs, separated

Preheat oven to 350°F. Stir together oat flour and milk over boiling water. When well blended, stir in grated cheese and stock. Add cloves and cook 20 minutes, or until smooth and creamy. Cool slightly.

Add some of the cooled liquid to beaten egg yolks, return egg-yolk mixture to pan and blend well. Beat egg whites until quite stiff and fold in. Bake soufflés in oiled custard cups for 30 minutes. Serve immediately.

YORKSHIRE PARKIN

You may notice that I'm slipping in a few of my family's Yorkshire favorites. Here's another. Parkin is a dryish, cakelike gingerbread, usually eaten at teatime, and a particular favorite on Guy Fawkes Day. The English version uses black treacle. I have substituted molasses.

¾ cup brown sugar

½ cup butter

1 cup dark molasses

1 egg

2 cups milk

2½ cups rolled oats

1½ cups whole wheat flour

1 teaspoon ground ginger

1 teaspoon baking soda

Preheat oven to 350°F. Melt sugar, butter, and molasses over low heat. Beat egg well, blend with 1 cup of the milk, and add to molasses mixture. Combine oatmeal, flour, and ginger in a large bowl and stir in molasses mixture. Beat well, then add remaining milk in which baking soda has been dissolved. Stir until blended, then pour into a well-greased 9 × 14-inch baking pan. Bake for 1 hour. Cool slightly and cut into squares.

VARIATION: Replace butter with ¼ cup vegetable oil, 1 cup applesauce, and use only 1 cup milk.

OAT WAFERS

1 cup oat flour

½ cup whole wheat flour

½ teaspoon salt

2 tablespoons brown sugar

¼ teaspoon baking soda

¼ cup vegetable oil

⅓ cup boiling water

Preheat oven to 425°F. Mix dry ingredients together, pressing out any lumps. Melt butter in the boiling water and combine the mixtures. Roll or press out on a well-greased cookie sheet to ⅛ inch thickness; cut into 1-inch squares. Bake for 10–12 minutes, or until slightly brown and crisp.

WHITE PUDDINGS

From a colonial cookbook:

Take 3 pintes of milke and when it is boyled put in two quarts of great oatmeal bruised a little, and stirr it over the fire till it be ready to boyle then take it off and cover it close all night, 3 pound of suet minced small put in with 3 grated nutmeggs, and youlks of 8 eggs, 2 whites and a little rose-water, a pound of sugar and a little grated bread, currants and creame as you think fit, this quantity will make 3 or 4 dozin.

A fine pudding can be made by substituting oat groats in a recipe for rice pudding, adding milk or cream as necessary, and extending the cooking time by half.

OATMEAL CANDY

7 cups brown sugar	3 teaspoons grated fresh ginger
1 cup molasses	3 cups rolled oats
3 cups water	

Cook sugar, molasses, and water together in a large heavy pan until the syrup forms a hard ball if dropped in cold water (260°F. on a candy thermometer). Remove from stove; stir in ginger and oats, blending well. Pour into greased pans. Cool and mark into squares. Cut before completely cold.

APPLE OAT CRUMBLE

4 tart apples, peeled and sliced

2 tablespoons lemon juice

¼ teaspoon cinnamon

¼ cup butter

⅓ cup packed brown sugar

1 tablespoon water

⅓ cup whole wheat or oat flour

¼ teaspoon salt

⅔ cup rolled oats

Preheat oven to 325°F. Butter a shallow 1-quart baking dish. Place apples in dish; sprinkle with lemon juice and cinnamon. Melt butter; stir together butter, sugar, flour, water, salt, and oats. Sprinkle over apples. Bake for 45 minutes. Makes 4 servings.

OLD-FASHIONED OATMEAL COOKIES

1½ cups whole wheat flour

1 cup oat flour

1 teaspoon baking soda

½ teaspoon salt

1 cup brown sugar

2 eggs, slightly beaten

1 cup melted butter

1 teaspoon vanilla

2 cups rolled oats

1 cup combined raisins and chopped nuts

Preheat oven to 375°F. Stir dry ingredients, making sure there are no lumps in the baking soda. Add eggs, butter, and vanilla; beat until smooth and creamy. Stir in oats, raisins, and nuts. Drop by teaspoonfuls onto greased cookie sheets. Bake for 15–20 minutes or until browned. Makes 3–4 dozen.

SOFT OATMEAL COOKIES

Just as there is a schism between creamy and crunchy peanut butter fans, so to between those who like their oatmeal cookies soft and those who like them crunchy. I happen to be a soft cookie freak, and this is *my* recipe. Everyone else around here seems to prefer crisp cookies; if you do, too, try the Old-Fashioned Oatmeal Cookies.

1 egg	½ teaspoon salt
½ cup melted butter	½ teaspoon cinnamon
½ cup honey	1½ cups rolled oats
1 cup wheat or oat flour	½ cup chopped nuts
½ teaspoon baking soda	

Preheat oven to 325°F. Beat egg; add other liquid ingredients and blend thoroughly. Stir dry ingredients together, making certain there are no lumps. Add to liquid mixture and mix well; stir in oats and nuts. Drop by teaspoonfuls onto a greased cookie sheet. Bake for 15–20 minutes. Makes about 2 dozen cookies.

BANANA OATMEAL COOKIES

When I was teaching elementary school, my second grade class made these cookies for a school open house and they were proclaimed excellent. If children raised on refined sugar and white flour enjoy them, they're worth recording!

½ cup nuts	1¾ cups rolled oats
½ cup honey	1½ cups whole wheat flour
½ cup vegetable oil	1 teaspoon salt
1 egg	¼ teaspoon ground nutmeg
2 large bananas	¾ teaspoon cinnamon

Preheat oven to 375°F. Grind nuts or chop them finely. Mix honey, oil, egg, and bananas. Add to the nuts and mix well. Stir together flour, salt, and spices.

Combine with the rest of the ingredients to make a relatively stiff batter. If too thick to spoon out easily, add a few teaspoonfuls of fruit juice; if too thin, add more flour.

Drop by teaspoonfuls onto a lightly oiled cookie sheet. Bake for about 15 minutes. Makes about 4 dozen cookies.

OATMEAL MACAROONS

¼ teaspoon salt
1 egg white
1 cup sugar

1 cup rolled oats
¼ cup grated coconut
½ teaspoon vanilla

Preheat oven to 350°F. Add salt to egg white and beat until stiff. Add sugar gradually, beating constantly. Fold in rolled oats, coconut, and vanilla, mixing well. Drop from the tip of a teaspoon to an oiled baking sheet. Bake for 10 to 12 minutes. Makes about 24 macaroons.

RYE

Sow wheat in dirt and rye in dust.
—Dr. Thomas Fuller's *Gnomologia,* 1732

Rye is a fairly recent member of the cultivated cereal family. The Egyptians did not grow rye, nor did the Sumerians, and it was only a weed to the Greeks. Pliny wrote about rye at the end of the Christian period, by which time the Romans had begun cultivating wild rye and harvesting its seed.

Rye in its present form was widely distributed throughout Europe during the Middle Ages and taken to Britain by the Saxons in A.D. 500. The basic bread of medieval Britain, and probably in continental Europe also, consisted of coarsely ground rye and pea flours, sometimes with a little barley flour mixed in. For several hundred years, rye was the major bread grain throughout Europe. Today Eastern Europe is the heaviest producer and user of this grain. Rye gained favor in Russia because it was able to tolerate the severe climate better than other grains. Large chunks of coarse black bread are still a common sight at Russian tables, where they are traditionally accompanied by *kvass*, a slightly alcoholic drink made from fermented rye. Rye eventually worked its way north into the Scandinavian countries, where it was made into a lighter, aromatic bread sweetened with honey instead of molasses.

Dutch settlers took rye with them to America and by 1850 many acres in Pennsylvania, New York, New Jersey, and Maryland were earmarked for its production. Today the Pennsylvania Dutch, descendants of German families, still serve rye frequently with their meals. The popularity of rye spread throughout the West as the frontier was pushed to the sea, but not necessarily because the pioneers thought so highly of black bread. Rye whiskey has always been one of the largest uses for this grain in America, even when a slice of bread would perhaps have quieted a noisy belly more effectively. It was distilled mostly by Irish and Scottish settlers, who probably discovered that the spirits were easier to transport and sell than the grain from which they were produced.

Rye isn't a very important crop commercially, if you compare its world production figures with those for a wheat, but it is important agriculturally because it grows where other grains won't—where it is too cold or too wet— and also because many people still prefer its dark, rich flavor to that of wheat or oats. You might include rye in your family's diet for much the same reasons. It costs about the same as wheat, it provides a change from other grains, and it tastes good. Rye has a low gluten content, which means that bread made from it will be heavier, will rise less, and will fill you up faster, Baked goods that do not rely upon yeast for their rising, however, such as cookies, cakes, or dumplings, can be made quite satisfactorily from rye flour. Try substituting it in a whole wheat recipe, or even one which calls for white flour (you might need a little bit more baking powder or baking soda in that case), and see how you like it.

Rye flour is often available in large grocery stores, and nearly always can be found in natural food outlets. Cracked rye and rye groats (whole grain rye) may be more difficult to locate, but it is worth the effort to have a supply of the whole grain at home so you can crack it or grind it into fresh flour whenever you want it. I buy my rye from a large natural foods store; feed stores will often carry it, and you can always inquire of the companies listed in the Sources section if you have difficulty finding a distributor.

You can also grow rye fairly easily. It will grow in nearly every type of soil and needs less rain than do wheat or oats. Planting, cultivating, and harvesting rye is done just like wheat, so consult that section for specifics. As with all other grains, some varieties grow better in one area than another, so check with local farmers or your agricultural extension agent before buying seed. Most rye is planted in the fall, often in the fields which were used first for corn, but if you have lots of water available, spring rye may be more practical for you. Rye and wheat used to be sown together in the same fields, probably because early farmers couldn't successfully eliminate the rye. Rye tends to mature somewhat earlier than wheat, but not early enough to make it possible to harvest the two grains separately. If you plant winter rye, make sure it's in the ground early enough to get well established before the cold weather sets in. Rye planted in August or September will ripen the following June or July.

Rye is subject to a particularly virulent fungus called ergot. This disease causes the developing grains to become large purplish or black masses which contain several highly toxic poisons. If the rye is badly affected, eating bread made from it can lead to a very painful death; mysterious epidemics in medieval Europe have recently been attributed to ergotism. All of which is to say, look closely at your grain before you harvest it. Walk in the fields and learn what developing rye looks like. If you have any doubts, take some grain samples to an agricultural extension agent for testing.

Rye is very soft, and like oats tends to clog a stone grinder. We generally use our steel-bladed mill and run the grain through twice for flour. Cracked rye makes a delicious breakfast cereal; it can also be combined with cracked wheat or oats for variety. Commercially marketed rye flour is often labeled "light" or "dark"; light has been bolted (sifted) and contains less bran. (In the U.S. almost any dark bread in which unbolted rye flour is a major ingredient goes under the name "pumpernickel," whether or not it bears much resemblance to its crumbly German cousin.) If you grind your own rye flour it will automatically be "dark," although its actual color is determined by the variety of rye you grow or purchase. Rolled rye is available in some health food stores, and makes an interesting change from rolled oats in cereal, meat loaf, or casseroles.

Store rye, as any grain, in a cool place, free from moisture and rodents. If protected from bugs and varmints, rye should keep for two or three years.

BASIC WHOLE RYE

1 cup rye groats   1 teaspoon salt
3 cups water

Bring ingredients to a boil, cover, and lower heat. Simmer until tender, about 45 minutes to 1 hour. Cooking time will be shortened if groats have been soaked overnight.

BREAKFAST RYE

2 cups water or milk   ½ cup raisins
1 cup finely cracked rye (sift out   1 teaspoon salt
   flour)

Bring liquid to a boil over medium heat; add rye, raisins, and salt; cover and reduce heat. Simmer for 15–20 minutes. Serve with milk and honey.

Leftover breakfast rye can be spooned onto a hot greased griddle, flattened, and fried like fritters. Good with sausages.

CREAM OF RYE

For those mushy cereal lovers, here's a homemade version of this favorite breakfast dish.

Pop 1–2 cups of rye groats as you would popcorn. Coarsely grind the resulting puffed grain. Bring to a boil 4 cups of milk for each cup of cracked grain; stir in 1 teaspoon salt. Gradually pour in cracked grains, stirring constantly to prevent lumps. Cook over low heat, stirring frequently to prevent sticking, until cereal thickens and absorbs all the water, about 10 minutes. Serve immediately (before it turns into glue) with milk and honey.

RYE PANCAKES

This is just a basic recipe; after you've tried it once, be imaginative and play around with it. Sometimes we add an extra egg, or thin it with more liquid, roll the pancakes after spreading with currant jelly, or sprinkle them with powdered sugar. Or you can eat them stacked like ordinary American pancakes—they're good that way, too.

1¼ cups rye flour	1 tablespoon honey
2 cups buttermilk	1 teaspoon baking soda
1 egg, beaten	1 teaspoon salt

Combine flour, buttermilk, and egg. Stir in honey and beat well. In a cup, stir together salt and baking soda, pressing out any lumps. Sprinkle over batter, then fold in gently but evenly. Bake pancakes on lightly greased hot griddle. Serve immediately; these are very light and do not keep well.

SCHWARZBROT

Rye flour is low in gluten, and breads made with all-rye flour will be heavier and more compact than those made with whole wheat or refined white flours. The classic German black bread was made with part rye flour and part coarser rye meal, and was risen with homemade yeast grown on potatoes. This recipe incorporates the old flavor with somewhat more modern ingredients. Make sure your flour is at least room temperature, do not sift it, and do not let the dough over-rise. When the bread is baked, slice it thinly, spread with a little fresh butter, and prepare your taste buds for a treat.

STARTER

1 quart water in which potatoes have been cooked, cooled to lukewarm	2 tablespoons yeast
	3 cups rye flour

Combine in large bowl, cover, and leave for 8–48 hours.

DOUGH

2 cups mashed potatoes	5–6 cups rye flour
1 teaspoon salt	
¼ cup malt syrup (see p. 45) or dark molasses	

When ready to bake, add potatoes, salt, and malt syrup to starter mixture. Mix well. Stir in flour until dough is too stiff to stir. Knead in the last of the flour on a floured board, incorporating only enough to have a smooth, workable dough. Knead well, until dough is smooth and elastic. Cover with a damp cloth and let rise 1 hour. Make into 2 medium or 3 small loaves, cover with a damp cloth, and let rise 30 minutes. Preheat oven to 350°F. Bake for 1 hour with a pan of water in the bottom of the oven (this crisps the crust). Turn out on a rack to cool.

BLACK RYE BREAD (BREAD MACHINE)

This traditional European bread recipe has been developed for use in a bread machine. Place the ingredients in your machine according to the instructions; usually that will mean placing the dry ingredients in first, then making a well in them for the liquids. This recipe makes a 1½-pound loaf. To adapt other recipes for your bread machine, see page 8.

1⅛ cups water
1½ tablespoons vegetable oil
¼ cup molasses
2 cups whole wheat flour
1 cup rye flour
1 teaspoon salt

3 tablespoons unsweetened cocoa
   powder
1 tablespoon brown sugar
1 teaspoon instant coffee
3 tablespoons vital gluten
2 teaspoons active dry yeast

SOUR MILK RYE BREAD

2 cups sour milk
2 tablespoons molasses
2 tablespoons butter
1 tablespoon salt

1 tablespoon yeast
¼ cup lukewarm water
3 cups whole wheat flour
3 cups rye flour

Heat sour milk, molasses, butter, and salt together in a saucepan until butter melts. Pour into a large bowl and cool to lukewarm. Dissolve yeast in ¼ cup lukewarm water (in the same cup used to measure the molasses). Add to milk mixture when it has cooled Stir in whole wheat flour; beat well, 300 strokes. Let batter stand, covered, 1 hour. Stir in rye flour, kneading when dough becomes too stiff to stir. Knead dough well, until smooth and pliable. Form into 2 loaves. Cover with a damp cloth and let rise 1 hour. Preheat oven to 350°F. Bake for 1 hour. Remove from tins or baking sheet and cool on a rack.

GERMAN PUMPERNICKEL BREAD

2 tablespoons yeast	1 tablespoon salt
1¾ cups lukewarm water	2 cups rye meal
3½ cups rye flour	about ¼ cup cornmeal

Dissolve 1 tablespoon yeast in ½ cup warm water. Stir in ½ cup rye flour. Leave overnight.

The next morning, add 1 cup warm water and 1 cup rye flour. Leave 4 hours more. Then add 1 tablespoon yeast dissolved in ¼ cup lukewarm water, salt, rye meal, and 2 cups rye flour. Mix together until the dough leaves the sides of the bowl. Knead thoroughly. Place in bowl, cover, and leave in warm place to rise for 1 hour. Form into 2 loaves, placed on a greased baking sheet which has been sprinkled with cornmeal; cover with a damp cloth, and let rise 30 minutes more. Preheat oven to 350°F. Bake for 1½ hours. Cool before slicing.

SWEDISH RYE BREAD

This is a lighter-colored and lighter-textured loaf than the other rye breads, good for sandwiches.

2 cups water	1 tablespoon crushed fennel seed
½ cup honey	2 tablespoons yeast
2 tablespoons butter	¼ cup lukewarm water
1 tablespoon salt	2 cups rye flour
2 tablespoons grated orange peel	4–5 cups all-purpose white flour
2 tablespoons crushed whole anise seed	

Heat water, honey, butter, and salt until butter melts. Pour into a large bowl and cool to lukewarm. Stir in orange peel, anise, and fennel. Dissolve yeast in lukewarm water (use the same cup used to measure the honey to speed the action of the yeast). When honey mixture has cooled, add yeast mixture. Stir in rye flour and 2 cups all-purpose flour. Beat vigorously, 300 strokes. Add remaining flour until dough can be worked with the hands. Turn onto a floured board and knead thoroughly. Form into 2 loaves and place in oiled bread pans. Let rise until bread is slightly above the tops of the bread pans. Preheat oven to 375°F. Bake for 40–45 minutes, or until golden brown and hollow-sounding when rapped. Remove from tins and cool on a rack.

RYE BAGELS

These are a little heavier than the whole wheat ones, but even more chewy. Bagels are often served with cream cheese and lox.

1¼ cups boiling water	2 tablespoons yeast
½ cup sour milk	¼ cup lukewarm water
3 tablespoons honey	2 cups rye flour
2 tablespoons salt	2–3 cups whole wheat flour

Combine boiling water, sour milk, honey, and 1 tablespoon salt. Cool to luke-warm. Dissolve yeast in ¼ cup lukewarm water; add to above. Stir in rye flour and beat well. Add remaining flour until you have a stiff but workable dough. Knead thoroughly. Shape into 12 balls. Poke a hole in the middle of each ball, pull gently to enlarge it, and work it into a doughnut shape. Place bagels on cookie sheet or baking cloth, cover, and let rise 30 minutes.

Preheat oven to 375°F. In a large kettle, combine 1 gallon water and 1 tablespoon salt. Bring to a boil. Boil bagels, 4 or 5 at a time, for 7 minutes, turning once with a slotted spoon. Place on ungreased cookie sheet. Bake for 30–35 minutes.

VARIATION: Poppy seeds can be pressed into these bagels just before baking.

CRACKED RYE KASHA

This is a very basic kasha. Add to it whatever you happen to have in your larder—mushrooms, celery, onions, green pepper, tomatoes.

1 tablespoon butter or margarine	3 cups stock (beef, chicken,
1 cup coarsely cracked rye	vegetable, whatever)
1 teaspoon salt	

Melt butter in a large, heavy skillet. Sauté rye in hot butter until slightly browned. Lower heat, add salt and stock, cover, and steam for 30–45 minutes, until all the liquid is absorbed and the rye is tender.

VARIATION: Kasha with Fruit: After the rye has cooled, stir in the following: ¼ cup slivered almonds, ½ cup chopped apple, and ¼ cup raisins. Mix together ¾ cup orange juice, 1 tablespoon cider vinegar, and 1 teaspoon honey. Add to rye mixture and serve on a bed of lettuce.

LAMB AND RYE SOUP

This was originally made with leftovers from the Sunday roast leg of mutton, but the milder flavor of lamb also tastes very good in combination with rye.

2 tablespoons butter	4 cups water or stock
½–1 pound cooked lamb, trimmed of	2 teaspoons salt (depending upon
fat and cut into cubes	your stock, you might want to
1 cup sliced fresh mushrooms	alter this)
1 stalk celery, sliced	1 teaspoon crushed rosemary
1 cup cooked rye (whole or cracked)	1 tablespoon chopped parsley

Sauté lamb, mushrooms, and celery in butter. Add rye, stock, and seasonings, cover, and cook over medium heat for 30 minutes.

RYE-STUFFED CHICKEN

2 cups cooked cracked rye

½ cup raisins or chopped prunes

1 cup chopped celery

1 teaspoon salt

1 tablespoon chopped parsley

1 teaspoon sage

½ cup (approximately) water or stock

1 whole chicken

Preheat oven to 325°F. Combine ingredients in a large skillet with sufficient water or stock just to moisten (about ½ cup). Stuff and truss chicken; place remainder of stuffing in an oiled casserole, cover and bake with chicken for ½ hour per pound of chicken. Remove stuffing from chicken and casserole, place on large serving platter in a low mound, and serve chicken pieces atop it.

RYE-HONEY REFRIGERATOR COOKIES

These are rather plain, wholesome cookies. Experiment with thicknesses; the thicker you cut them, the moister the cookie.

1 cup rye flour

1 cup whole wheat flour

½ teaspoon allspice

1 teaspoon ground ginger

1 teaspoon ground anise seeds

½ cup honey

2 tablespoons butter

1 tablespoon unsweetened fruit juice

Stir together flours and spices. Heat honey and butter just to the boiling point; stir in juice and add to dry ingredients. Work dough with your hands into a roll about 2 inches in diameter. Wrap with waxed paper or plastic and refrigerate overnight or freeze up to several months until needed.

Preheat oven to 325°F. Slice roll into cookies about ½ inch thick. Bake 7–10 minutes. These are best when slightly warm.

LEBKUCHEN

These honey cakes were traditionally made in Europe by the candlemakers—who, since they used beeswax in their trade, formed a guild with the beekeepers. One of my favorite parts of Christmas is enjoying Lebkuchen decorated with blanched almonds, a yearly gift from an Austrian friend. This recipe is her mother's, and is a little milder than the one we've enjoyed for many years. If you would like a spicier cookie, double each of the seasonings.

2¼ cups rye flour	1 teaspoon ground cloves
1 cup brown sugar	grated rind of 1 lemon
1 teaspoon ground ginger	2 eggs, beaten
1 teaspoon ground cinnamon	¼ cup honey

Stir together rye flour, sugar, and spices. Form a well in the dry ingredients, and place eggs and honey in it; stir flour into center and work into a dough, mixing with the hands when it becomes too thick to stir. Roll dough into a ball, cover, and refrigerate for ½ hour. Preheat oven to 350°F. Roll dough out on a lightly floured board to about ½ inch thickness and cut into stars, bells, diamonds, etc. Brush with a beaten egg and bake on a greased cookie sheet for 10–15 minutes. They should be golden brown when they are done. Decorate with hard sugar icing, blanched almonds, or candied cherries, or just leave plain. These keep well, and make beautiful Christmas tree ornaments.

PFEFFERNÜSSE

These "peppernuts" have long been one of my family's favorite cookies. Recipes differ throughout Europe, and I suspect there are as many different versions as there are cooks. Pfeffernüsse are traditionally served at Christmas, but we will eat them happily in summer, spring, winter, or fall.

3 eggs

juice and rind of 2 lemons

2 cups powdered sugar

2 cups rye flour

½ teaspoon ground cinnamon

½ teaspoon ground cloves

¼ teaspoon crushed cardamom seeds

¼ teaspoon crushed anise seeds

½ teaspoon ground nutmeg

½ teaspoon baking soda

¼ teaspoon salt

Preheat oven to 425°F. Beat eggs well. Gradually add lemon juice, grated lemon rind, and sugar. Stir together flour, salt, baking soda, and spices; add to egg and sugar mixture. Beat to form smooth, medium-soft dough. Chill thoroughly. Drop by spoonfuls onto a greased baking sheet and bake in the center of a preheated oven for 10 minutes. Dust with powdered sugar.

BANANA BREAD

¼ cup butter or blended butter (see p. 92)

⅔ cup maple syrup or molasses

3 eggs

2 cups ripe mashed bananas

⅓ cup water

1 teaspoon vanilla extract

2½ cups rye (or whole wheat) flour

¼ cup powdered milk

1 teaspoon salt

2 teaspoons baking powder

1 teaspoon baking soda

Preheat oven to 325°F. Cream butter and syrup together; add eggs and beat thoroughly. Stir in bananas, water, and vanilla. In separate bowl stir together flour, powdered milk, salt, baking powder, and baking soda, pressing out any lumps. Add to liquids, mixing well. Turn into an oiled loaf pan and bake for 1 hour. Cool slightly before removing from pan. Cool thoroughly before slicing.

SHOOFLY PIE

When I think of Shoofly Pie I remember lovely green countryside, anachronistic horse-and-buggy riders trotting along the main road, and tremendous Pennsylvania Dutch hospitality. If you're ever in Lancaster, Pennsylvania, visit the Farmers' Market and taste their version of this traditional dish. It can also be made with whole wheat flour, although the flavor suffers.

CRUMB CRUST
2½ cups rye flour
1 cup brown sugar
¼ cup blended butter (see Note)

Work flour, sugar, and butter together with a fork and your fingers until well mixed and crumbly.

NOTE: To make blended butter, beat together ¼ pound softened butter with ¼ cup sunflower oil until completely blended. Refrigerate in a covered container and stir before using. Makes 1 cup.

SYRUP FILLING
¼ teaspoon baking soda
¼ teaspoon ground nutmeg
¼ teaspoon ginger
¼ teaspoon ground cinnamon
¼ teaspoon ground cloves
½ teaspoon salt
¾ cup molasses
¾ cup hot water

Mix together baking soda, nutmeg, ginger, cinnamon, cloves, and salt. Add molasses and water and stir until well mixed.

Preheat oven to 450°F. To assemble pie, press half of the crumb mixture into a greased pie plate. Cover with syrup and sprinkle the remaining crumbs on top. Bake for 15 minutes. Lower heat to 350°F. and bake 20 minutes more. Cool slightly before serving.

PEACH RYE CRISP

4 cups sliced peaches, fresh or
   canned (well drained)
2 tablespoons honey
2 tablespoons lemon juice

1 cup rye flour
¾ cup brown sugar
1½ teaspoons cinnamon
¼ cup butter

Preheat oven to 350°F. Place peaches in a buttered 1½-quart baking dish and sprinkle with honey and lemon juice. Stir together flour, sugar, and cinnamon. Cut in butter with a fork until soft crumbs form. Spread this mixture over peaches. Bake, uncovered, for 30–35 minutes.

TRITICALE

KIRK: "Wheat. So what?"
BARIS: "Quadro-triticale is not wheat, Captain!"

It seems strange to me, but more people seem to have heard of quadro-triticale, which does not exist, than of triticale, which does. When David Gerrold was writing the script for "The Trouble With Tribbles," one of the most popular episodes of the television series *Star Trek*, he remembered reading about the man-made cereal grain, triticale, in a recent magazine article. At the suggestion of line producer Gene Coon, the name of the grain was futurized to "quadro-triticale"—the idea being that biological and genetic engineering would continue to develop the man-made grain over the next two centuries. In the episode, quadro-triticale was described by Mr. Spock:

> . . . a high-yield grain, a four-lobed hybrid of wheat and rye . . . a perennial, also, if I'm not mistaken . . . The root grain, triticale, can trace its ancestry all the way back to Twentieth Century Canada. . . .

Compared to wheat and other cereal grains that developed over thousands of years, triticale has come far as a crop in an extremely short time. In less than fifty years since the first commercial production, triticale has become firmly established as a crop in diverse markets worldwide. Created by genetically combining wheat and rye, triticale's grain yield potential and nutritional qualities are as good if not better than bread wheat, and it is better adapted to difficult growing conditions.

While only about 500,000 acres of triticale are grown annually in the U.S., over 6 million acres are grown worldwide. Proclaimed as a "miracle" grain crop in the 1960s, triticale receded into the background when unadapted varieties were brought into an area and failed to produce as expected. Current varieties, the result of aggressive breeding programs, are tolerant of soils which are acid, aluminum rich or alkaline, and resistant to foliar diseases so no fungicides are needed.

Triticale grains look like slightly shriveled grains of wheat, although I've been told that in the field the heads of triticale dwarf those grain-bearing parts of the wheat plant. Strictly speaking, triticale is not a hybrid (the result of a cross between two closely related species), but it did begin as one. It is the result of years of genetic research with numerous strains of wheat and rye, and combines the high lysine content and ruggedness of rye with the overall high protein content of wheat. Its gluten content is quite adequate, too, although more delicate than that of wheat, and its flavor, in my opinion, is even better than that of wheat, yet not so strong as that of rye.

Historically, rye and wheat have often been neighbors in the same fields, at least partly because rye is a very stubborn weed and tends to grow right along with wheat if not vigorously prevented from doing so. It was almost inevitable that wheat/rye crosses would occur, and probably no one paid much attention to them. Early farmers harvested whatever was out in their fields, and if rye grew with the wheat, or if some accidental cross grew along with them, it got harvested and threshed and made into flour right along with the wheat. Actually, there was probably little long-term effect on the flour, because hybrids usually will not produce seed, and if they do, the seeds rarely grow into new plants.

In the mid-nineteenth century, plant scientists in several parts of the world took up the challenge of creating a fertile rye/wheat cross. In 1876, A. Stephen Wilson wrote in the *Transactions of the Edinburgh Botanical Society* that he had succeeded in producing seedlings by manually dusting wheat plants with rye pollen. Unfortunately, all the new plants were sterile. About twelve years later a German botanist studying naturally occurring wheat/rye crosses noticed that some crosses produced seed—so now the seeds themselves became the object of research. It was found that for seedlings to be fertile, that is, to produce seeds which would result in new plants, their reproductive cell chromosomes had to be doubled—only doubled chromosomes could pair and split and reproduce themselves. Various doubling techniques were tried—different agents were applied to the plants and they were subjected to sudden temperature changes—but no method was consistently successful, until in the 1930s when it was discovered that inoculating colchicine, an alkaloid derived from the summer crocus, into young plants would cause their chromosomes to double.

Colchicine had been used previously as a treatment for gout, but now it was used again and again in the botanical laboratory to help scientists create a new food grain. After the young plants resulting from manual pollination were inoculated with colchicine, they matured and produced fertile seed. Unfortunately the most hopeful cross, between durum wheat and rye, pro- duced shriveled seed which would not grow. It took another technological development—that of the removal of the embryo of the shriveled seed to a culturing medium where it could be nurtured artificially—to make triticale into a viable grain. Embryo culture produced a plant which, after colchicine treatment, produced fertile triticale seeds which could then be grown success- fully without further intervention.

Many years of plant breeding were still to follow, when fertile strains would be crossed with other fertile strains to obtain third-generation plants with improved fertility, yield, and other desirable characteristics. The name triticale evolved during this time out of the combination of the genus names for wheat (*Triticum*) and rye (*Secale*). Two major centers for triticale research were the University of Manitoba in Canada and the International Maize and Wheat Improvement Center in Mexico, but seed exchanges among cooperating individuals from all over the world were also important, and the eventual result was several hardy strains of triticale which are now available on the commercial market.

One of the major motivations for the refinement of triticale has been to create a high protein, high yield, rugged grain that will grow in areas of the world which have difficulty successfully growing wheat. Wheat's outstanding characteristic, of course, is its gluten content, which is why we use its flour to make light breads and pastries. Rye, on the other hand, has a much lower gluten content, and breads made from rye flour tend to be heavy and crumbly. Earthly experiments with triticale flour were disappointing; they seemed to indicate that it was going to have rye's low gluten content. However, further baking tests have shown that excellent bread can be made from 100 percent triticale flour by using slightly different methods from those used for wheat. The gluten in triticale seems to be delicate, but not absent. Gentle rather than vigorous kneading, and allowing for only one rising rather than several, preserves the structure of the dough cell walls created by the bubbling of the yeast. I have substituted triticale flour into many recipes calling for wheat flour with excellent results. The one difference lies in the breadmaking technique.

Triticale grain and flour are now available in most natural foods stores.

Triticale seed is also available, or you can plant the grain you buy from natural foods stores, although that's an expensive way to go about it. Triticale is grown very much like wheat, so see that section for general information. If you do decide to plant it, however, it might be a good idea to contact one of the agronomists who have worked closely with triticale, who can give you any specific information you may need about soil, water, and temperature requirements. Seed and information can be obtained from the Triticale Growers and Marketers Association, G.P.O. Box 2218, Adelaide, South Australia 5001. Check the Internet for growers and seed sources, also.

TOASTED TRITICALE

Triticale can be prepared for breakfast cereal just like whole or cracked wheat (see page 28), but it is especially tasty when cracked and browned slightly before cooking.

1 cup triticale, very coarsely ground	2 cups water or milk
1 tablespoon sunflower oil	½ teaspoon salt

Sauté triticale in oil until lightly browned; stir in liquid and salt, lower heat and simmer, tightly covered, 15–20 minutes or until liquid is absorbed and grain is tender. Serve with more milk and sugar or honey.

SOUR CREAM WAFFLES

We make these waffles in an old-fashioned iron that you heat over the gas burner on your stove, but you can use an electric waffle maker. Sprinkle with powdered sugar they make a fancy dessert; spread with fresh fruit syrup they make a fine start to the day.

4 eggs	1 cup triticale flour
1 cup sour cream or yoghurt	1 teaspoon salt
¼ cup vegetable oil	1½ teaspoons baking powder

Beat eggs; stir in sour cream and oil. Stir together flour, salt, and baking powder. Fold into egg mixture only until blended. Spoon onto waffle iron, cover, and bake until iron stops steaming. Remove. Makes about 6 6-inch waffles.

TRITICALE TABOULI SALAD

This version of a traditional Middle Eastern dish makes a very refreshing lunch on a hot day. I enjoy the flavor of fresh mint; omit it if mint isn't one of your favorite foods and you'll find the taste is entirely different.

½ cup coarsely cracked triticale (wheat or bulgur may be substituted)
3 tomatoes, finely chopped
½ cucumber, finely chopped
4 green onions (scallions), finely chopped

¼ cup chopped fresh parsley
2 tablespoons chopped fresh mint
4 tablespoons olive oil
2 tablespoons lemon juice
1–2 teaspoons salt
¼ teaspoon freshly ground pepper

Cover triticale with boiling water and let soak while preparing vegetables. Drain thoroughly, toss all ingredients together, and chill for several hours. When ready to serve, drain again and serve on a bed of finely chopped crisp romaine lettuce.

100% TRITICALE BREAD

Triticale has a delicate gluten, so handle it as little as possible. It rises best the first time, which means it's a fast bread to make; you can begin just 2 hours before mealtime and have fresh hot bread for the meal.

1 tablespoon active dry yeast
¼ cup warm water
¼ cup clover honey
2 tablespoons vegetable oil

1½ cups water
1 teaspoon salt
3½–4 cups triticale flour

Dissolve yeast in ¼ cup warm water. Combine honey, oil, 1½ cups water, and salt in a large bowl. Stir in yeast mixture. Add flour a little at a time, kneading last part in with hands. Form into a loaf, place in a 4½ × 8½-inch bread tin, and allow to rise in a warm place until dough is just above the top of the pan.

Preheat oven to 450°F. Place tin in oven and immediately lower the temperature to 375°F. Bake for 55–60 minutes. Remove from bread tin; allow to cool slightly before slicing.

MOLASSES TRITICALE BREAD

2 cups dark beer

½ cup whole grain cornmeal

2 tablespoons butter or margarine

¾ cup molasses

1 tablespoon salt

2 tablespoons active dry yeast

½ cup lukewarm water

3 cups whole wheat flour

3 cups triticale flour

Heat beer in a medium saucepan until just about boiling; stir in cornmeal, butter, molasses, and salt. Stir until butter is melted, then pour into large bowl and cool to lukewarm. In cup used to measure molasses, dissolve yeast in ½ cup warm water. When mixture in bowl has cooled, pour yeast mixture, which should have bubbled considerably (if it didn't, try again) into bowl and stir in whole wheat flour. Stir vigorously for 5 minutes to develop gluten; add remaining flour, stirring and kneading to combine until dough is flexible and smooth. Set aside, covered with a clean cloth, for 20 minutes (this is when I usually clean up my mess). Divide into 2 parts, shape into loaves and place in warm location to rise for 1 hour (in bread tins or on baking sheet). Preheat oven to 450°F. Place loaves in oven and immediately lower the temperature to 375°F. Bake for 50–55 minutes. Remove from tins and let cool slightly before slicing.

SPINACH DUMPLINGS

My Austrian friend made spinach dumplings for me one day and I loved them, so I asked for the recipe. When I made them, however, I used triticale flour instead of the white flour which is generally used to make them in Europe. We both agreed that they are an entirely different thing, a little more chewy, a lot more tasty—and we like them this way. You can use whole wheat flour instead of triticale with just about identical results. These are also good made with spelt.

1 bunch (10–12 leaves) fresh spinach, washed and chopped	½ cup milk
	2–4 quarts water with
2 eggs	1–2 tablespoons salt added
½ teaspoon salt	Butter
1¾ cups triticale flour	Grated Parmesan cheese

Put spinach through a food mill, or purée it in a food processor or blender with as little water as possible (I have put it into the blender with the eggs and milk, which works quite well). Stir together all ingredients. You should have a slightly stiff, but not dry, bright green dough.

Bring 2–4 quarts of water to a rapid boil in a large kettle or saucepan. Add 1–2 tablespoons salt. Wet a spoon and place tablespoonfuls of the batter into the water, wetting the spoon each time to keep the dough from sticking to it. The dumplings should sink to the bottom, then slowly rise to the surface. Cook for 10–12 minutes. Test for doneness by taking a dumpling out and slicing it. It should be moist, but not doughy. Drain.

Serve hot by stirring a little butter and freshly grated Parmesan cheese into the drained dumplings.

TRITICALE ZUCCHINI BREAD

This is a moist nut bread which keeps well. It slices better if you refrigerate it, tightly wrapped in foil or plastic wrap, for 24 hours before serving, but we rarely manage to do that.

1 cup brown sugar

1 cup butter or margarine

3 eggs

1 tablespoon lemon juice

2 cups grated zucchini

3 cups triticale flour

1 teaspoon baking powder

1 teaspoon salt

2 teaspoons ground cinnamon

1 cup chopped nuts

Preheat oven to 350°F. Cream sugar and butter; beat in eggs and lemon juice, then stir in zucchini. Stir together flour, baking powder, salt, and cinnamon, pressing out any lumps. Blend into zucchini mixture. Stir in nuts and turn into a well-greased loaf pan. Bake in a 350°F. oven for 1 hour, or until a cake tester inserted in the center of the loaf comes out clean.

TRITICALE APPLESAUCE SPICE CAKE

1 egg

⅓ cup vegetable oil

½ cup honey

2 cups triticale flour

1 teaspoon baking soda

1 teaspoon salt

1 teaspoon ground cloves

1 teaspoon ground cinnamon

1 cup raisins

1 cup applesauce

Preheat oven to 350°F. Beat egg; add oil and honey and beat until creamy. Stir together flour, baking soda, and spices; add to first mixture and beat well. Stir in raisins and applesauce. Pour into an oiled and floured cake pan. Bake for 40–50 minutes, or until a cake tester or toothpick inserted in the center comes out clean. Cool slightly before serving.

KATH'S TRITICALE CHOCOLATE CAKE

Dr. Kath Cooper has been breeding spring-type triticale varieties in Australia since 1982. She released the triticale variety "Abacus" in 1992. When she is not busy in the breeding laboratory or the grain fields, she develops recipes using her favorite grain. This is one of my favorites.

1½ cups triticale flour
¼ cup cocoa
2 teaspoons baking powder
½ teaspoon baking soda
½ cup sugar

¼ cup golden raisins
1 cup milk
3 tablespoons canola oil
2 eggs, beaten

Preheat oven to 325°F. Spray an 8-inch cake tin with vegetable oil. Mix together flour, cocoa powder, baking powder, soda, sugar, and raisins. Combine milk, oil, and eggs and stir into dry ingredients. Spoon into pan and bake for about 40 minutes, or until cake tester inserted into middle of cake comes out clean.

PEANUT BUTTER COOKIES

¼ cup butter or canola oil
½ cup brown sugar
1 beaten egg
½ teaspoon vanilla extract

½ cup peanut butter
1½ cups triticale flour
1 teaspoon baking soda
¼ teaspoon salt

Preheat oven to 325°F. Cream together butter and sugar; add egg, vanilla, and peanut butter. Beat until smooth. Stir together flour, baking soda, and salt, pressing out any lumps. Blend into creamed mixture. Shape into balls and place on greased baking sheet; flatten with fork. Bake until dry to the touch (10 minutes, more or less, depending on size).

TRITICALE CARROT COOKIES

This is a recipe we make for the Easter Bunny, and the whole family enjoys them on Easter morning.

2 tablespoons butter or margarine	½ teaspoon ground cinnamon
1 cup maple syrup or honey	½ teaspoon grated nutmeg
2 eggs	2 teaspoons baking powder
1 teaspoon vanilla extract	½ teaspoon baking soda
1 cup grated carrots	1 cup raisins
2 cups triticale flour	½ cup chopped nuts
½ teaspoon salt	

Preheat oven to 350°F. Cream together butter, syrup, and eggs. Add vanilla and carrots and blend thoroughly. Stir together flour, salt, cinnamon, nutmeg, baking powder, and baking soda, pressing out any lumps and mixing well. Add to creamed mixture; stir in raisins and nuts and beat until well mixed. Drop by teaspoonfuls onto a greased baking sheet. Bake for 10–15 minutes, or until slightly brown.

MULESHOE GINGERBREAD

This is a low-fat version of a recipe from Muleshoe, Texas, where they grow a lot of triticale. They eat a lot of gingerbread there, too.

½ cup water	2 cups triticale flour
2 tablespoons canola oil	½ teaspoon salt
½ cup brown sugar	1½ teaspoons baking powder
½ cup molasses	½ teaspoon baking soda
½ cup yoghurt	1 teaspoon ground ginger
1 egg, beaten	1 teaspoon ground cinnamon

Preheat oven to 350°F. Stir together water and oil, then stir in sugar, molasses, and beaten egg. Sift together flour, salt, baking powder, baking soda, and spices. Add to first mixture and beat until smooth. Bake in greased 8-inch pan for 30–40 minutes, or until cake tester comes out clean. Cool slightly, then cut into squares.

BARLEY

Let husky Wheat the haughs adorn
An' Aits set up their awnie horn,
An' Pease an' Beans, at een or morn,
      Perfume the plain:
Leeze me on thee, John Barleycorn,
      Thou King o' grain!
                  Robert Burns
                  1786

Barley, although little known or used in American kitchens, is one of the oldest cultivated cereals, and is still used extensively in many countries as one of the grain staples. The barley plant probably originated in the highlands of northern Africa and southeast Asia, and in fact still grows wild in its original form in those areas.

Barley was used as food both for people and for animals in ancient Egypt between 6000 and 5000 B.C. and in China by 2800 B.C.; it was the chief bread plant of the Hebrews, Greeks, and Romans, and was one of the grain staples in early Europe until it was replaced by rye and wheat. This grain has the distinction of having been written about in at least two holy books; it is frequently mentioned in the Bible, and references in a Chinese sacred work provide the evidence that barley was cultivated in the Orient four thousand years ago.

Barley was important in ancient times for other reasons than as a food, however. It was used as the basic unit of the Sumerian measuring system from 4000 to 2000 B.C. and was also the standard monetary currency in Babylonia. In 1700 B.C. Hammurabi's code of laws included prices for labor and commodities, many of which were paid in barley. Barley was as valuable to hoarders as to hungry people.

A reference librarian told me that several volumes found in the earliest Sumerian libraries contain incantations to sing to the rats and mice in storage silos, to prevent damage to the barley there. One can well imagine the dismay of a banker who discovered that his "gold" had been eaten by rodents!

Barley was being grown in Europe in the Middle Ages, and was brought to North America by British and Dutch colonists. The impetus behind the spread of barley to the West was not food, however, but beer. Beer is brewed from barley germinated into malt. Sir John Barleycorn, the personification of the spirit of barley or malt liquor, was popularized by Robert Burns in England. Innkeepers are often called by that name to this day, in honor of this versatile grain.

Since over a third of America's barley crop is grown for beer brewing, it would be a sin to omit some discussion of this process. The softer varieties of the grain, which are lower in protein, are preferred for malting, and several types of barley have been developed with this purpose in mind. To make malt, the grain is soaked, then germinated to develop enzymes. (This can also be done to increase the vitamins and improve the keeping quality in the flour which can be made from the dried, sprouted grain.) Heating and drying the sprouted barley stops enzyme growth, and the barley is then mixed with other grains to produce a mash; malt enzymes reduce the starch in the mixture to simple sugars, and the whole thing is fermented by yeast and made into alcoholic beverages, malted milk products, and malt syrup.

Breweries were established in Massachusetts by 1646. By then the colonists had already become quite adept at using the native corn for their breads, and since barley did not grow quite so well as corn, it never was used heavily as a bread or cereal grain in the colonies. (Even in the brewing of alcoholic beverages, corn was preferred to barley, and corn whiskey, rather than beer, was the common American drink until some time after the Revolution.) Later immigrants from Northern Europe introduced hardier, winter varieties of barley to the colonies, but by this time wheat, oats, and rye were being successfully raised, and the resulting crops of barley were used primarily for animal feed.

But barley as a food is what we are interested in here. Barley cultivation spread both east and west from its Near Eastern cradle. Westward, as I have said, its main use became as malt. Eastward, however, barley became an important food grain. Asiatic people have for centuries used barley like rice, served as an accompaniment to meat or fish; in Japan it is generally pearled (hulled and milled to remove some of the brown outside layers), while in China it is often ground into flour with lentils or beans and made into bread. In Tibet, Buddhist monks have traditionally carried a bag of parched barley flour to mix with yak milk into a porridge called *tsampa*, and in Ethiopia a similar preparation is made from toasted barley flour and goat milk. When it is inconvenient for some reason (such as during a journey) to prepare a hot meal, the flour and milk dough is often rolled into small pellets and eaten raw with a beverage.

A grain of barley is not very different from one of wheat. It consists of two outer husks (together called a spikelet) surrounding the aleurone-covered endosperm, or starchy part, and smaller embryo, or germ. The protein is found in the aleurone cells, which unfortunately are usually removed in milling to prepare barley for human consumption. The result of this milling is called pearled barley, and it is the only form of barley found in most grocery stores.

Less than one-tenth of the barley grown in the United States today is used for human food, and of that, nearly all of it is pearled for use in soups and baby cereal. Specialty and health food stores often carry barley flour, but that is usually also made from pearled barley. It is possible to buy natural brown barley, which has been hulled but not pearled, and this form of the grain has most of the aleurone layer intact and is worth searching for. If you grind your own flour from this form of the grain, your resulting baked products will be significantly higher in protein, vitamins, and minerals than they would be if made from pearled barley flour.

Barley can be grown easily by the small farmer or homesteader, but most people who plant it do so with the intention of feeding it to their animals. Growing barley is not a problem; as with wheat, oats, and rye, the difficult part is threshing, winnowing, and milling. But it *can* be done, using the same techniques described for the other small grains (see Wheat section).

The barley plant is very dependable and adaptable to most soil conditions. Its major weakness is failure in acid soil, which may have been the cause of its lack of success in the colonies. Barley has been found growing on the hot, dry plains of northern India and inside the Arctic Circle, so temperature extremes and short growing seasons do not seem to damage it. It grows most successfully in not-too-humid areas where the ripening season is long and reasonably cool. It produces best in well-drained, fertile deep loam soils, yet it lodges (falls over) if there is too much nitrogen in the soil. A critical balance must be achieved in the soil content: the more nitrogen in the soil, the more protein in the ripened grain (which is what you want for a food grain), but if there is too much nitrogen the stalks weaken and give way.

A soil test can be done by your local agricultural extension agent to help you achieve the correct balance of nutrients. This is also the person to contact about the best variety of barley to plant in your area (there are about two thousand different varieties) and when to plant and harvest. Hull-less barley does exist, but is not produced commercially in this country because it has a low yield, and therefore it may be hard to find. I would think it worth some effort on your part to locate the seeds from a hull-less variety if you can, however, since threshing chores will be considerably lightened if you grow that type.

Since barley has a shallow root system, it must be sown early to get the benefit of natural soil moisture. In order to get the seeds into the ground early enough, prepare the soil in the fall, then just disk or rake before planting as early as the soil can be worked. One planting guide I read said between March first and May fifteenth, but in some areas barley can be planted almost anytime; where I live farmers plant shortly after Christmas. Check with farmers and others who know your area best. They can also tell you how much seed your land can support—six to eight pecks per acre is usually considered about right if you are broadcasting by hand. If you have access to farm equipment and can plant in rows, put them about eighteen inches apart.

Harvest your crop when the grain is fully ripe, which means when the straw is completely yellow and when the kernels feel dry to the touch and snap when bitten. To store without rotting, barley should have a moisture content of no more than 13 percent, which can be measured by (you guessed it) your local agricultural extension office. Store all grains in a cool dry place, in bug-proof and rodent-proof containers.

BARLEY WATER

In England, this beverage is used as the universal cure-all. My mother's version doesn't include wine, but this one was given to me by a lady who ran a boarding house, and she says the wine is crucial. She said it would cure just about anything from indigestion to pneumonia. Try it—who knows?

Cook ¼ cup barley in 6 cups water for 2–4 hours. Strain, reserving barley for soup. To liquid (there should be about 3 cups) add:

½ cup red wine (preferably port)   1 tablespoon lemon juice
⅓ cup honey

Serve warm.

BARLEY GRUEL

Porridges are found in nearly all cultures, made from nearly all grains. This one, named gruel along with many others, is traditionally served to invalids or to hangover sufferers. Don't wait for that kind of an excuse, though. Served with fruit and honey, this is an excellent breakfast cereal.

1 cup coarsely cracked barley, soaked   2 cups water
    overnight   ½ teaspoon salt

Bring water and salt to a boil. Add barley, cover, and cook over low heat for 10 minutes, or until moisture is absorbed. Serve with honey and milk, perhaps topped with fresh fruit.

BARLEY GRIDDLE CAKES

1 cup barley flour
2 teaspoons baking powder
½ teaspoon salt
2 eggs

1 cup buttermilk or sweet milk plus 1
tablespoon lemon juice
1 teaspoon vegetable oil

Stir together dry ingredients, pressing out lumps. Beat eggs slightly; add with buttermilk and oil to flour. Bake on hot greased griddle.
One cup cooked barley may be added with 1 more egg.

MEAT AND BARLEY SALAD

1 cup leftover cooked meat, chopped
or cut into small strips (pot roast,
chicken, mild sausage, etc.)
½ cup chopped onions or chives
1–2 cups cooked barley
½ cup fresh seasonal vegetable (such

as cucumber, bell pepper,
asparagus, peas)
juice of 1 lemon
1 tablespoon vegetable oil
1 teaspoon salt

Stir together ingredients and chill thoroughly before serving.

SCOTCH BROTH

The classic barley soup.

bits and pieces of mutton or
lamb and bones
½ cup barley
½ cup chopped onion
1 cup chopped or sliced carrot
1 cup chopped turnip

1 cup chopped celery
1 leek, chopped
½ cup peas—fresh, frozen, or canned
salt, pepper, thyme to taste
2–3 quarts water or stock

Combine meat and vegetables with water or stock in large soup pot. Simmer 1–2 hours, until meat and vegetables are tender. Taste to adjust seasoning.

LAMB STEW

A bit meatier than Scotch broth, but then a bit more expensive, too.

2 pounds lamb, cut from bone
and trimmed
2 tablespoons vegetable oil
2 quarts water
½ cup barley
3 stalks celery (including leaves),
chopped

2 leaves lettuce or spinach, chopped
1 medium onion, coarsely chopped
¼ cup chopped parsley
2 cups assorted vegetables, chopped
2 teaspoons salt
½ teaspoon pepper

Sauté lamb in 2 tablespoons oil; add 2 quarts water, bring to boil and simmer, covered, 1–2 hours, until meat is tender. Add remaining ingredients and simmer another hour. Serve.

BARLEY SOUP

This recipe was adapted from Ellen Buchman Ewald's *Recipes for a Small Planet*. Consult her book for many other recipes using barley and other grains.

1½ cups barley

2 quarts vegetable or meat stock

4 eggs

2 tablespoons barley flour

2 cups plain yoghurt

2 tablespoons chopped mushrooms

2 tablespoons butter

1 tablespoon salt

¼ cup chopped fresh herbs (parsley, marjoram, basil, etc.)

Cook barley in stock until tender, about 1 hour. Drain, reserving liquid. Let cool.

Beat eggs in a large saucepan and stir flour into them gradually; stir in yoghurt and 1 quart cold stock. Continue to stir, placing over high heat, until soup thickens but does not boil.

Stir in barley, mushrooms, butter, and salt. Simmer 10 minutes. Sprinkle with fresh herbs just before serving.

BARLEY CHICKEN

4 tablespoons vegetable oil

1 medium onion, chopped

2 stalks celery, chopped

1 cup barley

3 cups soup stock, vegetable or meat

2- to 3-pound chicken, cut into serving pieces

1 teaspoon salt

½ teaspoon pepper

1 medium-size can stewed tomatoes

Heat 2 tablespoons oil in a Dutch oven or large saucepan. Sauté onion and celery until tender; add barley and sauté 2 minutes more, stirring constantly. Add stock and bring to boil. Stir, cover, and simmer for 40 minutes.

Preheat oven to 350°F. Brown chicken in remaining oil; arrange on cooked barley, sprinkle with salt and pepper, and cover with tomatoes. Cover and bake for 30–40 minutes, until chicken is tender.

KRUPNIK

This vegetable and barley soup is a Polish Scotch Broth. When I first tasted it, a ham bone was the basis for the stock, although that is not the usual choice. Mutton, lamb, beef—the dish changes, of course, but the dill and sour cream provide a distinctive flavor no matter what the meat.

4 dried mushrooms	6 peppercorns, crushed
1 soup bone with meat, about 1 pound	1 teaspoon salt
	¼ cup barley
2 quarts water	3 medium potatoes, diced
1 large carrot, chopped	1 cup sour cream
1 large onion, chopped	3 tablespoons chopped fresh dill

Cover mushrooms with lukewarm water and soak for 20 minutes. Drain and slice, reserving liquid. Boil soup bone in 2 quarts water. Skim off fat and add carrots, onion, peppercorns, salt, and barley. Cook, tightly covered, over low flame for 1½ hours. Remove bone from soup when cooked and cut meat from bone, discarding fat and gristle. Return meat to pan, along with mushrooms, reserved liquid, and potatoes. Cook slowly, adding more liquid if necessary, until tender, about 30 minutes. Stir in sour cream and dill and serve. Serves 6–9.

BARLEY AND SHRIMP CASSEROLE

1 tablespoon light oil
3 cups cooked whole barley
1 small white onion, sliced
1–2 cloves garlic, finely chopped
1 teaspoon curry powder
1 tablespoon chopped parsley
1 tablespoon chopped mint or fresh
    basil, in season

½ cup chicken broth or vegetable
    stock
1 large ripe tomato, chopped
½ pound cooked shrimp, peeled
½ pound fresh hulled or frozen peas
    or snow peas

Preheat oven to 350°F. Heat oil in heavy skillet. Stir in barley, onion, and add garlic. Cook, stirring, until evenly coated with oil. Add curry powder and leaf seasonings and continue cooking until onion and garlic are tender. Stir in broth, tomato, shrimp, and peas. Turn into a 1½-quart casserole and cook for 15–20 minutes (5 minutes in microwave on High), or until peas are tender. Serve immediately.

FRESH MUSHROOM CASSEROLE

¼ cup vegetable oil
1 medium onion, chopped
½ pound fresh mushrooms, cleaned
    and sliced

1 cup barley
2½ cups beef or vegetable stock
1 teaspoon salt
¼ teaspoon pepper

Sauté onion and mushrooms in oil until tender; stir in barley and sauté until slightly brown. Add stock and seasoning; mix well. Cover tightly and cook over low heat for about 1 hour, until barley is tender and liquid is absorbed.

This casserole is good topped with grated cheese.

HOPPIN' GEORGE

One day when I went to make some Hoppin' John, which is made with rice and black-eyed peas (page 265), I discovered I was out of rice. Not wanting to disappoint my three-year-old daughter (who I suspect actually liked the name at least as much as the taste of the dish), I substituted barley and suggested she make up a new name. Which she did. We soon discovered that we liked this version just as much as the original.

1 tablespoon vegetable oil
¼ cup barley
¼ cup minced onion
½ cup black-eyed peas
2½ cups meat or vegetable stock

2 tablespoons bacon bits or chopped, cooked bacon
½ teaspoon salt or 1 teaspoon onion salt

Sauté barley and onion in oil until barley is slightly brown. Add black-eyed peas, stock, and seasoning, cover tightly and simmer until tender, about 1 hour.

BARLEY WITH NUTS

1 cup barley
1 tablespoon vegetable oil or butter
2 cups vegetable or meat stock

½ teaspoon salt
½ cup chopped or whole cashews, peanuts, or almonds

Brown barley in oil or butter, then add stock and salt and cook over low heat, tightly covered, until tender, about 1 hour. Stir in nuts, cover pan again, and simmer 5 minutes more. Serve.

STUFFED CABBAGE LEAVES (GOLABKI)

This Polish stuffed cabbage is delicious. Try it when you feel like offering up something exotic.

1 cup barley
1 large, firm head green cabbage
1 large onion, chopped
½ cup mushrooms, chopped
3 tablespoons butter
1 tablespoon lemon juice
salt, pepper, paprika to taste

½ cup parsley, chopped
1½ cups beef or vegetable stock
2 tablespoons flour (whole wheat or barley)
1 cup sour cream
2 tablespoons fresh chopped dill

Cook barley in 2 cups water for 1 hour, or until tender. Pull off and discard any wilted or tough outer cabbage leaves; cut out core to about 3 inches. Cook cabbage in salted water for 10–15 minutes, or until leaves become pliable. Separate leaves from head gently and carefully cut out the tough part of the rib from each leaf.

Sauté onion and mushrooms in butter until tender and limp; add lemon juice and seasonings, barley (reserve liquid for soup stock), and parsley. Mix well, remove from heat and spoon onto leaves, rolling up and folding in edges to securely hold the stuffing. Fasten each leaf with toothpicks or tie with string. Place in a large Dutch oven or saucepan, cover with stock and cook slowly, covered, about 1½ hours, or until leaves are quite tender. Remove stuffed leaves and keep warm. Stir flour into stock and cook, stirring, until smooth. Add sour cream and dill and heat through. Pour sauce over stuffed leaves. Serves 8–10.

MOCK CORNISH PASTY

What do you do if you promised yourself Cornish pasties for supper (see page 34) and you discover you're out of potatoes? Where we live you can't just run down to the corner store, so you look to your cupboard instead. We like this version so well that we are sharing it with you.

FILLING

2 cups cooked barley

1 medium onion, chopped

1 bouillon cube dissolved in ¼ cup
    water

1 tablespoon chopped parsley

1 teaspoon salt

½ teaspoon pepper

½ teaspoon sage

Combine ingredients in small saucepan, cover, and simmer over low heat while preparing crust. If you're using a frozen pie crust, simmer for 15–20 minutes.

PASTRY CRUST

3 cups whole wheat flour

1 teaspoon salt

½ cup butter

2 eggs

Preheat oven to 400°F. Stir together flour and salt; cut in butter. Beat eggs slightly and stir into mixture with a fork. Mixture will be slightly sticky, and since egg sizes differ, you may need to add more flour to get the right consistency. Turn dough onto a well-floured surface and with floured hands and floured rolling pin press and roll into a flat piece about ¼-inch thick. Cut circles about 6 inches in diameter (a cereal bowl makes a good cutter). Place ¼ cup filling on one side of each circle, wet edges with water, fold in half and seal, crimping with fingers or fork. Make 3 vertical slashes in the pasty to permit steam to escape. Place pasties on greased baking sheet, brush with egg or milk, and bake for 30–35 minutes. Cool slightly before serving, or you'll burn your mouth.

These are good served with a little tomato ketchup or steak sauce to dip into as they are eaten. Makes 6 to 8 pasties.

BARLEY FLOUR PIE CRUST

⅔ cup barley flour
⅓ cup whole wheat flour
½ teaspoon salt

3 tablespoons vegetable oil
¼ cup ice water

Preheat oven to 400°F. Stir together flours, salt, and oil. Add ice water gradually, stirring with fork until mixture balls up. Shape with fingers and press into a greased pie plate; this dough does not roll out well. Bake for 10 minutes. Makes 1 9-inch shell.

SUMERIAN FLAT BREAD

I'm not in communication with the spirits of ancient civilizations—but this recipe seems a probable approximation of what was baked by those ancestral peoples. It's good, too, especially with soup or cheese.

1 cup finely ground barley flour
½ cup sesame seed flour (use a metal-
   bladed flour mill, or nut grinder;
   the oil in the seeds will glaze a
   stone wheel)

1 teaspoon vegetable oil
¼ cup finely minced onions
½ teaspoon salt
¼ cup cold water
4 teaspoons whole sesame seeds

Preheat oven to 400°F. Stir together the barley flour and ground sesame seeds. Add oil, onions, and salt and mix well. With a fork, stir in water a little at a time, mixing until dough leaves sides of bowl and holds together. Work dough with your hands until it is soft and pliable, break into 4 balls and roll out ¼-inch thick. Cut into even circles (a cereal bowl makes a good guide), pressing 1 teaspoon whole sesame seeds and ¼ teaspoon salt into the rounds with the rolling pin. Bake for 15 minutes.

BARLEY BREAD

Barley has practically no gluten-forming proteins, so bread made with this grain will be rather heavy. However, sliced thinly, it is a delicious departure from the ordinary sort of bread.

¼ cup honey	1 tablespoon salt
2 tablespoons yeast	2 tablespoons vegetable oil
¼ cup lukewarm water	5–5½ cups barley flour
1¾ cups milk	

Dissolve honey and yeast in lukewarm water. Scald milk and place in mixing bowl; add salt and oil and cool to lukewarm. Stir in yeast and honey mixture, then stir in 3 cups flour and beat well to develop air bubbles and what gluten there is. Add remaining flour, kneading with hands until smooth and elastic. Shape into 2 loaves on a cookie sheet, cover with a damp cloth, and let rise 1 hour. Dough will rise slightly, but will not double in bulk. Preheat oven to 325°F. Bake for 1 hour.

BARLEY NUT BREAD

2 cups barley flour	2 tablespoons vegetable oil
2½ cups whole wheat flour	2 eggs
4 teaspoons baking powder	1¾ cups milk
2 teaspoons salt	2 cups chopped nuts
¼ cup honey	

Preheat oven to 325°F. Stir together flours, baking powder, and salt. In another bowl, blend honey, oil, eggs, and milk. Beat liquid ingredients into the dry ones until smooth. Fold in nuts. Pour into greased bread pans and bake for 45 minutes. Makes 2 loaves.

BARLEY MUFFINS

2 cups barley flour	2 eggs
2 teaspoons baking powder	½ cup honey
1 teaspoon baking soda	½ cup milk
1 teaspoon salt	

Preheat oven to 400°F. Stir dry ingredients together, pressing out lumps. Beat eggs slightly, blend in honey, and stir into flour mixture. Beat thoroughly, adding enough milk to make into a smooth batter. Pour into muffin tins, slightly greased. Bake for 20–25 minutes. Split and serve with butter.

BARLEY PUDDING

This is obviously a variation on my mother's English rice pudding, but we find it a delightful one. Hulled barley will remain chewy; if you prefer it more mushy, add 1 additional cup milk or cream and cook longer, or soak barley overnight before cooking.

2 cups barley	½ teaspoon salt
6 cups milk, or milk and cream combined	¾ cup honey
	whipped cream or yoghurt
1 cup raisins	

Preheat oven to 325°F. Combine ingredients in well-buttered large baking dish. Bake, uncovered, for 3 hours. Stir several times during first hour to keep barley from settling. If pudding seems dry toward the end of the baking time, add more milk. Serve with whipped cream or yoghurt.

BARLEY APPLE PUDDING

This is a pleasant variant on barley pudding.

1 cup stewed apples	½ teaspoon grated nutmeg
2 cups cooked barley	½ teaspoon ground cinnamon
juice of 1 lemon	2 eggs
¼ cup honey	

Preheat oven to 350°F. Stir apples, barley, lemon juice, and honey together in large bowl. Add spices.

Separate eggs. Beat yolks until creamy; stir into mixture. Beat whites until stiff; fold in. Turn pudding into buttered 1-quart baking dish. Bake for 35–40 minutes.

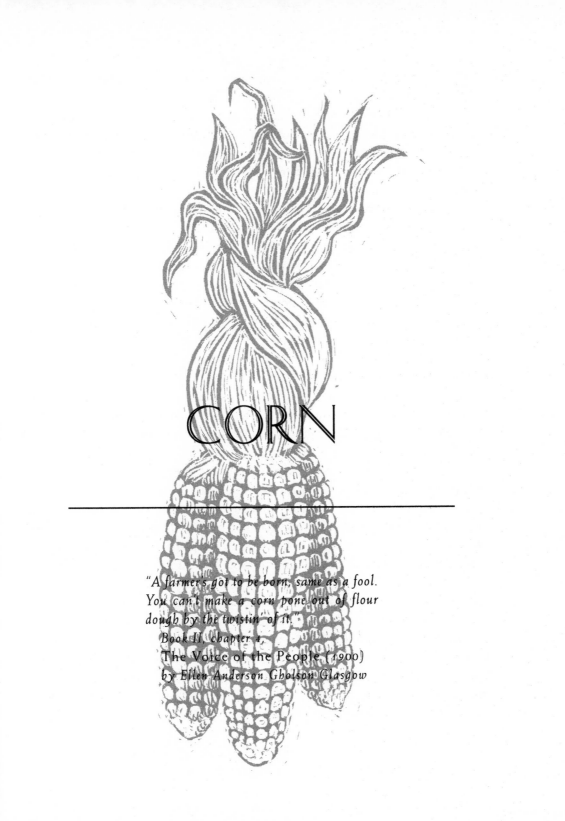

CORN

"A farmer's got to be born, same as a fool.
You can't make a corn pone out of flour
dough by the twistin' of it."
Book II, chapter 4,
The Voice of the People (1900)
by Ellen Anderson Gholson Glasgow

The grain which we in America know as corn was already the staple in the New World when Europeans arrived in the fifteenth century. Although it will be called corn throughout this section and this book, I should mention that if you ask for corn in England you may be given wheat, and that if you request maize, by which term it is known in most of the world, it will undoubtedly be assumed that you mean to feed it to your pigs, for that is where most of this grain goes in Europe.

According to archaeologists, corn grew wild in southern Mexico nine thousand years ago. The Indians of South and Central America had been using corn as their grain staple for so long that by the time Europeans arrived they had no record of where it had come from. The wild form had disappeared by this time and had been replaced by many cultivated varieties which grew in a wide range of climate and soil conditions all over the western hemisphere. American Indians thought so highly of this grain that it became a part of their religion. "Seed of Seeds," "Sacred Mother," and "Blessed Daughter" are only a few of the terms used for corn by these earliest users.

When Columbus was introduced to corn growing in Cuba in 1492, he mistook it for a plant native to Europe and reported to the people of Spain that the Indians ate the fruit of the wild sorghum. Sorghum does resemble growing corn, and since sorghum was mostly fed to animals, the Spaniards ignored the new grain.

But the English, who were struggling through their first hungry winters in Jamestown and Plymouth, soon learned the value of this hardy plant. Indians native to the area shared their crops and taught the colonists how to grow their own. One of the earliest planting manuals quoted from an Indian gardener: "When the oak tree leaves are as big as mice ears, plant the kernels of corn. Put a small fish in between them. Round the soil into a little hill." The fish helped to decompose and fertilize the soil, which was not usually plowed before planting. For a month after planting every dog in the colony would hobble around with one forepaw fastened to its neck to prevent it from digging up the fish.

These early planting methods were primitive, but they worked, and before long three crops a year were being grown in Plymouth. Indian corn became the mainstay of Virginia and Massachusetts for many years. There is even a plaque in Truro, Massachusetts, in honor of the corn plant, inscribed with the words of William Bradford, Governor of Plymouth Colony:

> And sure it was God's good providence that we found this corne, for else we know not how we should have done.

Although they did not immediately adopt corn for use in their own countries, the English, Spanish, and Portuguese distributed corn and techniques for its cultivation and preparation during their many voyages of exploration. Africa and India were introduced to corn about the same time, early in the sixteenth century, and Magellan took Indian corn with him to the East Indies and the Philippines, from whence it spread to the mainland of eastern Asia and New Zealand. Corn reached Japan and China by 1575.

The scientific name of corn is *Zea mays*, given to the plant by the Swedish taxonomist Linnaeus in the eighteenth century. The word Zea is from the Greek word for cereal, which is believed to have come from the verb meaning "to live."

In addition to the ways of preparing corn with which we are generally familiar and which will be covered later, some rather interesting uses have been made of this grain. There were no dairy animals in Plymouth colony until 1624, but during that earliest period a substitute for milk was made from crushed fresh corn mixed with the juices from boiled hickory nuts and chestnuts. It was heated for babies and served cold to older children. Indian children sucked a kind of sugar from the fresh corn stalks, made the husks into dolls, and chewed on the silklike tassels as farm children would later chew on stalks of grass.

The Maoris of New Zealand have adopted the custom of soaking corn ears in water for six months or so before eating the by-then thoroughly rotten grain. They may have learned this by way of the Peruvians, who also soak and ferment their grain before cooking. The slimy, strong-smelling kernels are then crushed, boiled to make a gruel, and fried or eaten warm with milk and sugar. In India, corn flour is sometimes used in baking, and the whole grains are often parched on beds of hot sand to improve keeping quality until later soaking and cooking.

Soaking dried kernels of corn seems to have been an almost universal practice, probably because of the tough nature of the earliest varieties grown. In Mexico, charcoal or lime was added to the water to help loosen the skins while the grains were soaked or boiled. The kernels were then rubbed between the hands to remove the loose skins, and crushed with a stone to form a paste, with water added as needed to make a dough which could be kneaded into patties (these became tortillas) and cooked on a stone griddle over the fire. Eventually someone noticed that the whole cooked grain was tasty even without crushing or grinding, so the first hominy was discovered. American colonists adopted from the Algonquin Indians the technique of soaking corn kernels in a weak wood-lye solution. Unfortunately, the bran and oil-rich germ were washed off along with the skin of the kernel and this *tackhummin*, as it was called, was deficient in protein, fiber, and vitamins compared to whole grain corn.

In the late seventeenth century, observers in Guatemala noted that cornmeal was cooked in a jar set within another jar or bowl of boiling water. This early use of a double boiler may be surprising, but the slow cooking produces a much smoother, more uniform gruel, which is far superior to cereal which has been merely boiled. This technique, by the way, will work with any grain.

These various ways of preparing corn are a tribute to its adaptability to various needs, as valuable a characteristic as its adaptability to growing conditions. Although originally found growing undomesticated, corn as we now know it could probably not make it in the wild, though it grows just about anywhere with a little help. Domestication has developed a sturdy husk, which while it protects the kernels from animals and frost, also prevents them from dropping to the ground when dry, and germinating, so that the entire ear usually rots if left in the field until the rains.

Growing corn in the family garden or on a small homestead is a very straightforward and worthwhile project. Because corn can be grown successfully in nearly every part of the United States, it is an ideal choice for the noncommercial grower. Numerous varieties are available; consult major seed catalogues and choose one which is right for your climate and soil type.

There are six major types of corn, classified mostly by their uses and the form of the kernel, or seed. The kernels are lined up in rows along the seed head, or cob, of the corn plant. Each plant may contain several cobs, called ears when they are on the plant, each (with the exception of pod corn) enclosed in a leafy husk, lined with strings of corn silk. Each kernel is made up of four main parts, in differing proportions. The outside is protected by a strong hull. Within the hull lies the hard starchy layer, or endosperm, and inside this shell are the softer starchy layer and the nutritious germ. Yellow and white varieties exist for most types, and are identical except in the pigment and vitamin A content. White corn, missing the pigment, also contains virtually none of the vitamin.

In *pod corn* each kernel is wrapped in an individual husk. Except as a curiosity, and as a probable ancestor of other varieties, pod corn is of little importance to us.

Flint corn is thought to be like the corn found growing in North America in 1607. Each kernel has a hard starchy outside, or endosperm, completely surrounding the softer interior and germ, and the kernels are difficult to grind. Flint corn is now grown almost entirely for animal feed.

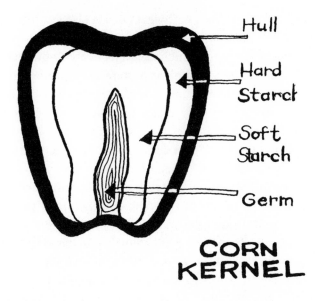

Hull

Hard Starch

Soft Starch

Germ

CORN KERNEL

Dent corn is a high yield corn developed for commercial production in the United States. The kernels of this type have the endosperm along the sides, with the soft part being in the center and along the top. Its name comes from the fact that when it dries, the soft part shrinks, leaving an obvious dent in the top of each grain. Dent corn is primarily used for animal feed, although corn-meal and corn flour are also ground from this variety.

Flour corn kernels are made up almost completely of soft starch, with a very thin endosperm on the sides. They are easy to grind into flour or meal (the difference between the two is only in the coarseness), but are difficult to locate. Generally flour corn is grown by American Indians for home use, and they keep their seed from year to year. Diligent searching of seed catalogues might reap some reward, but it would help if you knew someone who had seeds to sell you.

Popcorn is grown in great quantities for sale to entertainment industries. The kernels have a much higher percentage of hard endosperm than those of the other types, which makes them explode more easily upon heating, but they are nearly useless as food grains.

Sweet corn is the type with which we are most familiar. The kernels of this type have such a large proportion of sugar to hard endosperm that they wrinkle and shrivel up when they dry. Very small grains are produced, and they are pretty useless except for their one purpose in life—to be eaten "green," or immature and tender, preferably roasted or steamed just a few minutes after picking, with plenty of melted butter. Sweet corn is also cut from the cob and canned or frozen, although unless done very carefully this removes part of the nutritious corn germ, or embryo, which contains nearly a quarter of the protein of the kernel, and the only complete protein. The protein in the remainder of the kernel is deficient in two amino acids, tryptophan and lysine.

Generally, sweet corn is the only major type available in seed catalogues intended for small farmers and homesteaders, and most of these varieties are fine for eating fresh and frozen. If you desire corn which can be dried for meal and flour, however, you will need to search for a satisfactory variety and this may not be too easy to find. Some varieties of sweet corn can be adapted to this purpose, and seed companies can recommend them, but you might prefer to locate a feed store and purchase some dried flint or dent corn to use for seed. (Nichols Garden Nursery, 1190 North Pacific Highway, Albany, Oregon 97321, sells three varieties of flour corn, one of which is Black Aztec, an Indian corn. Hopi blue and Hopi white are available from the Redwood City Seed Co., P.O. Box 321, Redwood City, CA 94064.) Feed corn can also be purchased to grind at home, but be certain that it has not been treated with fungicide or insecticide. Generally corn which is sold to be fed to very small animals or birds and poultry has not been treated, but do ask the seed dealer or have it tested at your local agricultural extension office.

Yellow corn is preferable nutritionally, since it has a large amount of vitamin A, while the white varieties contain nearly none. However, many cornmeal afficionados, particularly those who grew up in the South, will talk your ear off about the tender, flavorful delicacies which can be made only from white corn. I guess that decision will have to be yours. Blue corn is specific to Arizona and New Mexico, and available in Native American stores and some specialty shops.

After choosing your seed, consider where you will plant and begin preparing your garden. Corn will grow well in a wide variety of climates and diverse kinds of soil, but a deep, dark silty loam with good drainage, abundant moisture, and moderately high temperatures will give the best yield. Sandy soils don't work so well because they retain moisture for a very short time and also tend to be low in the essential nutrients. If your soil is sandy, build it up with compost and fertilizer. Compost will also help if you have clay soil, because it will improve the drainage and give the roots more room to grow.

Corn takes large amounts of nitrogen, phosphorus, and potassium from the soil. Rotating your corn with oats or clover, if you have animals to feed, or with peas and beans if you don't, will help to return these nutrients to the soil.

Soaking the corn seed for two or three days before planting speeds germination, as does thoroughly preparing the seedbed and planting into damp soil. Plant at least four rows, two to three feet apart for best pollination, about ½-inch deep.

Sweet corn and field corn (corn to be dried for flour) can be raised side by side. Be sure to label your rows well, however. Biting into what you think is a sweet roasting ear can be a disappointment if it turns out to be a blander-flavored field variety—and leaving stalks of sweet corn in the field to dry is a waste of good eating. The meal ground from most varieties of sweet corn is too sweet for general use, and hardly worth grinding, since the kernels shrivel so badly.

Water only lightly until the plants break the surface of the soil, and don't pack the soil too tightly. Give plenty of moisture once the young plants have broken ground. Paper cups with the bottoms cut out can be placed over the young plants to keep rodents and cutworms away, or the seeds can be planted in a trench 6–8 inches deep, then covered with strips of cheesecloth until the seedlings reach the top of the trench. When the ears begin to form and the silk has appeared, applications of mineral oil to the end of the cobs will reduce damage from earworms. Don't apply oil before silk forms, or you will hinder pollination.

Native people in dry parts of the American continent generally stored corn in the husk on the stalk to prevent damage by rodents; they simply removed the ears as they needed them. (Remember, though, that early settlers considered corn to be inedible until it was dry. You can also store corn on the stalk if you live in a dry climate and are drying it for grinding.) Even if the ears were husked immediately and allowed to dry, they were usually stored whole in storage bins with plenty of ventilation. This is still a good method of storage. An inexpensive corn crib can be made from slim logs crisscrossed as in a log cabin and covered with plywood or some other waterproof sheeting.

In damper parts of the continent, ears were tied together after husking and hung over beams or on walls to dry (the modern East Coast practice of hanging several dried ears of corn on the front doors of homes in the autumn probably comes from this). Shelled corn was stored in baskets, pots, bags, or bark boxes. Shelling methods varied. The ears might be placed on the ground or on a blanket and beaten with clubs. Or the dried ears might be rubbed against a tightly fastened disk of corn cobs. Corn, when properly dried, will release its kernels with a minimum amount of scraping or beating, so be certain to dry your corn thoroughly. In the 1970s, the Department of Agriculture put out a bulletin, *Drying Shelled Corn and Small Grains*, FB 2214, which, although intended for commercial growers, contained some useful information about drying your own grain. It is now out of print, but may be located in your public library. Newer publications are available from the National Agricultural Library in Washington, D.C.

The harvesting of a field of grain is an enormous job if you try to do it yourself, but referring back to old traditions may help. Why not have a "corn shuckin'" party, where your freshly picked corn is husked by friends. Set a minimum number of ears, which must be husked and turned in for a meal, or hide a six-pack in the pile of unhusked ears. Half a dozen people picking and husking corn will make short work of the task, and will probably have a good time, too.

Grinding the corn for kitchen use is the next step. Most grinding chores in early America were performed with mortar and pestle, tools copied from the native people. Small spice mortars and pestles were made of brass, bell metal, or marble; larger mortars, such as the ones used for corn, were used with wooden or iron pestles. This combination for making home-ground cornmeal was one of the two basic requirements for Virginia households, the other being the iron cooking pot.

I, for one, would not begin to grind my corn in a mortar and pestle, but the equipment is available in boutiques or antique stores if you want to try it. The stone grinding mill is ideal for this purpose, either hand or electrically powered, and adjustable enough to grind very coarse meal for polenta, medium meal for cornbread, and fine flour for tortillas or tamales. Corn is too hard for most food processors, so I don't recommend using them. Set your grinder for a coarse meal first, then adjust gradually until you reach the consistency you want. Some people prefer to run the grain through two or three times, adjusting the mill for a finer and finer grind between passes, rather than to try for fine meal or flour in one pass, which tends to be a bit hard on the arm if you are using a hand-powered mill. One cup of dried corn yields about one and a half cups of meal, so take that into consideration when you are preparing your grain. Any excess meal or flour should be refrigerated and used in less than a week, because the oil contained in the germ will turn rancid if left too long.

If you prefer to purchase cornmeal, it is quite inexpensive and if you shop carefully you should be able to obtain meal just as nutritious as that which you prepare at home, although you will have less control over the texture. There are a few terms to be aware of, however, and you should read labels carefully. Most cornmeal sold in ordinary grocery stores is labeled "degerminated," which means exactly that—the nutritious germ has been removed to keep the cornmeal from spoiling on the shelf. The reduction in texture of the resulting baked products, not to mention the loss of protein and trace mineral quality, is so great, however, that nearly all recipes calling for cornmeal in modern cookbooks also include wheat flour to give body and value. Do *not* buy degerminated cornmeal. Sometimes "bolted" cornmeal is available; this has been sifted to produce a finer grind, but not degerminated. This is certainly preferable to the degerminated type, although since most of the bran gets sifted out, is still not very satisfactory for cooking uses.

The cornmeal to look for is stone ground *whole* cornmeal. Sometimes the bag will indicate that it has been "water ground," which isn't really necessary, but the implication is that if the grinding stones were powered by water, the mill is a small one and the miller is likely to be concerned about the quality of the product. Water ground cornmeal costs a little more, but it is well worth paying extra for if you can find it. Whole grain cornmeal can be obtained from most health food sections of large grocery stores, from health food and natural food stores, and from the sources listed in the back of the book.

Whole grain cornmeal, like any other ground whole grain, contains the germ and oil released in grinding, and will spoil if left too long. It keeps for several weeks in your refrigerator, but the flavor begins to deteriorate after that. Here is another advantage to grinding your own—you can grind just as much as you need.

POPCORN

This ancient grain was cultivated by the Incas and used to decorate bodies for burial. It is still available in various colors, some natural, some achieved by food coloring. Introduced at the first Thanksgiving dinner by the Native American brave Quadequina, it has been a favorite snack of American children of all ages ever since. It is now the mainstay of the American film industry.

Popcorn can be easily prepared at home with no special equipment.

Heat 1 tablespoon oil in a large, heavy saucepan over moderate heat. Sprinkle ¼ cup popcorn evenly on the bottom of the pan. Immediately cover pan tightly. Shake pan every few minutes to prevent kernels from sticking and burning. When popping sounds subside, pour popcorn into bowl, sprinkle with salt and stir in melted butter. Enjoy.

The popping action takes place when moisture within the corn kernel expands with heat and explodes the grain. If popcorn has not been stored properly, it will dry out and will not pop well. Should you encounter this problem, soak your corn for a few minutes in warm water. Drain thoroughly, and pop as usual.

ZUNI SUCCOTASH

Succotash was originally corn and kidney beans; sometimes it contained bits of meat, too, all cooked together in bear grease. The Narragansett Indians called this native dish *misickquatash*, and it was shortened to suquahtash by the colonists—a word which stuck, although it changed in its spelling through the years.

Other Indian groups developed dishes made from corn and beans, such as the following recipe from the Zuni.

1 cup fresh cut corn or cooked dried sweet corn	1–2 tablespoons sunflower seed meal or flour
1 cup cooked dried beans	Salt and pepper to taste
1 cup cooked meat, cut in cubes	

Cook corn, beans, and meat together in water to cover until tender. Thicken with sunflower seed meal and season with salt and pepper. Continue cooking until thick and soupy.

PIKI

This delicate Hopi bread is made from blue corn ground very finely and mixed with boiling water. The dough is spread thinly on a heated slab which has been well oiled (traditionally with crushed squash or sunflower seeds). It bakes quickly and as it separates from the griddle, the wafer-thin bread is peeled off and folded or rolled to eat.

Proportions vary from baker to baker, but if you would like to try this bread, begin with the amounts below, then vary as necessary to obtain satisfactory results. Don't be discouraged if your first results are somewhat less than spectacular; Hopi women spend most of their girlhood learning the art of piki-making.

2 cups very fine cornmeal made from blue corn (see Note)
1 cup boiling water

1 cup cold water in which 2 tablespoons ashes of burnt juniper have been mixed (use plain water if there are no junipers near your home)
cold water

Stir boiling water into cornmeal, stirring out lumps. Strain ash water slowly into cornmeal mixture, stirring constantly. Add sufficient cold water to make a thin pancake-like batter. Pour the batter quickly by tablespoonfuls onto a hot greased griddle. When piki begins to brown and separate from the griddle at the edges, remove with a pancake turner and roll up. Keep warm in a covered basket until all are done. Piki is also good dusted with powdered sugar.

NOTE: Blue corn may be replaced with yellow or white corn if you live outside the Southwest, but the results will be different. Check the Sources section if you want to try the real thing.

ATOLE

The Aztecs and Mayans made drinks out of balls of dough made from *masa harina*, a flour made from dried, lime-soaked parched corn. The dough was wrapped in a leaf or a corn husk while stored (for example while traveling), then broken up and stirred into water. Sometimes the atole was boiled, or flavoring was added, such as chile, honey, herbs, or chocolate. Indians in Mexico still drink atole.

Wash 2 cups corn kernels and boil in water to cover. When they are tender, and fill the room with their aroma, they are done. Drain, cool, and pulse in a food processor, or put through a food mill or meat grinder, or grind in a mortar and pestle with enough water to make a light dough.

Dissolve 1 cup atole dough in 8 cups water. Strain out any lumps, and place over medium heat with 1 stick cinnamon. As mixture comes to the boil, stir constantly, and continue stirring until smooth and creamy. Add ¾ cup sugar and cook until dissolved. Serve in large mugs.

TORTILLAS FROM SCRATCH

If you want to make tortillas the authentic way, begin with 2 pounds of corn kernels, 2 ounces of powdered lime (available from hardware stores), and 3 quarts of water.

Wash the corn, add lime and water, and boil until the kernel skins loosen. Remove from heat and cool. Rub handfuls of the kernels between the palms of your hands until the skins are loosened and removed. Wash kernels thoroughly in cold water to remove lime. You now have *nixtamal*—grind it in a food mill, meat grinder, or large mortar and pestle into a soft dough. Divide into small balls and work each into round flat disks about 7 inches in diameter and very thin. You can use a tortilla press for this.

In Mexico tortillas are baked on a *comal*, an ungreased clay or iron baking griddle, over a flame. Any griddle or large heavy skillet will work well, however. Bake on one side until tinged with brown and fragrant, then turn and bake on other side. Keep warm in a basket covered with a cloth. Serve hot.

TORTILLAS

Tortillas may also be made from *masa harina*, or you can use your own dried corn ground very fine (preferably in a stone mill rather than in one with metal blades). Toast the corn first to improve the flavor.

1 teaspoon salt	1 cup boiling water
2 cups corn flour or *masa harina*	

Stir the salt and flour together; pour the water over the mixture, stirring rapidly with a fork until well mixed. Work dough with hands, then form into 12 balls. Flatten each ball with your hand, then press and roll into a thin circle. Bake on slightly greased griddle until dry and speckled with brown; turn tortillas and bake other side. Keep warm with a towel until all are finished, and serve immediately.

COLONIAL CORN PUDDINGS

One of the most common ways of preparing cornmeal in the American colonies was to boil it in some way with liquid and serve it in bowls. The form and the name changed many times over the years and across the miles, but there were basically a half dozen varieties of this dish. *Hasty pudding* was originally made with equal parts milk and water and boiled quickly, forming a rather coarse gruel; this was also called *loblolly* (for a modern recipe for this dish, see following page). *Suppawn* was a thick porridge of cornmeal and milk, also cooked rather quickly, and often allowed to cool before eating either with milk and sugar or fried in deep fat. Today's *cornmeal mush* was probably originally suppawn, but the dish known by that name in early America was thinner, more watery, and was usually cooked more slowly, perhaps over boiling water (as in a double boiler) to obtain a creamier, smoother texture. Mush was nearly always eaten with sweetened fruit or honey. *Indian pudding* was mush with molasses and seasonings added in the cooking instead of afterward, and usually was boiled in a bag or steamed. Another dish borrowed from the native people was *samp porridge*, which was cooked for days with meats and vegetables. This concoction became very stiff in the cooking, and was often eaten in chunks, much like scrapple or sausage.

CORNMEAL MUSH

1 cup whole cornmeal　　　　　　1 teaspoon salt

1 cup cold water　　　　　　　　4 cups boiling water

Stir together cornmeal, cold water, and salt. Pour boiling water into the top of a double boiler and slowly stir cornmeal mixture into boiling water over medium heat. Place double boiler pan over water and cook mush, covered, 20–25 minutes, or until thickened. Stir occasionally. Serve in bowls with molasses, maple syrup, sorghum syrup, or honey.

VARIATION: FRIED MUSH. Pour prepared cornmeal mush into a loaf pan which has been oiled and preheated in a hot oven (this crisps the edges and makes the mush easier to remove from the pan). Refrigerate mush overnight. To serve, remove mush from pan, slice thickly, and fry in hot oil. Serve with maple syrup.

HASTY PUDDING

The colonists made many warm gruels and porridges to help them cope with drafty houses and chilly mornings. The traditional hasty pudding was a favorite because, as the name implies, it was cooked up quickly.

1 cup whole cornmeal　　　　　　½ teaspoon salt

4 cups water

Stir cornmeal and 1 cup cold water together. Bring 3 cups water and salt to a boil and stir in cornmeal mixture gradually, being careful to keep it from lumping. Cook over low heat, stirring occasionally, until very thick (10–15 minutes). Serve with butter and honey, maple syrup, molasses, or cream. Makes 6–7 servings.

INDIAN PUDDING

This is a traditional colonial Thanksgiving dessert, and has become a traditional treat at all our family holiday meals. It takes its name not from the Native Americans at the first fall feast, but from the cornmeal, which was known by the early settlers as Indian meal.

½ cup whole cornmeal	1 egg, beaten
⅓ cup brown sugar	¼ cup dark molasses
¼ teaspoon salt	1 teaspoon cinnamon
¼ teaspoon baking soda	½ teaspoon grated nutmeg
3 cups milk	½ teaspoon ground ginger
2 tablespoons butter or margarine	1 cup heavy cream

Preheat oven to 325°F. Combine cornmeal, sugar, salt, and baking soda in a medium saucepan. Add 1½ cups milk and the butter; bring to boil, stirring constantly, and remove from heat. Beat together egg, molasses, spices, and remaining milk; stir into cornmeal mixture. Pour into ungreased 1-quart baking dish. Bake, uncovered, for about 1½ hours, or until tip of knife inserted 1 inch from center of pudding comes out clean. Serve in bowls with cream.

SPOON BREAD

1 cup whole cornmeal	2 tablespoons butter or vegetable oil
3 cups milk	4 eggs
1 teaspoon salt	

Preheat oven to 350°F. Cook cornmeal in milk until thick—about 5–7 minutes after it comes to a boil. Add salt and butter and cool to lukewarm. Meanwhile, separate eggs. Beat whites until stiff, and beat yolks until creamy. Stir yolks into lukewarm mixture, then fold in whites. Pour into greased 1½-quart baking dish and bake for 35 minutes, until firm and slightly brown. Serve hot. Makes 6–8 servings.

CORNBREADS

Ash cakes and hoe cakes, johnnycakes and corn pones were the first corn-breads. Ash cakes were, as the name implies, baked in the ashes of a fireplace. native Americans wrapped the cakes in leaves, while colonists placed them inside cloths on the hearth and covered them with hot ashes. Hoe cakes were baked on the flat end of a hoe or other farm implement, often in a fire built in the open fields.

CORN PONES

My dictionary says a "pone" is an oval-shaped loaf of cornbread, which doesn't help much with the meaning, but since *apan* is the Delaware Indian word for "baked," one can assume that a corn pone is baked corn. That still doesn't explain the traditional oval shape, but it's a nice bit of trivia to drop at parties.

4 cups whole cornmeal	¼ cup vegetable oil
1 teaspoon salt	1 cup boiling water

Preheat oven to 325°F. Stir together cornmeal and salt; add oil and mix thoroughly. Gradually pour water into mixture, stirring with a fork until dough sticks together to form a lump which leaves the sides of the bowl. Work dough with hands into 12–15 oval loaves about ½ inch thick. Bake on a greased baking sheet for 30–40 minutes.

JOHNNYCAKES

Johnnycakes were originally "journey" cakes, and were made in advance to take on trips.

An early New England recipe:

Scald one pint of milk and put to three pints of Indian meal and a half pint of flour. Bake before the fire until done.

Here is a more precise one:

2 cups whole cornmeal	1 cup milk
1 teaspoon salt	1–3 tablespoons boiling water
4 tablespoons butter	

Cream cornmeal and salt with butter. Add milk, then 1 to 3 tablespoons boiling water to make a moist batter. Drop by large spoonfuls onto a hot greased griddle and flatten with the back of the spoon. Fry until firm and brown-tinged on the bottom, then turn and fry other side. Serve hot—good with butter and honey.

Or another recipe, this one made with water instead of milk, which allows the corn flavor to come through more strongly:

1 cup whole cornmeal	1 tablespoon butter
2 cups water	½ teaspoon salt

Preheat oven to 350°F. Stir ingredients together in saucepan. Cook until mixture thickens, stirring constantly. Cover pan; cool. Shape into 4 3-inch squares. Place on greased baking sheet and bake until crisp, about 40 minutes. Serve hot.

HUSH PUPPIES

When homesteaders get together for a neighborly meal, there always seem to be lots of dogs around. That is probably exactly what happened in early America, when folks were standing around a big kettle of oil, waiting for the corn cakes to cook. The early settlers discovered, as we have learned our-selves, that tossing a few tidbits to the pack keeps them quiet. Notice that when the frying's done, the pack of people quiets down quite a bit, too!

2 cups whole cornmeal	2 eggs
1 teaspoon baking powder	½ cup milk or yoghurt
1 teaspoon salt	oil for frying

Stir together cornmeal, baking powder, and salt, pressing out lumps. Beat together eggs and milk, then combine with dry ingredients, forming into balls about 1 inch in diameter. Cook in ½ inch of hot oil, until golden brown. Drain on paper towels and serve hot.

HOMINY

Hominy is treated, soaked, deskinned corn kernels. It is readily available in most supermarkets, or try making it yourself with the following recipe.

4 heaping tablespoons baking soda	8 cups dried corn kernels
4 quarts water	

Dissolve soda in water, using a ceramic or enameled pan (not metal). Add the corn, adding more water if necessary to cover. Soak overnight. The next day, bring to boil, reduce heat, and simmer until the hulls loosen from the grain, about 3 hours. Drain corn and wash several times, until soda taste is com-pletely gone. Rub hulls off between the palms of your hands.

Hominy may be frozen, canned (using pressure canning techniques for low-acid foods), or dried in a very low oven and kept in airtight containers. To cook, cover with boiling water and simmer gently about four hours, or until tender.

SCRAPPLE

I had been enjoying this sausage-like dish for many months before someone pointed out that the name came from the fact that it was made out of the left-over scraps at hog-butchering time. Don't let that get to you, though; it is delicious, especially with maple syrup.

½ pound beef or pork liver
½ pound boneless pork
8 or more cups water
1 teaspoon thyme

½ teaspoon powdered sage
½ teaspoon black pepper
1½ cups cornmeal
1 cup cold water

Cook meat slowly in 8 cups water for 1½–2 hours until tender. Add water to cover if necessary. Cool, reserving broth, and chop meat finely, pulse in a food processor, or put through food mill or meat grinder. Measure 3 cups broth and add seasonings. Mix cornmeal with 1 cup cold water. Add meat to broth and bring to boil, then add cornmeal gradually, stirring constantly until mixture is thick and bubbling. Add more cornmeal if mixture does not thicken well. Pour into a greased loaf pan and chill overnight.

To serve, slice scrapple ½ inch thick, dredge with flour, and brown quickly on both sides in hot buttered skillet. Serve with maple syrup and griddle cakes.

HOMINY ENCHILADAS

1 large onion, chopped	½ teaspoon oregano
2 tablespoons vegetable oil	½ teaspoon basil
2 tablespoons flour	5 pounds (or 2 2½-pound cans)
1 medium can whole or stewed	hominy
tomatoes	¼ cup butter or margarine
2 tablespoons chile powder	1½ cups grated cheddar cheese
1 teaspoon salt	

Preheat oven to 325°F. Sauté onion in oil until tender. Stir in flour, then add tomatoes and seasonings. Bring to boil to thicken, then simmer slowly for 10 minutes.

Sauté hominy in butter until lightly browned. Layer half the hominy, half the cheese, and half the onion mixture in a lightly greased 1½-quart baking dish. Repeat, reserving ½ cup cheese for the top. Bake for 30 minutes. Serves 6–8.

TANGY CORNMEAL MUFFINS

There are as many cornbread and cornmeal muffin recipes as there are cooks in the South, but I restrained myself to my favorites. The plain yoghurt in this one gives it the distinctive flavor.

2 eggs, separated	½ teaspoon soda
1 cup yoghurt	1 teaspoon baking powder
3 tablespoons vegetable oil	½ teaspoon salt
1½ cups whole cornmeal	

Preheat oven to 425°F. Beat egg yolks, yoghurt, and oil together. Stir together cornmeal, baking soda, baking powder, and salt, breaking up any lumps; add to egg-yolk mixture. Beat egg whites until stiff, and fold lightly into batter. Bake in hot greased muffin tins for 20 minutes. Makes 1 dozen muffins.

HOMINY CHEESE BAKE

Hominy grits, or just "grits," as they are called in the South, are broken pieces of dried hominy. If you prepare your own hominy and dry it, you can crack it coarsely in a flour mill to cook into a porridge-like consistency and serve with sausages or scrapple. Grits can be purchased in most grocery stores in the cereals section, however, and since they are not strictly a "whole grain" even when prepared at home, there is no advantage nutritionally to doing this one yourself.

1 teaspoon salt	1 cup finely chopped celery
5 cups water	½ cup finely chopped onion
1 cup hominy grits	1 cup sliced mushrooms
2 cups grated mild cheese	1 cup diced cooked meat
3 tablespoons butter or margarine	2¼-ounce can sliced olives

Bring salted water to a boil. Slowly add grits, stirring constantly. Cover and simmer, stirring occasionally, 25 minutes. Add 1 cup of cheese and stir until melted.

Preheat oven to 325°F. Heat butter in skillet and sauté celery, onion, mushrooms, and meat 3–5 minutes. Make a layer of half the grits in a buttered 2-quart baking dish. Add meat mixture and cover with remaining grits. Cover with remaining cup of cheese and sprinkle with olives. Bake 20–25 minutes. Makes 6 servings.

CHEESY CORN MUFFINS

1 cup whole cornmeal
½ teaspoon salt
½ teaspoon baking soda
1 beaten egg

2 tablespoons vegetable oil
1 cup yoghurt
1 cup grated cheddar cheese

Preheat oven to 425°F. Mix dry ingredients, stirring out lumps. Add remaining ingredients and mix only until smooth. Bake in preheated oiled muffin tins for 20 minutes. Makes 10–12 muffins.

GREEN CHILE CHEESE CORNBREAD

3 eggs
2 cups buttermilk, yoghurt, or sour cream
2 tablespoons vegetable oil
2 cups whole cornmeal
½ teaspoon salt

1 teaspoon baking soda
4 roasted, peeled, chopped long green chiles (2-ounce can)
1–2 cups grated sharp cheddar cheese

Preheat oven to 450°F. Mix together eggs, buttermilk, and oil. Stir together dry ingredients, pressing out lumps; add to liquid. Stir in chiles and all but ¼ cup of the cheese.

Heat oiled 10-inch cast-iron skillet or baking pan in oven. Pour in batter; top with ¼ cup more grated cheese. Bake 25–30 minutes, or until set and slightly brown on top. Or, using a glass baking dish, cook in a microwave on High for 5 minutes, then bake for 10 minutes in a 400°F. oven. Cool slightly before cutting into wedges and serving with lots of butter.

CORNMEAL BREAD

Rub a piece of butter the size of an egg into a pint of corn-meal. Make it into a batter with 2 eggs and some new milk. Add a spoonful of yeast. Set it by the fire an hour to rise. Butter little pans and bake it.

The Virginia Housewife
1 8 2 5

From my own Virginia experience comes the following recipe, courtesy of the National Park Service employees at a water-powered corn mill they operate near Alexandria.

2 eggs
2 cups buttermilk
1 teaspoon baking soda

2 cups whole cornmeal
½ teaspoon salt

Preheat oven to 450°F. Place 10-inch oiled skillet or oiled muffin tin in oven for 5 minutes before baking. Combine ingredients in any order; stir to blend. Pour into preheated pan. If you are using a skillet, bake bread for 25–30 minutes, or until a toothpick inserted in center comes out clean. Bake muffins for 15–20 minutes.

GRIDDLE CAKES

Also from the National Park Service comes this recipe for 100% cornmeal pancakes.

1 cup whole cornmeal
1 cup canned hominy, drained
3 eggs, slightly beaten
½ teaspoon salt

1 cup buttermilk
¼ cup melted butter or vegetable oil
1 heaping teaspoon baking powder

Combine ingredients in any order, stir to blend. Bake on hot griddle until browned; turn and bake other side. Serve with butter and pure maple syrup. Delicious!

ANADAMA BREAD

The story goes that the farmer had a lazy wife who served him cornmeal mush for breakfast every day, and often for lunch, too. When she began to serve up mush three times a day, the farmer finally got desperate and started adding odds and ends of other ingredients to her offering, just for variety. He eventually arrived at this popular bread recipe, and, having no hard feelings toward his wife, named it after her.

1 cup whole cornmeal	1 tablespoon salt
2½ cups boiling water	2 tablespoons active dry yeast
3 tablespoons vegetable oil	¼ cup lukewarm water
½ cup sorghum syrup or molasses	5–6 cups whole wheat flour

Stir cornmeal gradually into boiling water; add oil, sorghum syrup (or molasses), and salt and beat well. Set aside to cool. Dissolve yeast in water (if you use the cup used to measure the sorghum, the yeast will bubble faster); stir into lukewarm cornmeal mixture. Stir in 3 cups flour; beat well to develop gluten. Add remaining 2–3 cups flour, working the last flour in by hand when dough becomes too stiff to stir. Knead thoroughly, turn dough into oiled bowl, and let rise, covered with a damp cloth, in a warm place until double in bulk—about 1 hour. Punch down, form into 2 loaves, and let rise again until almost double. Preheat oven to 375°F. Bake for 40–45 minutes.

TAMALES

Tamales are like Mexican hot dogs. The outer covering is not edible, however, but is used simply as a wrapper for the dough and meat filling. If corn husks are not available where you live, use aluminum foil.

24 clean dried corn husks

FILLING
1 pound beef or pork, cut from bone
1½ teaspoons salt
4 cups water
1 clove garlic, finely chopped
2 tablespoons bacon fat, shortening,
    or margarine (not oil)

1–2 hot green chiles, chopped
1 tablespoon chile powder
1 tablespoon ground cumin (*cominos*)

DOUGH
3 cups corn flour or *masa harina*
2 teaspoons salt
⅓ cup melted bacon fat, shortening,
    or margarine

Separate corn husks; soak in warm water until soft (or overnight). Keep damp until ready to use by covering with a wet cloth.

Cook meat in salted water until tender, drain broth, and reserve. Chop meat finely, pulse in a food processor, or run through a food mill or meat grinder.

Sauté garlic in fat until soft; stir in chiles, chile powder, cumin, ½ cup broth, and meat. Stirring constantly, cook until thick, about 15 minutes.

Combine corn flour, salt, and melted fat in a bowl. Stir in 2 cups of broth. Knead until dough holds together, adding more broth or flour to obtain the right texture. Cover with damp cloth until ready to use.

Place a corn husk flat on working surface. Spread about 1 tablespoon dough over half the heavy end of the husk. Shape dough with your hands into a rectangle. Place 1 tablespoon of meat in the center of the dough; roll the husk like a jelly roll and fold up both ends to enclose filling. Tie with string or a strip of corn husk. Form 24 tamales.

Steam tamales piled on a rack in a large kettle for 45 minutes, being sure that the water does not contact husks. The *masa* coating should be firm and come loose easily from husks. To serve, unfold the top and sides of husk, place on a platter.

TAMALE PIE

This was a favorite of mine when we lived in the Southwest.

DOUGH
1 cup whole cornmeal
4 cups boiling water
1 teaspoon salt

FILLING
1 pound ground meat (beef, pork, lamb, or turkey)
1 onion, chopped
1 tablespoon vegetable oil

1 8-ounce can tomato sauce
1½ cups soup stock or boullion
½ teaspoon pepper
1 teaspoon salt
1 tablespoon chile powder
1 cup cut corn—fresh, frozen, or canned
½ cup chopped green pepper
1 2¼-ounce can sliced olives, drained

Sauté meat and onion in 1 tablespoon oil until meat is browned and onion is tender; drain any excess fat. Add tomato sauce, stock, pepper, salt, chile powder, corn, green pepper, and olives. Cover pan and simmer for 20 minutes. Meanwhile prepare dough. Add the cornmeal gradually to boiling water, stirring constantly. Continue stirring and cook slowly for 10 to 15 minutes, or until thick. Set aside.

Preheat oven to 375°F. Grease a 1½-quart baking dish. Spread a layer of cornmeal mixture on the bottom and up the sides. Pour meat filling into dish; spoon more cornmeal over the top, smoothing to form a crust. Bake for 30 minutes, or until top is firm and lightly browned.

CORNMEAL WAFERS

2 cups finely ground whole cornmeal
1 teaspoon salt

¼ cup vegetable oil
water to moisten (about ¾ cup)

Preheat oven to 400°F. Stir together cornmeal, salt, and oil. Gradually add water, stirring with a fork, until dough can be worked. Knead slightly, then press onto well-greased cookie sheet. Roll with cylindrical glass or rolling pin until flat and very thin. Score with knife or pastry wheel into squares the size you want your crackers to be. Place in oven, then immediately reduce heat to 325°F. After 20 minutes, reduce heat again to 250°F., and continue baking until thoroughly dry and slightly browned. Watch carefully, as these burn easily.

CORNMEAL ONION LOAF

1 cup whole cornmeal
1 teaspoon salt
2 teaspoons baking powder
½ cup milk

2 eggs, beaten
¼ cup chopped onion
2 tablespoons vegetable oil
1 cup boiling water

Preheat oven to 375°F. Combine cornmeal, salt, and baking powder, pressing out any lumps. Add milk, eggs, and onion; beat well. Stir in oil and boiling water. Bake in loaf pan for 40 minutes, or until puffed and golden-brown. Onions will rise to top.

TUNA FESTIVAL

This is one of those dinners you can pull out of the cupboards and put together in half an hour.

2 cups vegetable or whole wheat noodles
4 cups salted water
1 tablespoon butter or margarine
1 tablespoon whole wheat flour
½ cup milk
1 #10 can cut corn or hominy

1 7-ounce can tuna or bonita or 1 cup cooked rice
1 4½-ounce can chopped green chiles
1 4-ounce can chopped mushrooms
2 cups grated cheddar or longhorn cheese

Boil noodles in 4 cups salted water. Melt butter in large skillet. Stir in flour and cook 2–3 minutes. Slowly stir in milk and cook until thickened and smooth.

Preheat oven to 350°F. Drain cans of corn, chiles, and mushrooms, adding liquid to sauce. Stir cheese into sauce. Mix drained noodles, corn, tuna or rice, chiles, and mushrooms together in 2-quart baking dish. Add cheese sauce. Bake for 15–20 minutes.

CORNMEAL CHEESE WEDGES

⅔ cup whole cornmeal
2 cups milk
1 cup grated cheddar cheese
1 tablespoon butter or margarine

¾ teaspoon baking powder
½ teaspoon salt
2 eggs, separated

Preheat oven to 350°F. In medium saucepan, stir cornmeal into milk and heat slowly, stirring constantly until thickened. Stir in cheese, butter, baking powder, and salt. Remove from heat. Gradually add a little of the hot mixture to slightly beaten egg yolks in small bowl; beat well and return to saucepan (this is to prevent curdling). Beat egg whites until stiff; fold into cornmeal mixture. Turn into greased 9-inch pie pan. Bake 40–45 minutes. Cut into wedges to serve.

THREE-GRAIN SOUP

In parts of the Tyrol and Italy, corn is sometimes mixed with wheat and rye in soups and breads, and the combination is also used occasionally for polenta. Try it in the following hearty soup.

2 pounds lamb (shoulder or neck)	1 small turnip, chopped
4 quarts cold water	4 medium carrots, chopped
¼ cup coarsely cracked corn	2 stalks celery, chopped
¼ cup coarsely cracked wheat	1 medium onion, chopped
⅛ cup coarsely cracked rye	3 teaspoons salt

Wipe meat with a damp paper towel and place in a large soup pot. Cover with cold water, bring to a boil, and simmer, covered, for 1 hour. Skim fat from broth, or refrigerate overnight and lift fat from top before reheating. Add grains and chopped vegetables, season with salt, simmer for another hour, and serve. Serves 8.

CORNMEAL COFFEE CAKE

1 cup whole wheat flour	2 eggs
2 tablespoons brown sugar	1 cup milk
3 teaspoons baking powder	3 tablespoons vegetable oil
½ teaspoon salt	½ cup fruit preserves
1 cup whole cornmeal	brown sugar

Preheat oven to 425°F. In mixing bowl, stir together dry ingredients, pressing out all lumps. Blend eggs, milk, and oil; add to dry ingredients. Stir just until smooth (do not overbeat). Turn into greased 9-inch pie plate. Spoon preserves over batter; crumble sugar on top. Bake for 20–25 minutes, or until cake begins to shrink from edges of pan. Cool slightly; cut into wedges and serve hot.

POLENTA

This is the staple dish of northern Italy, and although it begins much the same as our own Southern cornmeal mush, somehow it comes out differently. The cooking of polenta is still a daily ritual in many Italian kitchens. Traditionally made in a copper pot, it now is often stirred in a large stainless-steel pan sitting on a modern stove, but the old criterion for "doneness" hasn't changed: simmer and stir until the spoon will stand by itself in the mixture.

1 cup cornmeal   3 cups chicken stock

Grind cornmeal to medium coarseness. Bring to a boil 3 cups chicken stock, then slowly stir in corn. Reduce heat and cook slowly, stirring often, until thick, about 20 minutes. Spoon into serving dish or bowls and top with butter and grated cheese. Polenta is usually served with meat and gravy.

Polenta may also be spooned into a mold and allowed to cool slightly before unmolding onto a plate, or it may be refrigerated in a loaf pan, sliced while still cold, and fried until crisp before serving.

MAMALIGA

Here is the old trusty cornmeal mush again, this time as the staple of Romania. The primary difference is in how it is served, usually with sour cream or yoghurt.

1 cup whole cornmeal   2½ cups salted water

Combine cornmeal and cold salted water. Bring slowly to a boil and simmer gently, stirring constantly, until thick, 12–15 minutes. Invert onto a plate.

Serve with sour cream, yoghurt, grated cheese, melted butter, gravy, or topped with eggs.

KENKE

This is yet another version of cornmeal mush, which in parts of Africa is called Mealie Meal Porridge. Kenke is made from fermented corn dough and steamed in corn husks. In this version, yoghurt is used to introduce a culture which is allowed to grow for 8 to 24 hours before cooking the dough.

4 cups boiling water	2 teaspoons salt
4 cups whole cornmeal	2 cups boiling water
2 tablespoons yoghurt	

Stir 4 cups boiling water into cornmeal, stirring rapidly to prevent lumps. Cool to lukewarm and stir in 2 tablespoons plain yoghurt. Cover with a damp cloth and leave overnight.

When ready to prepare kenke, add 2 teaspoons salt to the dough and stir dough into 2 cups rapidly boiling water, stirring constantly until mixture has thickened. Spoon onto squares of aluminum foil, folding sides and ends to make rectangles. Place on rack inside large kettle of boiling water; steam for 2 hours. Cool slightly, until dough easily pulls free from foil. Serve hot or cold. Makes 12 kenke.

RICE

What is the matter with Mary Jane?
She's perfectly well and she hasn't a pain
And it's lovely rice pudding for dinner again!
What is the matter with Mary Jane?
When We Were Very Young, 1924,
"Rice Pudding," by A. A. Milne

Rice is the staple food crop of over half the world's people. About 200,000,000,000 pounds a year are produced, most of it in Asia; most of the people in China, India, Pakistan, Japan, Korea, Taiwan, Sri Lanka, Indochina, Thailand, Indonesia, the Philippines, Malaysia, and Madagascar eat rice every day. In the United States we grow about one percent of the world crop, and eat only part of that. Someone estimated that each person in the Far East eats four hundred pounds of rice every year, while less than ten pounds a year are eaten by the average American. Which is not to say that we should all run out and start gobbling rice. First of all, the form in which most of that rice is eaten—highly polished—is not especially nutritious. Secondly, rice becomes boring as a steady diet. Most people who eat rice for breakfast, lunch, and dinner would just as soon have a little more variety, but for economic and cultural reasons do not have that option. Rice can, however, add nutrition and variety to western diets if eaten in its unrefined form and balanced with appropriate other foods.

Rice is nearly always eaten whole, boiled or steamed, and served in either sweetened or salted versions with fruit or with meat, fish, and vegetable accompaniments. It can also be ground into flour and used for baking. Rice flour is light colored and can be used as a replacement for white flour in many egg-rich recipes. A wine called *sake* is made from rice in Japan; in India a similar drink is known as *arrack*.

Nearly five thousand years ago in China, the sowing of the first rice was part of an important annual religious ceremony. The Emperor planted the first and best seeds, followed by other members of his family who planted several different kinds of rice nearby. For many years it was thought that rice originated in China, but it is now believed that the wild grass Nivara, a native of India, is the ancestor of the modern cultivated varieties.

Buddhism was an important factor in the spread of cultivated rice from India through China, Japan, and most of Asia. Alexander the Great took rice to Europe with him when he returned from his invasion of India, but it was not cultivated there until centuries later. It was unknown in the New World when colonists arrived, although its wild cousin was flourishing in the Great Lakes region. Virginia colonists tried to grow rice in the mid-seventeenth century, but were not very successful. Planters in South Carolina renewed attempts about fifty years later, and for about two hundred years rice was grown quite heavily in the Southern states.

Rice thrives in warm, humid areas and requires abundant water. Its wild ancestors grew in lakes and swamps, and cultivated varieties have retained this need. During most of their growing season, rice plants must be submerged in from one to eight inches of water, a condition achieved in the U.S. and other wealthy countries by irrigating carefully leveled and dammed fields. When the rice is ready to ripen, the fields are drained and the grain is picked and harvested by machine, just like other cereals. Most of the world, however, uses time-honored, labor-intensive planting and harvesting methods. Since it is possible to grow rice on small farms, and since you might decide to try it, I have described the necessary steps in some detail below.

First broadcast the seed rice into a carefully spaded and raked nursery bed, thickly enough to just about cover the ground. (To speed germination, some farmers soak their seed for up to 30 days in cool, circulating water before planting.) Cover the rice seeds with a thin layer of soil or sand and thin straw mulch and keep this layer in place until the plants are about three inches tall. At that time the seed bed can be flooded, or normal watering can be continued until the plants are ready for transplanting, when they are about six inches high. During this early germinating process it is very important that the bed be kept well watered and free from weeds. The temperature of the soil and water are critical; 75°F. To 85°F. is the most effective for germination and strong root formation. To raise the temperature of well or stream water, Asian farmers usually dig out a shallow warming pond through which the water is run before being routed onto the seed bed.

Rice plants are transplanted about forty to forty-five days after seeding, by which time the nursery plot is becoming quite crowded. Make a paddy by digging trenches and forming dikes with the removed soil to enclose a level area. On level ground the paddy can be quite large—10 to 15 feet on a side—but if your land is sloping, contour the paddy to the form of the ground, or make several small paddies. Before transplanting, the soil should be soaked so that it is quite muddy (both in the seed bed and in the paddy) to prevent damage to the roots. Press each plant carefully into the mud of the paddy, pressing soil firmly around each one.

Most farmers keep their paddies flooded continuously to a depth of at least one inch, although if there is adequate water available there are some advantages to draining the water out at night (for example, mosquitoes cannot breed). In order to keep the paddy flooded, you will need to use a soaker attachment to a hose and adjust the water flow carefully so that the water soaks in slowly without overflowing your dikes.

When the plants are about fifteen inches high, the paddies are drained, hand weeded, and cultivated with a hoe, then flooded again until two weeks before harvest. Four to six months after planting, the heads of rice are golden and heavy and ready to cut. You usually use sickles for this task, and bundling, drying, threshing, and winnowing follow the same pattern as for wheat. The hulls, however, are tough and adhere quite firmly to rice grains, and must be milled off. Primitive methods of milling included pounding the rice with a large wooden hammer or using a wooden mortar and pestle. Neither method was very efficient, but since effective milling removed not only the hulls but also the bran, germ, and endosperm, the undermilled rice retained much of the valuable protein, fiber, vitamins, and minerals it might otherwise have lost. More effective milling methods now exist even in countries where rice is farmed by hand—not all of which have to result in an overmilled product. Many farmers own gasoline-powered milling machines or take their harvest to a large commercial mill for processing.

It was noticed in 1890 that plantation workers in Sarawak, fed on imported white rice, developed a form of malnutrition known as *beriberi*, while their families, who remained at home and consumed freshly husked rice processed by primitive methods, did not. For many years the mystery continued, until it was learned that beriberi was caused by a vitamin B deficiency. By that time millions of people whose primary food was white rice had suffered the debilitating disease. Beriberi did not appear when brown rice was substituted into the diet, nor when vitamin B was added to polished (thoroughly milled) rice.

There are ways of treating rice, methods used for generations in India and other parts of Asia, which cut down the nutritional loss in milling. One of these methods is parboiling, which consists of soaking, steaming, and drying the rice before milling to drive the water-soluble vitamins and minerals from the bran into the grain so that they will not be worn away. In the United States this process is used to make converted rice. Other methods include fermenting the grain and steaming it.

If you decide to try growing rice, contact your local agricultural extension agent for details about locating germination-tested seed and about the nutrient requirements of your soil. According to David Spiekerman and Junsei Yamazaki (*Organic Gardening and Farming*, December 1975), it is possible to grow over six thousand pounds of rice on one acre of land using hand methods, so it might be worth trying if you or your friends eat a lot of this grain.

You can purchase converted rice in most major grocery stores, and that might be a good first step to brown rice, since it contains more minerals than polished rice, and is similar in appearance. My bet, however, is that once you have tried unpolished, undegerminated (brown) rice you will be hooked. The unpolished grain bears little resemblance to the pallid white rice you've usually eaten, and to my mind that's all to the good. Large grocery stores usually carry small boxes of brown rice, but to purchase it at a more reasonable price or in larger quantities, try a natural foods store.

Rice is susceptible to many diseases and varmints, and is often treated quite heavily with fungicides and pesticides, so this is one grain where I would recommend you try to seek out an organically grown product. If you are unsure about the rice you are buying—ask. At least it will make your dealer know that you care. If you can't find it anywhere else, track down growers and ask them where you can buy it.

Brown rice takes longer to cook than either converted or conventional polished white rice, but the resulting product is rarely ever gummy. All the recipes in this section, with the exception of the wild rice recipes, assume you are using whole grain brown rice. If you substitute converted rice, shorten the cooking time appropriately.

Rice flour is occasionally available in the import section of large grocery stores or in natural foods outlets. It is so easy, however, to make fresh flour in a grain mill or nut grinder that it seems silly to buy the refined product (which is what most commercial rice flour is—ground polished rice) when you can have the whole grain one in just a few moments. Rice is soft, and very easy to grind. If you have any difficulty with gritty pastry, cookies, pancakes, or whatever, try grinding the flour finer or combining the liquids with the flour and bringing to a boil before adding other ingredients.

As with all recipes in this book, these are intended to simply give you the feel of using the grain. Rice is a particularly variable grain. Experiment freely with whole rice and rice flour, and you will find that there are many more flavors than you could have ever imagined.

WILD RICE

Wild rice, or *Zizania aquatica* as the botanists call it, is not a rice at all, but a tall aquatic grass which is a distant relative of cultivated rice. It grows naturally in China, Japan, and parts of North America, particularly in the Great Lakes region. It was the staple grain of the Chippewas and even now grows primarily on their land.

Attempts to cultivate this beautiful grass commercially have so far been unsuccessful, and the old methods of harvesting it are still the most common ones. You can pick it yourself if you have a canoe or rowboat and live in the right part of the country. Here are the instructions:

Pull the ends of the six-to ten-foot reeds into your boat and hit them sharply with a stick so that the grains fall into the boat. Try to have them fall into a box but don't expect to get them all. Spread the rice out to dry in a warm place or parch it in a large kettle, stirring constantly. This keeps the damp rice from spoiling, and helps to loosen the hulls. Winnow out the husks through a sieve or rub them between your hands and blow them away.

Make sure, by the way, that before you go to all this work, you know the ownership of the land you are on. The money which comes from the harvesting and distribution of wild rice forms most of the income of the Chippewa Nation, and I doubt it would be taken kindly were you to be caught poaching.

An easier way to enjoy wild rice is to buy a box of it at the grocery store. Its scarcity makes it a rather expensive commodity, but if you treat it as a rare luxury, the cost can be overlooked. To the best of my knowledge, no one has attempted to polish wild rice, so here is one whole grain product which can be purchased without difficulty. Enjoy.

BASIC BROWN RICE

1 cup brown rice	2 cups water or stock
1 tablespoon vegetable oil	1 teaspoon salt

Sauté rice in boil until translucent, stirring constantly to be sure it doesn't stick. Bring water or stock to boiling and stir into rice; add salt, cover, and simmer over very low heat for 40–50 minutes. Check at 30 minutes; if rice seems too dry, add ¼ cup or so boiling water. Do not stir rice once it begins to puff; serve with a bamboo paddle or wet wooden spoon to prevent sticking.

RICE FLOUR PANCAKES

2 cups finely ground rice flour
4 teaspoons baking powder
1 teaspoon salt

2 cups milk
2 eggs
1 tablespoon vegetable oil

Stir together flour, baking powder, and salt, pressing out any lumps. Beat together milk and eggs; add to flour mixture. Stir in oil. Let stand ½ hour before baking. Drop by large spoonfuls onto a hot, lightly greased griddle. Bake until dry on top; turn and bake other side. These are particularly good with fruit toppings.

RICE SALAD

2 cups cooked brown rice
1 2¼-ounce can sliced olives
¼ cup French or other creamy salad
    dressing

¼ cup finely chopped celery
¼ cup chopped tomato

Stir ingredients together; chill thoroughly. Serve by spooning onto a bed of crisp lettuce.

RICE BREAD

Boil 6 ounces rice in a quart of water till it is dry and soft. Put it into 2 pounds of flour, mix it well; add two teaspoonfuls of salt, two large spoonfuls of yeast, and as much water as will make it the consistency of bread. When well risen, bake it in the molds.

The Virginia Housewife
1825

163

RICE CRACKERS

The two most important things about making crackers are: Roll them very thin and dry them thoroughly. I make my crackers directly on the baking sheet, and dry them in a medium warm oven for close to half an hour. Textures differ depending on the moisture content of your ingredients, the humidity on the day you make them, and your oven, so experiment until you find the right combination of temperature and time for each batch.

2 cups cooked brown rice
2 cups whole wheat flour
1 tablespoon salt

¼ cup sunflower oil
approximately ½ cup water

Preheat oven to 425°F. Stir together rice, flour, and salt with a fork. Add oil, and stir thoroughly, until oil has darkened the flour evenly. Add water gradually, and add just enough to allow you to press dough together into a moist, but not sticky, ball. Sometimes you will need a little more or less water. Roll out on buttered baking sheets until quite thin (this much dough makes about 2½ full-sized baking sheets worth of crackers). Brush with the beaten yolk of an egg and sprinkle with salt. Cut into squares or rectangles with a very sharp knife.

Place baking sheets into preheated oven and immediately lower the temperature to 350°F. Check at 20 minutes. If the edges are quite dry and crisp at that point turn off oven and let crackers dry inside the oven until it cools. If the edges are not yet crisp, let crackers bake a little longer. Lift crackers from baking sheet with a spatula and let dry on a cookie rack, or turn them over on the baking sheet so that the bottoms can dry thoroughly. Place in an airtight container to store.

BROWN RICE RISOTTO

This is a very moist rice dish, but should not be gummy. The best way to prevent gumminess is to serve at once.

1 medium onion, finely chopped
1 clove garlic, finely chopped
2 tablespoons vegetable oil
1 cup brown rice
3 cups chicken stock, heated
3 tablespoons fresh parsley, finely chopped

¼ teaspoon powdered saffron (or 6 saffron stigmas dissolved in 2 tablespoons stock)
½ cup grated Parmesan cheese

Sauté onion and garlic in oil until translucent. Add rice and cook for 3 minutes more, stirring constantly. Dissolve yeast, parsley, and saffron in stock. Pour 1 cup of stock into rice mixture and simmer gently, adding rest of stock gradually as liquid is absorbed and stirring frequently to prevent sticking. Rice should be tender in about 30 minutes. Stir in half of the cheese, top with the remaining cheese, and serve.

LAMB PILAF (PILAU)

Each culture seems to have a favorite dish made from its staple grain. The cracked wheat version is called bulgur, the buckwheat one is called kasha. Cornmeal mush, Tuo Zaafi, couscous, oatmeal—all have formed the basis for meals in different countries. So it is with pilaf, also known as pilau. Originally made by cooking rice in meat juices, pilaf can be cooked in water or any type of stock and dressed up with shredded or chopped meat, nuts, fruits, and herbs in hundreds of different ways. The Persians served it with kebabs— pieces of meat and vegetables that had been skewered and cooked over open coals. In India, pilau is frequently flavored with curry spices or saffron. This recipe and the following one are two ways of preparing similar dishes; use them as jumping-off points for your own creations.

4 tablespoons vegetable oil	1 teaspoon grated nutmeg
1 pound lamb, cubed	1½ teaspoons ground cumin
1 medium onion, chopped	1 teaspoon salt
1 clove garlic, chopped	¼ teaspoon pepper
1 cup stock	pinch saffron

Sauté lamb in oil until evenly browned; remove from pan and sauté onion and garlic in remaining oil. Return lamb to pan. Add stock and spices; simmer about 30 minutes. Meanwhile, prepare rice mixture:

6 small carrots, sliced	1 cup raisins
1 cup slivered almonds	1 tablespoon honey
1 cup stock	3 cups hot cooked brown rice

Cook carrots, almonds, raisins, and honey in stock until carrots are just tender, about 10 minutes. Drain, reserving stock, and stir into rice. Mound on a serving plate. Add stock to meat mixture if desired; pour over rice and serve at once.

GREEN PEA PILAF (PILAU)

1 onion, sliced	¼ cup slivered almonds
¼ cup vegetable oil	½ cup seedless raisins
2 cups brown rice	1 cup green peas, fresh or frozen
1 teaspoon salt	4 cups water or stock

Sauté onion in oil until tender. Remove with slotted spoon to plate. Sauté rice until translucent; add salt, almonds, raisins, and liquid. Cover tightly and steam over very low heat 40–50 minutes, or until rice is tender and liquid is absorbed (add ¼ cup water if rice seems dry; do not stir). Lightly stir in peas; cook 5 minutes more. Serve in a mound, sprinkled with sautéed onion rings.

STUFFED GRAPE LEAVES

I once thought of Dolmath, or stuffed grape leaves, as an exotic dish beyond my reach, but they aren't as hard to make as I thought. The grape leaves themselves can be purchased at Middle Eastern specialty shops.

1–1½ pounds tender grape leaves
salted water
2 large onions, chopped
2 tablespoons vegetable oil
1½ cups brown rice
2½ cups water

½ cup chopped parsley
½ teaspoon fresh mint
juice of one lemon
1 teaspoon salt
¼ cup chopped pine nuts

Boil grape leaves for 2–3 minutes in salted water, then spread on a clean board or cloth to dry. Sauté onions in oil; add rice and 2½ cups water. Cover tightly and simmer for 20 minutes. Remove from heat and stir in remaining ingredients. Keeping the shiny side of the grape leaves on the outside, put about 1 teaspoonful of filling on each leaf and fold each one lengthwise, one side over the other. Fold ends down and place folded-side down in a large saucepan. Place packages on top of each other in several layers in the pan until all the filling is used. Put a plate on top to keep them from rising up, and pour water into the pan to cover. Cover pan tightly and steam for 45–50 minutes, or until rice is thoroughly cooked.

STUFFED ZUCCHINI

Remember that year you grew zucchini and were eating it twice a day for a month? Well, we did that, too, and we collected lots of recipes together. This one is for the end of the season, when the zucchini are getting out of control and growing two feet long. By then they're so tough you really need to take the seeds out to eat them, and so we devised this mixture to fill up the hole.

2 large zucchini

salt and pepper

Halve lengthwise 2 large zucchini. Scoop out seeds and pulp. Parboil shells 3–5 minutes. Drain and sprinkle with salt and pepper.

1 medium onion, chopped	1 cup cooked brown rice
1 clove garlic, finely chopped	¼ cup chopped nuts
2 tablespoons vegetable oil	1 teaspoon salt
1 cup cooked lentils	½ teaspoon pepper

Preheat oven to 350°F. Sauté onion and garlic in oil until tender. Combine with lentils, rice, nuts, and seasonings. Heap into zucchini. Bake for 25 minutes, or until squash is fork-tender. Really huge ones may take longer.

RICE-STUFFED SQUASH

2 cups brown rice	2 acorn, butternut, or other winter
4 cups water or stock	squash
1 teaspoon salt	½ cup grated cheddar cheese

Preheat oven to 350°F. Cook rice in salted water or stock over low heat, tightly covered, for 45 minutes. Meanwhile cut squash into halves, remove seeds, and turn cut-side down in a pan containing ¼ inch of water. Bake 30 minutes. Turn right-side up, stir cheese into rice, and heap into squash halves. Return to oven for 15 minutes.

SOPA ARROZ (RICE SOUP)

This is one of the *sopas secas*, or dry soups, of Mexico. We first encountered Sopa Arroz in Oaxaca, and were rather surprised to discover that this rice "soup" was not a soup at all in our sense of the word, since the soup stock had been entirely absorbed by the rice.

1 cup brown rice
1 clove garlic, finely chopped
1 small onion, finely chopped
2 tablespoons vegetable oil
2 tablespoons finely chopped parsley

1 long green chile, roasted and
  peeled (or canned), chopped
2¾ cups chicken stock
1 teaspoon salt

Sauté rice with garlic and onion in oil until golden-brown. Drain off excess oil. Add parsley, chile, stock, and salt. Cover tightly and simmer for 45 minutes, or until all liquid has been absorbed.

VARIATION: After sautéing rice, add 1½ cups tomatoes and 3 cups liquid. Cook as above for 40 minutes, then stir in 1 cup cooked shrimp and steam for 5 more minutes. Serve immediately.

CHICKEN RICE SOUP

This is the last stage in what we generally call "no-residue chicken" at our house. The first stage is to cook a chicken. Save the bones, gravy, neck, giblets, stuffing, whatever is left after the meal. Boil these leftovers in 2 quarts of water or vegetable stock for 2 hours, or 30 minutes in a pressure cooker. This can be done in the evening after your chicken dinner, or any time thereafter. Strain stock, then strip any meat off the bones by hand. Discard bones (if they were pressure cooked, they can be run through a food mill or grinder and fed to your animals).

1 cup brown rice	1 teaspoon salt
1 tablespoon vegetable oil	4–6 cups chicken stock
2 stalks celery	1 teaspoon thyme
¼ cup chopped parsley	½ teaspoon sage
1 medium onion, chopped	¼ teaspoon pepper

Sauté rice in oil until translucent; add celery, parsley, and onion and cook until tender. Add stock and seasonings; lower heat, cover, and simmer for 30 minutes.

Add to this any chicken meat cleaned from the bones, and canned tomatoes, chopped squash, fresh corn, etc.—in other words, any fresh, frozen, or canned vegetables you have on hand that appeal to you. Cook 10 more minutes. A quarter cup of white wine added just before serving improves the fragrance—and makes a plain, hearty soup seem just a little exotic.

RICE/NUT STUFFING

This stuffing is particularly good for out-of-the ordinary things, like Cornish game hens, ducklings, or fish.

1 medium onion, chopped	1 cup chicken stock
3 tablespoons vegetable oil	¼ cup raisins
⅓ cup pine nuts or almonds	½ teaspoon salt
½ cup raw brown rice	¼ teaspoon sage

Sauté onion in oil until soft; add nuts and rice and sauté until light brown. Lower heat and stir in stock, raisins, and seasonings. Cover and cook slowly 45 minutes to 1 hour, or until rice is tender and liquid is absorbed.

SAFFRON RICE

Some version of this recipe is included in every collection of Near Eastern, Middle Eastern, and Far Eastern dishes. The orange stamen of the saffron flower is used to give it the distinctive color.

1 tablespoon vegetable oil
1 cup uncooked brown rice
2 cups vegetable or meat stock
1 teaspoon salt
¼ teaspoon pepper

¼ teaspoon powdered saffron (or 6 saffron stigmas dissolved in 2 tablespoons stock)

Sauté rice in oil until translucent. Add other ingredients. Cook, tightly covered, over low heat 45 minutes to 1 hour. Serve with a vegetable or meat dish.

KEDGEREE

This recipe is supposed to have come originally from India, but the people who serve it in England think of it as a native dish. It doesn't really matter where it originated—it's very tasty. The fish usually used is called Finnan Haddie where I come from, but you'll probably find it faster if you call it smoked haddock. It's the yellow-orange fish you may have seen in the meat section of your grocery store and wondered about. You can also used smoked cod.

1 pound smoked haddock or cod, poached in water to cover 10 minutes
3 cups cooked brown rice
¼ cup melted butter (see Note)
1 tablespoon curry powder

¼ teaspoon cayenne pepper
¼ teaspoon freshly ground black pepper
4 hard-boiled eggs, finely chopped
2 tablespoons finely chopped parsley

Remove fish from water and drain thoroughly; with two forks, break into bite-sized flakes, removing any bones. Gently blend with rice in top of double boiler; heat through while preparing sauce.

Stir together melted butter and seasonings; stir in eggs and blend thoroughly. Fold into rice and fish mixture. When well blended and warm, turn onto serving plate. Garnish with parsley.

NOTE: This dish is just not the same without the taste of butter! Reduce your fat somewhere else today.

EGGPLANT (AUBERGINE) CASSEROLE

5 tablespoons olive oil
3 medium peeled tomatoes, sliced
   (see Note)
2 cups uncooked brown rice
4 cups chicken or vegetable stock

2 medium eggplants
flour for dredging
¼ cup Parmesan cheese
¼ cup fresh parsley, chopped

Preheat oven to 350°F. Sauté tomatoes in oil until golden brown. Stir in rice and stock; lower heat and cook, covered 45 minutes to 1 hour, or until rice is tender. Slice eggplants ¼-inch thick, flour lightly and fry in hot oil until browned and tender. Drain, and arrange in large, shallow baking dish. Cover with rice mixture. Sprinkle with cheese and parsley. Bake for 25 minutes. Serves 6–8.

NOTE: To peel tomatoes, plunge them into rapidly boiling water for 1 minute then into cold water. The skins will come off easily.

RICE AND VEGGIES

A standby in many college-student homes, this vegetable dish has become a regular at our house. The vegetables change according to what is in season, but the yoghurt and sesame seeds are there to complement the protein in the rice. If you omit them, add something else, such as cheese or a large glass of milk, if you want to make a meal out of this mixture.

1 cup yoghurt	½ cup vegetable oil
1 tablespoon chopped fresh dill weed	1½ cups uncooked brown rice
1 tablespoon chopped fresh parsley	3 cups vegetable or meat stock
1 tablespoon sesame seeds	1 cup raw green peas or lima beans
1 large red onion, coarsely chopped	1 cup sliced carrots
2 cloves garlic, finely chopped	1 cup sliced or diced squash

Stir together yoghurt, dill, parsley, and sesame seeds. Refrigerate until ready to use. Sauté onion and garlic in oil until tender. Add rice and sauté until translucent. Lower heat, add stock, cover, and cook 30 minutes. Stir in vegetables and cook, covered, 15 minutes more, or until rice is tender and all liquid has been absorbed. Add ¼ cup more liquid during cooking if mixture dries out before becoming tender. Stir in yoghurt sauce.

SHRIMP JAMBALAYA

2 cups cooked small shrimp	1 teaspoon thyme
1 small onion, chopped	1 teaspoon salt
¼ cup butter	¼ teaspoon pepper
3 cups cooked brown rice	dash cayenne pepper
1 16-ounce can stewed tomatoes	parsley to garnish
1 medium bell pepper, chopped	

Sauté shrimp and onion in butter until shrimp is golden pink and onion is tender. Stir in rice, tomatoes, and bell pepper; add seasonings and heat until thoroughly warmed. Spoon onto serving plate; garnish with parsley.

SPANISH RICE AND MEATBALLS

1 pound ground meat
1 medium onion, chopped
1 egg
1 tablespoon vegetable oil
2 bell peppers, chopped
1 cup celery, chopped

1 clove garlic, finely chopped
1 1-pound can tomatoes
1 tablespoon chile powder
1 cup brown rice
2 cups water

Combine ground meat, onion, and egg; make into 12 meatballs and brown in oil in a heavy skillet. Remove with a slotted spoon and set aside. Drain excess grease, leaving only enough to sauté peppers, celery, and garlic. Return meatballs to pan and add remaining ingredients. Cover and cook over low heat for 1 hour. Serves 4.

HASH BROWN RICE

2 cups cooked brown rice
1 cup chopped roasted peanuts
½ cup sunflower seeds
2 eggs, beaten

1 medium onion, chopped
1 teaspoon salt
1 teaspoon sage or thyme

Combine ingredients in a medium bowl; moisten with a little water if mixture seems dry. Spoon into a well-oiled skillet and press flat with the back of a spatula. Fry 8–10 minutes, or until crisp and brown; turn and fry other side until crisp.

WILD RICE CASSEROLE

1½ cups wild rice	4 cups stock
2 tablespoons vegetable oil	2 teaspoons salt
1 medium onion, chopped	½ teaspoon pepper
1 cup chopped celery	1 teaspoon thyme
1 cup sliced mushrooms	1 teaspoon marjoram

Preheat oven to 375°F. Sauté rice in oil until translucent, about 3–5 minutes. Add onion, celery, and mushrooms; sauté until tender. Turn into an oiled baking dish; stir in remaining ingredients. Bake for 1½ hours, or until rice is tender and moisture is absorbed. If rice dries out before becoming completely cooked, add ¼ cup wine or stock.

BROWN AND WILD RICE PILAF

This is a less expensive way to enjoy wild rice; its unique flavor comes through, but the dish goes farther than when made with only wild rice.

½ cup wild rice	3 cups water or stock
1 cup brown rice	½ teaspoon salt
1 tablespoon vegetable oil	
½ cup sliced, sautéed mushrooms (or	
1 4-ounce can sliced mushrooms	
with liquid)	

Sauté wild rice and brown rice in oil until translucent; add mushrooms and liquid they were cooked in, stock, and salt. Seasonings may be added to taste. Cover and simmer slowly for about 1 hour, or until rice is tender and liquid is absorbed.

WILD RICE STUFFING

We enjoy this stuffing in our Easter goose. This recipe makes enough to stuff a nine-pound bird.

1 cup wild rice	½ cup chopped onion
1 tablespoon vegetable oil	1 cup pine nuts
3 cups chicken stock	¼ cup vegetable oil
2 teaspoons salt	2 tablespoons chopped parsley
4 cups sliced fresh mushrooms	
1 cup chopped celery	Goose (if you are using stuffing now)

Preheat oven to 450°F. Sauté wild rice in oil for 3–5 minutes. Add stock and salt; simmer, covered, until tender, about 1 hour. Sauté mushrooms, celery, onion, and nuts in ¼ cup oil until onion and mushrooms are tender and nuts are browned. Stir in cooked wild rice and parsley.

Put goose in oven breast-down, lower temperature to 350°F. Roast goose 1 hour without stuffing. Take out of oven, stuff and truss, and return to oven breast-up. Goose should be cooked ½ hour total per pound.

ORANGE RICE

1 cup orange juice	2 tablespoons honey
1 cup milk	1 cup plain yoghurt
1 cup uncooked brown rice	1 can mandarin oranges, chopped
¼ teaspoon salt	

Bring juice and milk to a boil; liquid will curdle. Stir rice and salt into boiling mixture, lower heat, and simmer, covered, 1 hour. Stir in honey and cool. Stir yoghurt and oranges into rice just before serving.

RICE FLOUR COOKIES

½ cup butter or vegetable oil
4 tablespoons honey
½ teaspoon vanilla

1 egg
1 cup finely ground rice flour
1 cup chopped nuts

Preheat oven to 350°F. Cream butter and honey until light; beat in vanilla and egg. Stir in rice flour and nuts. Chill dough overnight for several hours. Roll into 2 dozen balls; put on well-greased baking sheet and press flat with the bottom of a glass. Bake for 12–15 minutes.

CHINESE ALMOND COOKIES

1 cup finely ground rice flour
¼ cup sugar
½ teaspoon baking powder
¼ cup butter, softened
1 egg

1 teaspoon almond extract
1–2 teaspoons water
blanched whole almonds
milk or egg yolk for glaze (optional)

Preheat oven to 350°F. Stir together flour, sugar, and baking powder, pressing out any lumps. Beat in butter and egg. Add almond extract and enough water to make a rollable dough. Roll dough into balls and place on greased baking sheet; flatten slightly with the bottom of a glass (or roll out ½ inch thick and cut out with round cutter) and press an almond into the center of each cookie. Cookies may be brushed with milk or a beaten egg yolk for glazed, brown effect. Bake for 20 minutes.

BANANA RICE BREAD

2 cups finely ground rice flour
1 teaspoon salt
4 teaspoons baking powder
½ cup butter
1½ cups mashed bananas (2 large ones)

4 tablespoons honey
1 egg
½ cup nuts

Preheat oven to 350°F. Stir flour, salt, and baking powder together, pressing out any lumps. In separate bowl, cream butter, bananas, and honey. Beat in egg, then add dry ingredients; stir in nuts. Turn into a small well-greased loaf pan and bake for 30 minutes, or until a toothpick inserted in the center of the loaf comes out clean.

BROWN RICE PUDDING

1 cup brown rice
6 cups milk
1 cinnamon stick
½ cup honey

½ teaspoon grated nutmeg
2 eggs
1 teaspoon vanilla extract

Preheat oven to 325°F. Cook rice in milk with cinnamon stick until tender, about 1 hour. Stir often to prevent sticking. Remove cinnamon stick and pour pudding into baking dish. Stir in honey and nutmeg. Beat eggs and fold in. Bake for 30 minutes, or until firm. Stir in vanilla just before serving. Serve with heavy cream.

MILLET

All kinds of good food are ready;
Rice, broom-corn, early wheat,
  mixed with yellow millet;
Bitter, salt, sour, hot and sweet;
There are dishes of all flavors.

The poem on the previous page, a third century B.C. Chinese poem, "The Summons of the Soul," proclaimed the desirability of a variety of textures and flavors in eating. Any twentieth-century cook who wants to bring variety to the diet of his or her family should remember to give millet a try.

Like sorghum, millet has been relegated to the lowly ranks of birdseed in the United States, though millions of people in Asia and Africa eat it daily. Often called the "poor man's cereal," millet tends to be looked down upon by those who see it only in their pet birds' dishes, yet this grain's pleasant flavor caught our family off guard when we first tasted it, and we have since found a permanent niche for it in our diet. Millet is a more nearly complete protein than any of the other grains, is particularly high in minerals, and is easily digested, so adding it to your diet makes sense.

Millet has been used for food as far back as history can record. In preliterate India and ancient Egypt it was grown on poor soil and with little water, and used to make bread. Pliny, writing nearly two thousand years ago, recorded that Sarmatian tribes commonly mixed millet meal with mares' milk, or with blood from a horse's leg.

Millet was a staple in China before rice became the staple grain, and in Asia today several forms of millet are used in cakes, cookies, and puddings. The national bread of Ethiopia, *injera*, is still made from a fine flour ground from millet. In India flat thin cakes, called *roti*, are often made from millet flour, and used as the basis for meals. In fact millet is one of the staple grains of India. In eastern Europe millet is used in porridge or kasha, or is fermented into a beverage.

According to one historian, millet was planted in the early colonies and used like corn. Today, however, it is one of the least popular American grains, though it is generally available in natural food stores, or the health food sections of large grocery stores. The millet purchased from these sources comes hulled. Since it has a very hard hull (that's what the canaries leave behind in their dishes), this is definitely the preferred way to buy it, although you can also get unhulled millet from feed dealers. Hulled millet comes whole and cracked (one manufacturer even sells it puffed for breakfast cereal); recipes calling for whole millet mean whole *hulled* millet. If you cannot find millet near your home, try writing to one of the companies listed in the Sources section.

You can grow millet if you wish. Finding the seed is the hardest part; growing it is fairly straightforward. The most common kinds of millet are pearl millet (also known as cattail millet, bulrush millet, bajra, and candle millet), foxtail millet (Italian millet), and pro-so (broomcorn millet or hog millet).

Contact major seed companies for information. I buy foxtail millet at a feed store and plant that; if you live in the north central states, where most of the millet is grown in the United States, you should have no difficulty finding it, but in other areas you may need to depend on a mail-order source.

Plant millet in well-worked soil after the last frost—from late May to early July—and treat about the same as you would corn, except that you should broadcast or drill your seed rather than planting in hills. Millet can be grown fairly far north, but it won't grow well anywhere until the soil is warm. In Africa the seed is often sown on the soil surface, then covered with a layer of manure, which heavy rains wash into the earth. The lesson is that millet needs nutrients even though it grows in arid and semi-arid conditions, so build up your soil as you would for any other crop. Millet has the ability to go dormant if water becomes unavailable, then continue growth when it rains again, but it will grow best if water is provided throughout the growing season. Water well until the plants are about six inches high, then just water occasionally.

As the heads begin to ripen, prepare for visits from the birds. Our philosophy is to plant extra for the wild creatures; that way we fret less and still get a good harvest. If you'd rather outsmart the birds, cut the heads a few days before they are ripe and sun dry them under gauze.

Threshing is time-consuming, but soul-satisfying; people have been doing it for centuries. Since you probably don't live near a millet huller, consider the following methods: You can take the seed heads from the stems and lay them on the ground, then drive a car or walk a horse over them. Or you can separate the seeds out from the stem and rub them between your hands. It helps to have leather hands or leather gloves for that method (I've tried it). Still another method, the one still in use in many parts of the world, is to pound the seeds in a hollowed-out log with a mallet or the end of a stick. We've had pretty good luck with the car driving method. The grains which defy us go to the chickens.

Winnow the grain by pouring it slowly from one container to another, or holding it over your head and pouring it slowly to the ground. The seeds will remain; the lighter husks will blow away. If there is no wind, an electric fan will work every bit as well as nature.

Millet is quite resistant to rotting and to insects, and can be stored for over two years if it is kept dry. But don't let the birds or mice get into it!

BASIC COOKED MILLET

Millet is a very tiny, delicate grain. It can be cooked to resemble mashed potatoes if you stir it frequently (if you *really* want it to resemble mashed potatoes press it through a food mill or meat grinder after cooking), or it may be made fluffy and ricelike by steaming without stirring.

4 cups water	1 teaspoon salt
1 cup whole millet	

Bring water to a boil; stir in millet and salt, lower heat and simmer, covered, 30–40 minutes, or until grain is tender and water is absorbed. Check at 30 minutes, but do it quickly and replace lid immediately so you don't lose steam. If it seems to be sticking, or too dry, lower heat and/or add ¼ cup water.

For a nuttier flavor, sauté millet briefly in 1 tablespoon oil in a saucepan, then add salt and 4 cups boiling water. Cover and steam as above.

TUO ZAAFI

This stiff millet porridge is the staple meal of many North Africans. We like to shred apples over a big bowlful, and sometimes we also add chopped nuts and raisins.

1 cup coarsely ground millet meal	½–1 teaspoon salt
3 cups water	

Mix meal with 1 cup cold water. Bring remaining water to a boil; stir meal/water mixture and pour into boiling water, stirring constantly to prevent lumps. Lower heat and cook, stirring frequently, until mixture thickens, at least 15 minutes. Use a bamboo paddle or wet wooden spoon to prevent sticking. Serve with honey or brown sugar and milk. Or, chill overnight and serve for breakfast.

VARIATION: Koko is a confection made from leftover Tuo Zaafi. Its texture varies with the amount of leftovers, the number of people around to eat it, and the length of time left to ferment. Experiment.

Add honey to leftover Tuo Zaafi until pleasantly sweet; stir and knead in enough fine millet flour to make a soft dough. Leave in a bowl overnight to ferment.

When ready to eat, break dough into a medium pan and stir enough boiling water into it to make a thin paste; stir thoroughly to blend and break up any lumps. Bring to a boil and simmer 5–10 minutes. Serve hot or cold with more honey.

MILLET BALLS

Millet balls are eaten in several parts of Africa. They can be prepared in at least two different ways. In some areas millet meal or flour is combined with salt and water to make a stiff dough that is formed into balls about 1½ inches in diameter. These balls are then cooked in water or soup like dumplings, dusted with rice or millet flour, and eaten along with the soup or alone.

The Nyaturu of Tanzania take handfuls of leftover porridge and roll them into balls, eating them dipped into a meat or vegetable relish. These are generally eaten in the morning, putting to good use the dried remains of the previous night's dinner.

COUSCOUS

Couscous is the bulgur of North Africa; it can be served with meat, vegetables, or fruit. The word is derived from an Arabic word meaning "to pulverize or crush," and is made by steaming finely cracked millet or wheat. You can buy prepackaged boxes of couscous in health-food and specialty stores, but these are seldom made with whole grains (they are usually semolina), so your best bet is to buy whole millet and crack it yourself. To get whole millet the right coarseness, run it through a grain mill with the blades quite far apart, so that each grain is cracked into two or three pieces. The authentic pan to use for this dish is a couscoussière, which is a large double boiler with holes in the bottom of the upper pan. It can be approximately by placing a metal colander inside a large saucepan in such a way that the water doesn't come into the colander; rest the handles on the rim of the larger pan or place the colander on a trivet. Line the colander with cheesecloth and cover the pan with lid or piece of aluminum foil.

2 cups cracked millet

1 cup water

2 pounds boneless lamb or mutton, cubed

1 medium onion, chopped

1 teaspoon powdered coriander

2 teaspoons salt

1 teaspoon crushed red pepper

¼ teaspoon saffron (or 6 saffron stigmas dissolved in 2 tablespoons stock)

1 teaspoon ground cumin

¼ cup vegetable oil

2 quarts water or stock

2 small carrots, sliced

1 cup diced yellow squash

1 cup sliced small zucchini

1 cup cooked black-eyed peas

Soak millet in water. Sauté meat, onion, and spices in oil; add 2 quarts of water or stock and simmer, covered, until meat is just tender, about 1 hour. Place moistened millet in top of couscoussière or perforated steamer, cover, and steam for 30 minutes. Meanwhile, add remaining vegetables and peas to stew and cook slowly. When millet is tender, rub the grains together gently with your hands, then turn it onto a serving platter and make a hole in the center of the mound; drain vegetables and spoon them into and over the millet. Serve meat with the liquid, which can be thickened with millet flour to form a gravy.

QUICK SKILLET MEAT LOAF

You don't have to make this in a skillet, but that's part of what makes it a fast dish for me—my cast-iron skillet is always on the top of the stove, so I don't even have to look for a baking sheet.

1 pound ground meat

1 egg

1 cup cooked whole millet

1 package enchilada sauce mix (or other spicy sauce mix you happen to have handy)

Combine ingredients on the baking sheet or in your skillet, by making a well in the meat. Knead into a loaf shape, place in preheated 350°F. oven, and bake for 1 hour. Cool slightly, slice, and eat.

MILLET-STUFFED SQUASH

Another in the continuing series of "what to do with all that zucchini we grew this summer."

1 medium onion, chopped

1 clove garlic, chopped

1 cup sliced mushrooms

1 tablespoon vegetable oil

2 cups cooked whole millet

2 tablespoons chopped fresh parsley

2 teaspoons oregano

2 teaspoons basil

2 eggs, slightly beaten

2 large parboiled zucchini or other summer squash, with seeds and some of the pulp removed

grated Parmesan cheese (optional)

Preheat oven to 350°F. Sauté onion, garlic, and mushrooms in oil until tender. Stir in millet and seasonings; cook 3–5 minutes. Beat eggs into mixture and mound into squash. Place in ½ inch of water in a shallow baking dish and bake 30 minutes. May be sprinkled with Parmesan cheese before or after baking.

MILLET SOUFFLÉ

2 cups cooked whole millet
½ teaspoon salt
¾ cup milk

½ cup grated cheddar cheese
3 eggs, separated

Preheat oven to 375°F. Stir together millet, salt, milk, cheese, and beaten egg yolks. Beat egg whites until stiff; fold in and pour into ungreased 1½-quart soufflé dish. Sprinkle a little more cheese on top. Bake for about 30 minutes, or until a knife inserted in the center comes out clean. Serve immediately. Lower oven temperature after 20 minutes if soufflé seems to be browning too fast.

TOMATO MILLET

3 cups cooked whole millet
1 medium onion, finely chopped
1 clove garlic, finely chopped
1 16-ounce can stewed tomatoes and liquid

1 cup raw green lima beans or cooked dried limas
2 teaspoons basil
2 tablespoons chopped fresh parsley

Preheat oven to 350°F. Combine ingredients in a 1½-quart baking dish. Bake for 1 hour.

INJERA

Injera is the national bread of Ethiopia, and is made on large, flat griddle-like pans directly over a fire. The batter is usually made from *teff*, a particularly fine sort of flour made from millet, and is left to ferment for several days, leavened with starter kept from a previous batch. It is poured onto the griddle in a large spiral, starting at the outside and working in, and results in a thin, flexible pancake-like bread from 9 to 13 inches in diameter. These are served with nearly every meal in Ethiopia, piled in a bowl or on a plate, and we have found them to be particularly good with soups and stews. Tear off a small piece as the Southwesterners do with flour tortillas, and use it as a utensil to scoop up your food.

1 tablespoon active dry yeast	3 cups finely ground millet flour
5 cups water	¼ teaspoon baking soda
1 teaspoon honey	

Dissolve yeast in ¼ cup of the water, which should be lukewarm, and stir in honey. When yeast is frothy and rising actively (about 5 minutes), combine it with the remainder of the water and stir in flour, blending until lumps are gone. Allow to ferment for 24 hours.

Just before making *injera*, stir vigorously, and fold in ¼ teaspoon baking soda, pressed against the side of a cup with the back of a spoon to eliminate any lumps. Bring a large, well-seasoned skillet to a medium heat; test with a small spoonful of batter. The bread should cook quickly without browning. When pan is heated, pour about ⅓ cup of batter onto it in a spiral, beginning at the outside and working quickly into the center. Cover pan and cook *injera* for about 1 minute. The bread should rise slightly, and can be removed easily with a long spatula. The top should be slightly moist; the bottom dry but not crisp or brown. Lift *injera* to a platter to cool, then stack cooled breads on a serving plate. Continue until all the batter is used. Makes 12–15 *injera*.

ROTI

This recipe for fresh homemade bread (which can also be made with whole wheat or sorghum flours) comes from Chetana, a cultural organization of Indian women in the Washington, D.C., area. Made much like tortillas, roti is best when rolled very thin and baked (not fried) on a super-hot griddle. This bread is often served with a pat of butter and eaten with spinach; we like it spread with cream cheese and rolled up.

1 cup water	1 cup millet flour
¼ teaspoon salt	

Bring water and salt to a boil; stir in flour and cover. When it has cooled enough to touch, turn it onto a well-floured board and knead well. Divide into 6 equal portions. With floured hands, knead each portion thoroughly and make a ball. Dust it with flour and roll into a 7-inch circle. If it sticks, dust it again with flour.

Preheat a flat frying pan or griddle (do not grease). Put the roti on it to bake. Turn several times, making sure it doesn't burn, and press the edges gently. It will slowly rise, forming two separate layers. The roti is done when it is deep golden brown and mottled with specks of dark brown.

WHEAT GERM/MILLET BREAD

1 cup coarsely cracked millet	¼ cup honey
½ cup wheat germ	2 teaspoons salt
1½ cups boiling water	2 tablespoons oil
1 tablespoon active dry yeast	3–4 cups whole wheat flour
¼ cup water	

Combine millet and wheat germ in a large bowl; pour boiling water over them and set aside. Dissolve yeast in ¼ cup water. Leave to rise while adding honey, salt, and oil to first mixture. When millet mixture has cooled, add yeast and half of the flour. Beat vigorously to develop gluten; add remaining flour until dough is smooth and workable; knead well. Set aside in oiled bowl, covered with a damp cloth, to rise for 1 hour, or until doubled in bulk. Punch down, form into 2 loaves, and place in bread tins or on a baking sheet. Let rise once more, about 1 hour. Preheat oven to 375°F. Bake for 50 minutes. Remove from tins or baking sheet immediately and let cool slightly before slicing.

FRUITED MILLET BREAD FOR BREAD MACHINE

This sweet bread recipe has been developed for use in a bread machine. Place the ingredients in your machine according to the instructions; usually that will mean placing the dry ingredients in first, then making a well in them for the liquids. This recipe makes a 1½-pound loaf that keeps well. To adapt other recipes for your bread machine, see page 8.

1 cup water	3 tablespoons whole millet
¼ cup lemon or orange juice	¾ teaspoon salt
1½ tablespoons vegetable oil	3 tablespoons vital gluten
3 tablespoons honey	2 teaspoons active dry yeast
2½ cups whole wheat bread flour	3 tablespoons chopped nuts or seeds*
½ cup barley flour	3 tablespoons raisins or sultanas*
½ cup millet flour	rind of 1 lemon or orange*

*Add after the first kneading cycle.

189

MILLET PUDDING

1 cup whole millet
4 cups milk
2 eggs, slightly beaten

½ cup honey
1 teaspoon vanilla extract

Heat millet and milk in the top of a double boiler and cook over boiling water, stirring occasionally, for 1 hour. Remove from heat; cool until lukewarm. Add eggs, honey, and vanilla and beat well. Cook for an additional 10 minutes. Serve immediately with thick cream or chill and serve topped with whipped cream and nuts.

ORANGE MILLET

This dish approximates a Chinese congee.

1 cup whole millet
4 cups water

⅓ cup brown sugar
1 11-ounce can mandarin oranges

Simmer millet in water, stirring occasionally, until tender, about 45 minutes. Remove from heat and let stand 15 minutes. Add sugar and oranges and bring again to a boil. Serve hot.

LEMON MILLET

5 cups water	juice and rind of 1 lemon
1 cup whole millet	¼ cup honey

Bring water to a boil in the top of a double boiler set directly over heat; then place top back in double boiler, over pot of boiling water, and stir in remaining ingredients. Cook, stirring frequently, until thick. Pour pudding into a mold. Refrigerate until set—at least 1 hour. Unmold by setting the mold for a moment in a bowl of warm water, then inverting it over a plate.

NINA'S MILLET PUDDING

Whenever I cook whole grains I cook a large potful then put whatever I don't use that night into the refrigerator. This recipe for cold millet pudding was introduced to me by an Austrian friend, and is delicious made either from scratch or with leftover cooked millet.

6 cups milk	1 cup chopped nuts
1 cup whole millet	1 cup currants or raisins
¼–½ cup honey	¼ cup shredded coconut
¼–½ cup heavy cream	

Cook millet in milk for 45 minutes to 1 hour, until tender. Refrigerate until thoroughly chilled. (Or use several cups of leftover cooked millet.) Stir in other ingredients. Served cold, this is refreshing and crunchy.

SORGHUM

As corn is the traditional cereal of the New World, sorghum grain is the staple of Africa and much of Asia. Although hardly ever eaten by human beings in America, this grain is one of the world's most important cereals. As late as 1959 it was third only to wheat and rice in the amounts consumed.

Most scientists agree that sorghum originated in Africa, but so many different varieties have developed that a detailed history is almost impossible. It is known that the Egyptians cultivated sorghums as long ago as 2200 B.C., and they were probably the major item in the diet at Nineveh on the Tigris River in Mesopotamia. A carving showing sorghum being used for food was found in an Assyrian ruin dating from around 700 B.C.

In the seventeenth and eighteenth centuries sorghum, then called guinea corn, was brought to the West Indies and the British colonies by slave ships traveling from Africa, and it was commonly seen growing in the South. Being more drought-resistant than corn, yet nutritionally very similar, sorghum is an ideal staple for arid places such as the southwestern United States, and has been introduced into many areas that are too dry or too hot for corn. In 1995, a biodiversity project in Ethiopia successfully introduced such traditional crops as sorghum and *teff* in place of newer hybrid grains that require pesticides and fertilizer.

Sorghum continues to be one of the major foods of the common people in much of Africa. It is ground each day in the home; as with corn in American culture, the entire grain is used in preparing flour and meal, and because of the presence of the germ, or embryo, would become rancid if not made fresh each day. In the Sudan and South Africa, sorghum is primarily eaten in the form of mush. Known there as *durra*, sorghum is planted with digging sticks in hills, and rarely gets very much water. The Africans also make beer from sorghum, and I understand that it's not bad.

In China and Japan, sorghum (called *kaoliang*) is grown where it is too dry for rice. The Chinese use sorghum much as they do rice, boiling the whole grain or grinding it into meal for bread or porridge. Sorghum wine is also a common use of this grain, and in fact nearly as much of the sorghum is grown for wine as is grown for food in China.

During World War I the United States Department of Agriculture promoted sorghum as a partial solution to the food shortage, and even published bulletins with recipes for its use. Grain sorghum disappeared from the shelves after the war, however, and today it is virtually unknown in American kitchens. Yet many thousands of acres are sown with sorghum each year (mostly for use as cattle feed), and you can buy it for less than ten cents a pound at feed and grain stores. It costs less than a third of the price of the lowest-priced wheat, and represents an unexploited treasure for the adventurous cook.

How does one go about exploiting this food resource? Living in an agricultural area, I simply drove to the nearest feed store and ordered five pounds each of the *milo* and *kafir* types, checking with the man who ran the store to be sure that they were free from pesticide residue (if the grain is being sold for poultry feed it is usually quite clean). Other sources of food-grade sorghum seed and flour include the Nebraska Grain Sorghum Board, the Kansas Grain Sorghum Board, and Jowar Foods of Hereford, Texas, 113 Hickory Street, Hereford, TX 79045. You might try growing your own if you have enough room. Seed can be purchased from feed dealers or, if you want certified (germination-tested, weed-free) seed, from major seed outlets. Look in your telephone book under grain or feed or seed, or talk to the local agricultural extension agent.

There are four major groups of sorghums, classified primarily by their uses, but only one group is of interest to us as a grain.

Forage or syrup sorghums are generally known as *sorgos*. These tend to have a luxuriant leaf growth, and rather sweet stalks. Cattle are often allowed to forage on these varieties, but they are primarily grown for the syrup which can be extracted from their stalks. Sorghum syrup is similar to maple syrup or a very light molasses, and is widely used in some parts of the United States as an unrefined substitute for sugar.

Grass sorghums (Johnson grass, Sudan grass) are grown strictly for pasture, hay, and silage—in other words, for animal feed.

Broomcorns are varieties of sorghum, which when cut and dried can be made into brooms and brushes. This type of sorghum has been grown in the United States ever since Benjamin Franklin plucked some seeds from an imported broom and planted them. It is also commonly grown in Eastern Europe.

Grain sorghums are the types which are used for food. The stalks of these varieties are not sweet, and the plants have been selected over generations for the size of the seed-bearing heads and for the strength of the stalks. The grain sorghums grown in the United States are classified into seven groups. Any of them is acceptable for use as human food, although in my opinion *kafir, milo,* and *durra* have the best flavors.

The *kafirs* (sometimes called kafir corn) come from South Africa. They have thick juicy stalks, large leaves, and cylindrical grain-bearing heads. The seeds are white, pink, or red, and are of medium size.

The *milos* are from east central Africa and have wavy leaf blades with a yellow rib down the center. The stalks are less juicy than those of kafir, and the seeds much larger. The seed-bearing heads are compact, bearded (they have a hairlike tuft of silk), and contain salmon-, pink-, or cream-colored seeds. Milos are generally more tolerant to heat and drought than kafirs.

The *feteritas*, from Sudan, have very few leaves and slender dry stalks. The seed-bearing heads are oval, compact, and contain very large white seeds.

The *durras*, from North Africa and the Near East, have bearded, fuzzy heads, large flat seeds, and dry stalks.

Shallu, once known as Egyptian wheat, is from India. It has tall, slender, dry stalks which have a tendency to lodge (fall over) with the weight of the seed heads, which contain white seeds. This variety is not a very popular commercial one because it matures late and doesn't yield very well.

The *kaoliangs* are from Asia. These varieties are tall and have dry, woody, slender and thinly leaved stalks, wiry rather compact seed-bearing heads, and bitter brown seeds.

Hegari, from Sudan, has chalky white seeds on nearly oval heads.

Sorghum should be planted after the soil warms up, usually not before May or June. The land to be sown should be well prepared, disked or plowed, and thoroughly freed from weeds, because sorghum seedlings are very small and get lost among weeds, making cultivation nearly impossible. If you are planting in a low rainfall area, use no more than two to four pounds of seed per acre, although if water isn't a problem your land can probably support four to five times that much. If you are broadcasting your seed, sow about 20% heavier than that. Milo should be spaced furthest apart, while hegari, feterita, and kafir, the most common other classes, can be as close together as 6 inches. If you have access to farm equipment, space your rows from 20 to 40 inches apart. Most sorghums available to the small farmer are hybrids, so if you are serious about growing this grain consult the sources of seed for more specific planting and cultivating information. Non-hybrid seeds can be purchased from some sources. Check with your local university extension agent or farm advisor.

Sorghum has a reputation for being hard on the land, because it takes both moisture and nitrogen from the soil in great quantities. The first problem isn't a problem if you have sufficient water, and you can take care of the second problem by planting legumes after sorghum, or by applying nitrogen at a somewhat higher rate than normal before planting another crop.

Do not allow your animals to forage on young sorghum. The leaves and stems of undeveloped plants release a substance known as prussic acid, a cyanide compound which even in very small quantities is fatal to cattle, sheep, and goats. After the plant is fully grown, cut, and dried, the prussic acid content has dissipated sufficiently to make the hay and fodder safe. The heads of growing sorghum contain very little prussic acid, and fully developed heads, even before drying, are not dangerous. Any regrowth after cutting, however, will be high in prussic acid.

Commercial growers harvest their sorghum with combines, but in Asia and Africa it is still cut with hand sickles or knives when the grain is not quite ripe. That is probably what you'll wind up doing. As with other grains, don't wait too long to harvest, or you'll lose most of your grain in the field. Cut the stalks when the seeds are still slightly unripe, and can be dented with a fingernail. Dry the heads on screens or tables away from the ground and varmints, then thresh with a flail or other device as for wheat.

Storage of sorghum grain can be a problem. If the grains are at all cracked during threshing, or if they are too moist, they will pack tightly and may heat up and spoil. Moisture and heat damage any grain, but sorghum seems to be particularly subject to this danger. Try to rig up some sort of ventilation system in your storage bins, at the very least a screened strip that passes through the grain in the bottom portion of the bins and is open to the outside, thus providing a flow of cool air to the grain at the lower end, rising upward to cool the warmer air at the top. All openings to the bin should of course be screened to keep out rodents.

Whole sorghum grain can be cooked just like rice, salted, and served with a main course, or vegetables; and stock can be added to make a kasha-like dish. The first time I served sorghum to guests, I held my breath, expecting negative remarks. After what seemed an endless wait, I received one comment I've never forgotten: "The birdseed . . . needs more salt!" The moral of this is— don't let the strangeness of any grain overwhelm you and keep you from experimenting with seasonings. Try recipes several times, keeping your family's preferences in mind when adjusting ingredients.

The recipes published by the Department of Agriculture in 1913 were primarily warmed-over cornmeal recipes, substituting kafir flour for cornmeal, and on the whole they are pretty bad. There is a yeast bread recipe, for example, which simply doesn't work, primarily because there is no gluten in sorghum. Those recipes may be one of the reasons that sorghum didn't catch on in this country. In preparing the following suggestions for the use of this grain, I've taken some ideas from traditional dishes served in Africa and India, and also played around with cornmeal recipes myself. Sorghum needs to be cooked a little longer than corn in those dishes, or it tends to settle out and layer.

Sorghum can be popped, like popcorn, although because the resulting confection is so tiny, it's not likely to catch on with movie theaters. Still, you might enjoy trying it. Use a very low heat, keeping in mind the small size of the grains. Pour enough oil in a pan to cover the bottom, warm slightly, add a tablespoon or so of sorghum, cover tightly, and shake over the heat. The grains should pop within a couple of minutes; if it takes longer than that, check to see if they have burned. If they have, lower the heat and try again. If they're just sitting there, try raising the temperature a little. A few tries and you should be an expert sorghum popper. Butter and salt—and enjoy. You can also use popped sorghum in place of bread crumbs in some recipes.

One note about sorghum when it is ground into meal: since grades and moisture content of sorghum differ greatly, cooking times may vary from the ones I have listed. Be flexible. If settling occurs, or one recipe seems to take considerably longer to bake than it should, try first combining meal and liquids in the top of a double boiler and cooking over water for 15 to 20 minutes before proceeding with the recipe as directed.

All the recipes in this section can also be made with millet, amaranth, and quinoa, although the cooking times may vary.

BASIC SORGHUM

| 1 cup sorghum grain (kafir, milo, | 4 cups water or stock |
| etc.), rinsed in clean water | 1 teaspoon salt |

Combine ingredients in medium saucepan and bring to boil. Cover, lower heat, and simmer for 45 minutes to 1 hour. The grains will remain slightly chewy. Adjust seasoning to taste.

Milo is somewhat larger than kafir and takes a little longer to cook. Be flexible when cooking sorghum, and alter cooking times as necessary.

You can prepare basic sorghum in a microwave. Combine all ingredients in a 2-quart casserole and cook at 50% power for 30–40 minutes.

Makes 4 cups cooked grain.

SORGHUM AND PEANUTS

2 cups sorghum (cooked)
2 tablespoons butter or vegetable oil
½ cup chicken stock

1 cup peanuts, shelled (raw or roasted)
salt and pepper to taste

Sauté sorghum in butter, stirring to separate grains. Lower heat; add stock and peanuts, and seasoning to taste. Cover tightly and simmer 20 minutes.

CAJUN KAFIR

2 cups cooked kafir (or other sorghum)
1 cup stewed tomatoes (reserve juice for later in recipe)
1 medium onion, chopped
½ bell pepper, cored, seeded, and minced

1 teaspoon habanero pepper sauce
½ teaspoon salt
½ teaspoon freshly ground pepper
1 teaspoon crumbled basil

Stir together kafir, tomatoes, onion, and pepper in large, heavy skillet. Cook over medium heat, stirring, until onion is tender. Add tomato juice and seasonings, cover tightly, and simmer 15 minutes.

VARIATION: Add sliced, cooked sausage or fresh shrimp.

SORGHUM LOAF

Originally a Depression recipe, this extended meat loaf is still used as staple in the homes of the grandchildren of the original author. The sorghum gives the loaf a distinctive, slightly sweet flavor.

1 pound ground meat (beef was the
    original; also try turkey)
1 cup cooked sorghum grain
1 8-ounce can stewed tomatoes (or
    two fresh tomatoes, chopped)
1 egg

2 tablespoons freshly chopped
    parsley
½ teaspoon dried basil
1 teaspoon salt
¼ teaspoon pepper

Preheat oven to 350°F. Blend ingredients in a large bowl, mixing with hands if necessary, then form into a loaf and place on cookie sheet in the middle of the oven. Bake for 1 hour. Slice and serve with a green salad or other vegetables for a balanced meal. Serves 4–6.

MIXED GRAIN STEW

½ cup wheat
½ cup sorghum
¼ cup oats, rice, or barley
4 cups water or chicken stock
1 onion, chopped
1 tablespoon vegetable oil

1 carrot, sliced
1 celery stalk, sliced
¾ cup milk
1 teaspoon salt
1 tablespoon freshly chopped parsley

Clean and soak grains overnight in 4 cups liquid. Boil grains in the water they were soaked in for 45 minutes. Sauté onion in 1 tablespoon oil; add carrot and celery, cooking until soft. Add vegetables, milk, and seasonings to grain. Cook, covered 10 minutes. Serve hot.

SORGHUM BREAD

2 cups sorghum flour
1 teaspoon salt
2 cups buttermilk

2 eggs
1 teaspoon baking soda

Preheat oven to 450°F. Place 10-inch oiled skillet or oiled muffin tin in oven for 5 minutes before baking. Stir together flour, salt, and milk in a saucepan. Cook over low heat, stirring frequently, for 5–10 minutes, or until stiff. Remove from heat and cool to lukewarm. Beat eggs and stir into cooled mixture; sprinkle baking soda over and fold in.

Pour sorghum mixture into pan; return to oven and bake for 20–25 minutes, or until a cake tester or toothpick inserted in the center of the loaf comes out clean. Bake muffins for 10–15 minutes.

SORGHUM PEANUT COOKIES

½ cup sorghum meal
2 tablespoons milk
¼ cup honey
2 eggs, slightly beaten
1 teaspoon baking powder

¼ teaspoon salt
1 teaspoon ground ginger
½ cup chopped peanuts
2 tablespoons butter

Preheat oven to 350°F. In medium saucepan over low heat or in top of double boiler, combine sorghum meal, milk, honey, and eggs. Stir together baking powder, salt, and ginger, pressing out any lumps. Add to sorghum mixture. Stir in nuts and cook over low heat or boiling water for 5 minutes. Stir in butter. Drop by teaspoonfuls onto a greased cookie sheet and bake for 10–12 minutes. Makes 1½ dozen soft cookies.

JOWAR BROWNIES

Jowar Foods, Inc., a new company based in Hereford, Texas, has developed a line of whole grain products made from a new variety of grain sorghum—Jowar. Jowar is the Hindi word used in India to describe grain sorghums used for food. The Jowar grain being produced in Texas is a hard white grain without any "off" flavors or colors, allowing it to be used in a broad range of foods, including breakfast cereals, Mexican foods, ethnic foods, and as a substitute for wheat or rice flour for those with food allergies. Jowar is gluten-free

1⅓ cups Jowar flour
1 cup sugar
7 tablespoons cocoa (or 4 tablespoons Hershey European Cocoa)
1 tablespoon cornstarch (or ½ teaspoon xanthan gum

1 teaspoon baking power
½ cup (1 stick) plus 2 tablespoons margarine, melted
2 eggs plus 1 egg white
1 teaspoon vanilla

Preheat oven to 350°F. Mix together Jowar flour, sugar, cocoa, cornstarch, and baking powder. Add remaining ingredients and mix until well blended and smooth (about 1 minute). Spread in a greased eight-by-eight-inch pan and bake for 30–35 minutes

SORGHUM GINGERBREAD

2 cups sorghum meal
2½ cups buttermilk
1 teaspoon salt
1 cup whole wheat flour
2 teaspoons ground ginger
1 teaspoon ground cinnamon

½ teaspoon ground cloves
1 heaping teaspoon baking soda
¾ cup honey
1 egg
2 tablespoons vegetable oil

METHOD I

Preheat oven to 325°F. Combine sorghum and buttermilk. In separate bowl, stir together dry ingredients, pressing out any lumps. Stir into sorghum mixture. Add honey, egg, and oil, and mix well. Bake for 50–55 minutes, or until a toothpick comes out clean.

METHOD II

Preheat oven to 350°F. Combine sorghum and buttermilk in the top of a double boiler; cook over hot water, stirring occasionally, for 15 minutes. Cool mush to lukewarm. Stir together dry ingredients, pressing out lumps. Add oil, honey, and egg to mush, stirring to blend thoroughly. Stir in dry ingredients until just blended. Bake 30 minutes, or until a toothpick comes out clean.

BOUZA

Bouza is a delicious pudding served in parts of Africa, often delicately scented with geranium water (see Note). The traditional way of preparing this dish includes pounding the sorghum dough, thinning with cream and pressing through cloths, blanching and skinning the nuts, and pounding them into a fine powder. The method below takes only a short time to make, yet results in a good approximation of the original.

1 cup very finely ground sorghum flour	1 cup shelled almonds
2 cups cold water	2 cups milk or cream
1 cup shelled filberts	½ cup honey

Stir together flour and water. Put through a sieve, pouring liquid into medium saucepan and discarding any sorghum remaining in sieve. Shred nuts by pulsing in a food processor, or in a mill or blender until very fine. Stir into sorghum and water mixture; slowly add milk or cream, stirring constantly to prevent lumps. Bring to a boil over low heat, stirring often. When mixture has thickened, stir in honey and serve. Bouza may also be chilled thoroughly in small bowls, and sprinkled with shredded nuts before serving. Makes 6 servings.

NOTE: Geranium water is sometimes available in food specialty shops. If you can find it, add 1 teaspoon to mixture after it has cooled slightly.

QUINOA

"Mother Grain" of the Incas

A long with corn and potatoes, this light and tasty grain (pronounced "keen-wa") was a staple of the Incas, and was imbued with sacred power. Championed by plant breeder Luther Burbank in the 1880s, today quinoa plays an important role in South American cuisine, and is imported and distributed to the North American gourmet health-food market, where it appeals to people seeking nourishing food that is high in fiber and low in fat. Since quinoa contains no gluten, it is also a useful ingredient for many people with gluten allergy. Several varieties of quinoa pasta are available, as well as the whole grain.

Quinoa is a good source of high-quality protein. The protein contained in quinoa is high in lysine, methionine, and cystine, three amino acids that are limited in most other grains and in soybeans. This grain is also a good source of iron, magnesium, phosphorous, and calcium, and, due to its small size, takes only 15 minutes to prepare.

Quinoa is a hardy plant, and the hardiest varieties grow at altitudes of up to 13,000 feet, in regions where the annual rainfall may be no more than two inches. Although it is a staple for millions of people, quinoa is still virtually unknown outside Bolivia, Chile, Ecuador, and Peru; before the Spanish conquest it was one of few native grains growing in the high soils of the Andes. An annual, broad-leafed plant, *Chenopodium quinoa* matures in 5 to 6 months, and the seed-laden stalks may be as tall as 12 feet. However, some varieties of quinoa will grow at lower altitudes and 12-inch-high stalks of the seed can be grown from grain purchased in food stores. You can plant the seeds purchased for food. For best results, sow seeds inside in small pots, then set outside like tomatoes when the plants reach about 6 inches tall. In Bolivia, where farmlands are too rocky to be plowed, quinoa is grown by simply digging holes in the ground with a stick and dropping in the seed. In a few months, and with a minimum of care, the quinoa matures into colorful stalks. Like their relatives of the *Amaranthus* family, quinoa plants are often brightly colored, yellow, red, and even magenta. Traditionally, at this point, the plants are uprooted, allowed to dry in the sun, and threshed by hand. You might want to cover the seed heads with cheesecloth to protect them from birds. To remove the seeds from the husks after maturity, simply rub the seed heads between your hands. The seeds are flat, round, and quite small. The starchy inside of the quinoa seed becomes translucent when cooked, with the outer digestible hull appearing like a tiny band around each one.

When harvested, most varieties of quinoa seeds are coated with a layer of soaplike substances called saponins, which render the cooked product bitter if not washed away. Researchers postulate that saponins deter insects and birds that normally feast in grain fields. Some saponin-free varieties exist, but are not are hardy, and are not yet common in the U.S. Most of the bitter saponins are removed from quinoa before it is sold to consumers, but to remove the remainder, soak the seeds for 5 minutes and then rinse until the water no longer foams. Flour ground from saponin-containing quinoa imparts a slight bitter flavor to the baked products; when saponin-free seeds are available, freshly ground quinoa flour can be added to a variety of recipes, or used as a partial wheat flour substitute. Quinoa seeds grind quickly into fine flour when placed in a nut and seed grinder, or coffee grinder.

Quinoa can be substituted for brown rice in many recipes, reducing the cooking time without sacrificing the nutritional content of the meal. It can also be used like cracked wheat or bulgur, offering a light, fluffy alternative grain for Middle Eastern dishes such as tabouli or pilaf. Easily digestible, quinoa is an ideal "first food" for young children.

BASIC COOKED QUINOA

1 cup quinoa   2 cups water

To cook quinoa, first soak and rinse the tiny grains thoroughly in cold water. This will remove the saponin, which may leave a bitter flavor and irritate the digestion. Combine 1 cup grain with 2 cups water in a medium-sized pan. Bring to a boil, then reduce heat and simmer, covered, until all the water is absorbed. This takes from 10 to 15 minutes. When cooked, quinoa is somewhat translucent, with a clear ring around each seed indicating the germ of the grain. Remove from heat and allow to steam for about 5 minutes. Fluff with a fork and serve. Serves 4.

VARIATION: A delicious breakfast cereal can be prepared by cooking quinoa as above, adding ½ cup raisins, ½ finely chopped apple, and 6–10 chopped walnuts or almonds to the grain as it cooks. Served with honey or molasses and milk, the high protein of this grain makes it a complete and substantial breakfast.

QUINOA SOUP

When I was in college I wanted to be an archaeologist. The closest I ever came to it was excavating a Spanish mission near the university campus. My dig foreman had lived for a time in South America, and recently he reminisced about their housekeeper and her quinoa soup. Pleasant memories, Joe.

Basically a vegetable soup, this recipe depends on the stock for its flavor. Traditionally the stock would be made from beef, although a rich chicken or vegetable stock will produce an equally delicious result.

8 cups meat or vegetable stock	½ teaspoon salt
3–4 cups chopped mixed vegetables (onions, carrots, peas, fava beans in season, squash)	½ teaspoon ground cumin
	½ teaspoon freshly ground black pepper
1–3 cloves garlic, peeled and chopped	1½ cups quinoa, thoroughly rinsed
2–3 fresh tomatoes, chopped, or 1 can (14.5 ounces) stewed tomatoes	

Bring stock to a boil. Add the chopped vegetables, garlic, tomatoes, salt, cumin, and pepper. Lower heat and cook for about 10 minutes, then add quinoa. Continue to simmer until the quinoa grains burst, about 20 minutes. Season to taste and serve.

QUINOA DULCE (SWEET QUINOA PUDDING)

1 cup cooked quinoa	1 teaspoon ground cinnamon
1 cup low-fat milk	1 egg, beaten
¼ cup honey	1 teaspoon vanilla extract

Combine cooked quinoa, milk, and honey in a medium-sized saucepan. Stirring gently, bring to a boil over low heat. Reduce heat, add cinnamon and beaten egg, stirring quickly. Add vanilla. This may be served immediately, or poured into a covered casserole and served later, when it will be slightly thicker. Also good cold.

VARIATION: Add raisins, grated coconut or other dried fruit, and/or chopped nuts.

QUINOA CRACKERS ("QUIN THINS")

If you have never made crackers before, this may take a little practice. In order for them to be crisp, it is important that they be rolled *very thin*.

½ cup quinoa meal (see Note)	1 tablespoon brown sugar
½ cup whole wheat pastry flour	2 tablespoons canola or corn oil
½ teaspoon salt	1 tablespoon honey
¼ teaspoon baking soda	4–5 tablespoons water

Preheat oven to 400°F. Mix together quinoa meal, flour, salt, baking soda, and brown sugar until well blended. Make a well in the center, and pour in oil and honey; mix to blend until the texture is somewhat like cornmeal. Add water until the dough can be pressed together in your hand. Add slightly more water or flour as necessary to produce a workable dough. Knead lightly. Lightly oil a baking sheet. Press dough into a flat shape in your hands, then place on baking sheet. Using a small rolling pin or a plastic tumbler, work the dough toward the edges of the sheet. The dough should be no more than ⅛ inch thick. Prick the dough thoroughly with a fork to prevent bubbles, score into squares and bake until lightly brown, about 12 minutes. Allow to cool 5 minutes before cutting along score marks. Cool 10 more minutes before removing from baking surface. Store in airtight container.

NOTE: Rinsed and toasted quinoa may be ground to meal in an electric nut and seed grinder or a dry blender.

QUINOA TABOULI SALAD

4 cups cooked quinoa, cooled
1 cup English cucumber, cubed
2–3 medium-firm ripe tomatoes,
    cubed
¼ cup fresh finely chopped parsley
¼ cup fresh finely chopped mint
    leaves

¼ cup chopped walnuts (optional)
2 cloves garlic, minced
¼ cup olive oil
½ cup lemon juice

Lightly stir together quinoa, cucumber, tomatoes, parsley, mint, walnuts, and garlic. Blend together olive oil and lemon juice. Pour over quinoa and toss well. Makes 4 servings.

QUINOA FRUIT SALAD

2 cups cooked quinoa
¼ cup celery, thinly sliced
1 6-ounce can mandarin oranges and
    1 tablespoon juice

¼ cup sliced almonds

Stir ingredients together and serve chilled in small bowls over torn lettuce. Makes 4 servings.

QUINOA "RICE" PUDDING

2 cups cooked quinoa
3 cups milk
½ cup honey
3 eggs, beaten
¼ teaspoon salt

½ cup raisins or sultanas (golden
   raisins)
½ teaspoon ground cinnamon
1 teaspoon vanilla extract

Preheat oven to 350°F. In a large bowl, stir together quinoa, milk, and honey. Add eggs, salt, raisins, and cinnamon, and mix gently. Pour into greased baking dish. Bake until set, about 45 minutes. To prepare in microwave, cook at 50% power for about 20 minutes. Stir in vanilla just before serving.

VARIATION: Add ½ cup shredded coconut, ½ cup ground or chopped almonds or walnuts.

BOLIVIAN ALMOND COOKIES

½ cup light honey
¼ cup sesame or sunflower oil
1 egg, beaten
1 teaspoon vanilla extract
½ teaspoon almond extract
2 cups quinoa flour (see Note)
¼ teaspoon salt

1 teaspoon baking soda
12 whole blanched almonds

GLAZE
1 egg white beaten with 1 teaspoon
   water

Preheat oven to 350°F. Stir together honey, oil, egg, vanilla, and almond extract. In a separate bowl, combine flour, baking soda, and salt. Make a well in the flour and pour in liquid mixture. Mix well. With oiled hands, shape dough into 12 balls. Place each ball on a baking sheet that has been coated with vegetable spray, and press 1 almond into the center of each. Brush lightly with egg-white mixture. Bake until golden, about 10 minutes.

NOTE: To make quinoa flour, place seeds in a nut grinder or coffee grinder and grind until fine.

BUCKWHEAT

De buckwheat cake was in her
mouth, de tear was in her eye;
Says I: "I'm coming from de South,
Susanna, don't you cry."

Buckwheat is often thought of as one of the cereals that is a member of the grass family or *Graminae*, but it is actually an herbaceous plant from an entirely different botanical family known as *Polygonaceae*, and its true relatives are sorrel, rhubarb, and dock. While the fruits of the buckwheat plant do look a lot like grains of wheat, rye, or oats, and belong with them nutritionally, the plant itself doesn't look at all like a grass. It is not tall and straight, but branching and weedlike, with heart-shaped leaves and white flowers that do a very good job of attracting bees, much to the delight of those of us who enjoy the dark honey made from their nectar. Its very name is a reminder of the plant's strange place in the botanical scheme of things; the word buckwheat comes from the Dutch word *bockweit*, meaning "beech wheat." This name reflects the fruit's physical resemblance to beechnuts and its nutritional similarity to wheat.

Buckwheat is thought to have originated in Asia. It grew in China in prehistoric times and was cultivated there at a very early date, and was introduced from that area into Eastern Europe and the Mediterranean by tribes migrating from Siberia and Manchuria. According to one historian, buckwheat was used by the ancient Phoenicians to make a refined flour which they called *far*; this became *farinha*, a staple of Mediterranean people (today farina is usually made from degerminated wheat).

In China, buckwheat was primarily used as a bread grain, but in Europe it was more commonly made into a porridge. The plant is shallow rooted and grows easily, and the soft triangular seeds could be cooked more quickly than other grains, thus saving fuel. Buckwheat was also ground into a coarse meal in some European areas to combine with more expensive wheat flour for making into pastries and breads. Many people in Eastern European countries still use buckwheat as a major part of their diet.

German and Dutch settlers brought buckwheat seeds with them when they immigrated to the New World, and planted many fields of it in what is now New York. The hardy and somewhat spunky plant then took off on its own and now grows wild in many parts of the country. It was adopted in the South during the 1800s as an inexpensive flour grain and eventually became the inspiration behind Stephen Foster's lyrics, quoted at the beginning of this section. Today, however, buckwheat is rarely eaten in America except by families with Eastern European roots, and very few farmers find it profitable to grow it for human use. It is mostly grown for animal feed, for honey, or to be plowed under as so-called green manure.

Buckwheat is therefore regarded as somewhat of a specialty food, and as such it tends to be difficult to find and about twice as expensive as wheat. Before planting an acre in buckwheat, however, or buying a fifty-pound bag of it from a feed store, try it out on your family. Buckwheat groats (as the fruits are generally called) are very distinctively flavored, quite unlike wheat, oats, or even rye. Buckwheat is one of those foods which people either love or hate, and while we like it a lot at our house, we've discovered by trying out recipes on our friends that the feeling is not universal. Health-food sections of large grocery stores and natural food stores usually carry buckwheat groats and buckwheat flour in two-pound or five-pound bags. Start with a small amount and try it out.

The way most people in America meet buckwheat is in pancakes. Personally, I think dumplings or cake would be a more interesting way to introduce this grain to your family. The easiest way to serve buckwheat is as the Russians do—cook the whole groats into a dryish porridge called kasza, or kasha, and eat it as a side dish with meat or as a breakfast cereal with milk and sugar. Kasha, like bulgur, can be used as the basis for many other dishes. But if you find buckwheat to your taste you may not want to overdo it. Some people who have eaten this grain at every meal have found themselves breaking out in a mild rash. On the other hand, since buckwheat is unrelated to the classic cereal grains, you can eat it even if you are allergic to wheat.

Buckwheat is a crop that can grow under adverse conditions, and is often found in out-of-the-way fields where nothing else will grow. This is a good grain to plant if your soil is poor, because it is forgiving, and will improve the soil, especially if you plow under the plants after harvesting the fruit. Buckwheat does best on well-drained soils, in cool, moist climates. A hard frost will kill it, however; it must be planted after all danger from frost is past. Actually, figuring backward twelve weeks from the first fall frost gives you a good planting date. This plant has what agronomists call an indeterminate growth, and will continue producing shoots, leaves, and fruit until finally killed off by the cold, but twelve weeks is ample for the major harvest to be ripe. Since buckwheat can be grown in hilly or rocky areas where other grains won't flourish, it is often treated as a catch crop (an extra crop sown to make land use more efficient), but keep even the edges of your planting away from other plants, as it will smother nearly anything.

As usual, drilling is the best way to plant if you can borrow someone's equipment, but you can broadcast four or five pecks per acre if you don't have access to machinery. Use slightly less seed if planting in rows. The major varieties of buckwheat are Japanese, Common Gray, Silverhull, Tartary, and

Tetraploid, although the last two are mostly used commercially to produce rutin, a drug used for the treatment of vascular disorders.

Harvest buckwheat when the earliest seeds mature in order to get the maximum amount of grain from the plants. Cut the plants, shock them, and dry them in the field for a week or ten days, then thresh like wheat. Store the whole groats in a cool, dry place and grind as needed.

BREAKFAST BUCKWHEAT

Known in parts of Europe as Black Polenta, this thick mush is typically served in a large mound which has been turned out onto a board. A hollow is scooped out in the middle and filled with melted butter. Each member of the family is then armed with a spoon, and the race is on, everyone eating a trough into the mound toward the butter. Another way to serve buckwheat mush is with crisply fried and crumbled bacon sprinkled on top, with hot bacon fat poured over the mound. One of my friends takes that version and smothers it with maple syrup. Or you can just pour a little honey on a bowlful of plain mush, cool it with some milk, and eat it like any other porridge.

4 cups water	1 cup finely cracked
1 teaspoon salt	buckwheat groats

Bring water to boil in a heavy pan (to get a nice mound shape, use the top of a double boiler), sprinkle in salt and buckwheat, stir once and simmer, covered, until just tender, about 10 minutes. Continue cooking, stirring constantly, until mush is smooth and stiff. Remove from heat; let cool slightly. If you want to serve in a large mound, place pan briefly in a pan of cold water, then invert over a plate and strike it with the heel of your hand to loosen the mush. To serve in individual bowls, just spoon out.

SOUTHERN-STYLE PANCAKES

2½ cups buttermilk

2 eggs

2 tablespoons vegetable oil or butter

3 tablespoons honey

1½ cups buckwheat flour

½ cup whole wheat flour

1½ teaspoons baking powder

½ teaspoon salt

Combine buttermilk, eggs, oil, and honey and beat well. Stir together flours, baking powder, and salt, pressing out any lumps. Add liquid ingredients, stirring only until blended. Bake on a slightly greased griddle until dry on top, then turn and bake on other side. Serve immediately with lots of butter and syrup. Makes 10–12 buckwheat pancakes.

YEASTED BUCKWHEAT PANCAKES

1 tablespoon active dry yeast

3 cups milk

3 cups buckwheat flour

Stir together; leave overnight in warm place.

¼ cup light molasses

¼ cup melted butter

½ teaspoon baking soda

1 teaspoon salt

In the morning, stir down bubbly batter and beat in molasses and butter. Stir together baking soda and salt, then sprinkle over batter and fold in. Bake pancakes on a hot, lightly greased griddle. Thin mixture with milk if you prefer a thinner pancake. Serve with butter and lots of maple syrup or molasses.

KASZA (KASHA)

Kasha is a mush made from whole or coarsely ground grains and is served as an accompaniment to meat meals in East European countries. Buckwheat groats classically have served as the basis of most kasha recipes.

1 cup buckwheat groats

1 egg, beaten

1 teaspoon salt

¼ teaspoon pepper

2 cups boiling stock

Over medium heat, stir groats, egg, and seasonings together in a heavy skillet until each grain is separate and dry. Add stock, stir once, and cover tightly. Cook over low heat for 15–20 minutes, or until grains are light and tender. You can stir in a little butter before serving if you like a moister kasha.

KASHA-STUFFED CHICKEN

1 egg, beaten

1 cup buckwheat groats

1 teaspoon salt

1 large onion, chopped

1 stalk celery and top, chopped

liver, heart, and gizzards of 1 roasting
    chicken, chopped

vegetable oil for sautéing

2 cups stock

1 cup dried pitted prunes

1 can mandarin oranges, chopped

1 whole roasting chicken

Combine egg, buckwheat, and salt in small bowl. Sauté onion, celery, and chicken parts until tender. Stir in buckwheat mixture and stock. Bring to a boil and simmer, covered, until tender, about 20 minutes. Meanwhile, boil prunes in water to cover until tender, about 30 minutes. Chop finely. Preheat oven to 325°F. Stir prunes and oranges into buckwheat mixture. Lightly stuff chicken and truss; put any remaining stuffing in greased baking dish and roast in oven with chicken. Cook chicken ½ hour for each pound of its weight.

KASHA CASSEROLE

2 tablespoons olive oil

2 medium onions, sliced

½ pound mushrooms, sliced

1 cup yoghurt or sour cream

4 cups cooked buckwheat groats

¼ cup chopped fresh parsley

Preheat oven to 325°F. Sauté onions and mushrooms in olive oil; stir with yoghurt into cooked groats. Turn into greased baking dish and bake for 30 minutes. Remove from oven, sprinkle with parsley, and serve.

RUSSIAN STUFFED MEATBALLS

1 pound ground meat

½ cup whole wheat bread crumbs

1 egg

1 teaspoon salt

1 clove garlic, chopped

1 tablespoon chopped fresh parsley,

½ teaspoon basil

½ cup cooked buckwheat groats

oil or vegetable shortening for frying

¼ cup water or stock

Combine all ingredients except buckwheat and oil. Form 12 small balls with the cooked buckwheat and add a layer of the meat mixture around these. Fry in hot skillet, turning frequently, until browned, about 10 minutes. Add ¼ cup water or stock and steam, covered, 15 minutes more.

STUFFED FRESHWATER FISH

One of the most common ways of serving buckwheat groats in Europe is as a stuffing for game and fish. If you come home from your next camping trip with 6 or 8 small trout or crappies, you might try this elegant way of serving them.

2 medium onions, chopped	1 teaspoon salt
6 tablespoons butter	¼ teaspoon pepper
2 cups cooked buckwheat groats	6 small fresh fish
2 hard-boiled eggs, chopped	additional salt
2 tablespoons chopped fresh parsley	½ cup fine dry bread crumbs
2 tablespoons chopped fresh dill	1 cup sour cream

Preheat oven to 400°F. Sauté onions in 3 tablespoons of the butter; add buckwheat, eggs, parsley, dill, salt, and pepper. Mix well. Clean fish and wipe them dry. Sprinkle cavities with salt and spoon stuffing inside. Arrange in buttered shallow baking dish. Melt remainder of butter; toast bread crumbs in it and sprinkle them over the fish. Bake about 10 minutes. Spoon sour cream over fish and bake 5 additional minutes.

NUTS AND GROATS

This kasha-like dish makes a very good stuffing for wild game.

1 cup buckwheat groats	½ cup chopped nuts
1 teaspoon salt	¼ cup chopped fresh parsley
2 cups boiling stock	½ teaspoon basil
1 medium onion, chopped	½ teaspoon thyme
1 tablespoon vegetable oil	

Cook buckwheat in salted stock for 5 minutes. Sauté onion in oil and stir into buckwheat. Add remaining ingredients, cover, and simmer for 5–10 minutes longer, or until groats are tender and liquid is absorbed.

BUCKWHEAT PIROSHKI

These little packages of buckwheat make tasty appetizers or can be served alone or with gravy, with the main course at an evening meal. Potato pastry is a little tricky to work with, but well worth a few tries. (*Piroshki* is the Polish word for them; in Russian it's *pirozhki*, in Yiddish *piroshke*.)

PASTRY
7 large potatoes, boiled and skinned
2 eggs
1 tablespoon butter or shortening
1 teaspoon salt
about 1 cup whole wheat flour

FILLING
1 egg, beaten
1 cup buckwheat groats
2 cups boiling water
2 large onions, diced
3 tablespoons vegetable oil
Egg yolk, beaten

For the pastry, mash potatoes; beat in eggs, butter, and salt. Add enough flour to enable you to roll out dough. Roll on floured surface to ¼ inch thick. Cut into 16 squares. If you have difficulties with pastry, as I do, roll the dough out on 2 floured cookie sheets. Cut into squares and take up with a spatula; place filling on sticky side and fold over as directed.

For the filling, stir egg and groats together over medium heat; add water and cook 20 minutes, covered. Sauté onions in and stir into buckwheat.

Preheat oven to 350°F. To assemble, place a small spoonful of filling in the center of each square. Bring the corners together in the center and press to seal edges. Brush with egg yolks. Place on greased baking sheet. Bake for 25 minutes. Serve hot or cold.

FRIED BUCKWHEAT MUSH (SCHMARRN)

This European dish is usually served by making a pile of the pieces of pancakes in a large bowl and pouring melted butter or bacon grease over it. Schmarrn is usually eaten with sausages or bacon.

1 cup buckwheat flour	½ cup milk
½ teaspoon salt	3 tablespoons vegetable oil
1 egg, beaten	

Beat together flour, salt, egg, and milk. Allow to sit for 10 minutes. Heat 1 tablespoon oil in large skillet, then pour in enough batter to cover bottom of pan and cook it over medium-high heat, breaking it apart with two forks as it cooks. Remove pieces to warm bowl and repeat until all of the batter is used. Serve hot.

Schmarrn may also be made into a dessert by adding ¼ cup sugar to the batter before cooking, and topping the pile of pieces with stewed plums.

BUCKWHEAT SOUP DUMPLINGS

These dumplings are not light like the English type, but rather should be firm (not doughy) when cooked. Experiment with size; obviously the larger dumplings need longer cooking.

3 cups buckwheat flour	stock or soup, boiling, in which to
1 egg, beaten	cook dumplings and serve with
1¼ cups hot water	them
1 tablespoon salt	

Combine ingredients and stir to blend well. Drop by tablespoonfuls into a kettle of boiling stock or soup. Cover and cook for 15 minutes. Serve with soup.

TYROLEAN BUCKWHEAT DUMPLINGS

The original recipe for these delicious dumplings came from Austria, where white bread cubes are used for a binder. We have used whole wheat bread and light rye with excellent results, so use whatever you have and see how it works.

4 cups cubed stale bread (about 4
    thick slices, ½-inch cubes)
4 tablespoons butter
¼ cup chopped chives
½ cup chopped fresh parsley
1 cup buckwheat flour

¼ cup whole wheat flour
2 eggs
¼–½ cup milk (or water)
1 teaspoon salt
water for cooking dumplings

Sauté bread cubes in butter until crisp; stir in chives and parsley, then remove from heat. Place flours in a bowl. Add bread-cube mixture and eggs and combine. Stir in milk (or water) slowly, adding only enough to make a stiff dough. Wet hands and form dough into 8 or 10 balls. Lift dumplings with a slotted spoon into a large kettle of rapidly boiling salted water. The dumplings will sink to the bottom, then rise in 1 or 2 minutes. Cook for 15–20 minutes. Remove from water and drain. Serve with goulash or sauerkraut (or soup or all by themselves). Any leftover dumplings can be sliced and fried.

SOURDOUGH BUCKWHEAT BREAD

STARTER

2 tablespoons active dry yeast
   softened in ¼ cup lukewarm water
2 cups lukewarm water

1 tablespoon honey
¼ cup buckwheat flour
¼ cup rye flour
¼ cup whole wheat flour

Combine ingredients and blend well. Cover and let sit in a warm place overnight.

1 tablespoon salt
½ cup lukewarm water
2 tablespoons honey
1 cup buckwheat flour
1 cup rye flour

3 cups whole wheat flour, or enough
   to make a workable dough
about ¼ cup cornmeal
milk or egg yolk for glazing loaf

In the morning stir down, and add salt, water, and honey. Add flours gradually, stirring vigorously to develop gluten. When all flour has been incorporated, knead well until dough is smooth and pliable. Oil bowl and turn dough in it to coat. Leave it to rise in a warm place, covered with a damp cloth. Let rise until almost double in bulk, 1½–2 hours. Punch dough down and form into 2 loaves. Place on baking sheet sprinkled with cornmeal. Cover and let rise until nearly doubled in bulk—about 1 hour. Preheat oven to 400°F. Brush loaves with milk or egg yolk. Bake for 35–40 minutes, or until the loaf sounds hollow when rapped with the knuckles. Makes 2 small loaves. Slice very thin to serve.

BUCKWHEAT MUFFINS

Baked buckwheat products have a grayish color which is displeasing to some people. This muffin recipe uses molasses for flavoring, and I find that it also improves the color of the resulting muffins.

1 cup buckwheat flour	¼ cup molasses
½ cup whole cornmeal	2 beaten eggs
2 teaspoons baking powder	1 cup yoghurt
1 teaspoon salt	¼ cup melted butter

Preheat oven to 375°F. Stir together dry ingredients; beat together liquid ingredients and combine with first mixture. Thin with a little milk if needed to make a pourable batter. Pour into muffin tins and bake for 25 minutes.

POTATO SOUP

2 quarts soup stock or water	1 tablespoon fresh parsley, chopped
6 potatoes, scrubbed and diced	1 teaspoon thyme
2 large onions, chopped	1 tablespoons salt
¼ cup buckwheat groats	2 cup cream or half-and-half
1 teaspoon fresh basil	

Cook potatoes, onions, groats, and seasonings in stock or water for 20–30 minutes. stir in cream and serve.

BLINI

Yeasted buckwheat pancakes are very popular appetizers in Russia. Sometimes they are stuffed and rolled or folded over, but most frequently they are served as the base for an open-faced sandwich, spread with melted butter, then with a piece of smoked, salted, or pickled fish or caviar, and topped with a dab of sour cream. Other fillings include mushrooms and cottage cheese. The traditional time for blini making is during the Maslenitsa, or "butter festival," the carnival week just before Lent.

1 cup lukewarm water	3 eggs, separated
1 teaspoon honey	1 teaspoon salt
1 tablespoon active dry yeast	3 tablespoons melted butter
2 cups warm milk	2 cups buckwheat flour
2 cups whole wheat flour	

Mix water and honey in large bowl. Dissolve yeast in mixture and add milk and wheat flour. Beat well and place in a warm place, covered, to rise, about 1 hour. Beat egg yolks until creamy; add salt, melted butter, and buckwheat flour. Stir into yeast mixture and leave again to rise for 1 hour. Beat egg whites until stiff and gently fold into mixture. Drop by spoonfuls onto a hot greased griddle or skillet and bake until dry on the top; turn and bake on other side. Continue until batter is used. Serve warm with smoked or salted fish.

A variation we like is to use about ½ cup less liquid; the blini rise while baking until they resemble English muffins. Split with forks and toast lightly. Spread with butter. Enjoy.

AMARANTH

The Grain of the Gods

*Immortal amaranth, a flower which once
In Paradise, fast by the Tree of Life,
Began to bloom, but soon for man's offence
To Heav'n remov'd, where first it grew, there grows,
And flow'rs aloft shading the Fount of Life.*
        —Paradise Lost, Book iii, line 353, 1667,
                                    by John Milton

Amaranth is a tiny grain that has been grown for thousands of years in Mexico, Central and South America, Nepal, and India. According to one researcher, it was first cultivated by cave dwellers in areas where it grew wild, but by the time Spanish conquistadors arrived in Mexico and Central America, amaranth had become a staple crop, as important as corn and beans to the Aztecs.

Historical records tell us that the Spanish conqueror Cortes commanded the Aztec people to stop producing amaranth in the sixteenth century. Before that time, thousands of acres were cultivated in order to produce and store sufficient grain for a year's use. In spite of the fact that people were killed or severely punished for disobeying this edict, some amaranth production continued in secret for use in religious ceremonies. Each year, farmers offered 200,000 bushels of this tiny seed to their ruler, Montezuma, as a tribute. In addition, according to legend, huge statues of honey-sweetened amaranth dough were fashioned in the shapes of individual gods to be honored during their festivals. At the conclusion of the festival, the idol was broken apart and eaten by the party-goers. The Aztecs believed that amaranth eaten under these conditions gave them mystical, almost supernatural energy and power.

Today's food scientists tell us that this grain is extremely nutritious. Among their discoveries: amaranth provides more and better quality protein, and more iron, potassium, phosphorus, and magnesium than other grains. Lysine, essential to body functions, is a limiting amino acid in many vegetable foods, and is also contained in a higher content in amaranth than in most cereal grains (nearly twice the lysine of wheat and three times that of corn). In addition, 100 grams of amaranth contains more of these minerals than an equal amount of milk. People who are allergic to the gluten in wheat and rye can eat amaranth as a whole grain or dishes made with amaranth flour with no ill effects.

On the downside, amaranth is low in leucine, another amino acid needed for body functioning. However, leucine is found in excess in most common cereal grains. Combining amaranth and corn or wheat flour, therefore, results in an almost "perfect" protein. Amaranth, a tall, broad-leaved plant—not a grass, like wheat, corn, rye, and other common grains—is extremely hardy. Amaranth plants grow easily, resisting flooding, drought, heat, and pests, and readily adapt to new environments, including some that are inhospitable to conventional cereal crops. Today amaranth grows wild and with human assistance in many poor areas of the world, where scientists have discovered it is often the food that keeps malnutrition at bay.

Since the early 1980s, Midwestern farmers have been growing amaranth, which has now been well integrated into the health-food market, although not yet into mainstream American kitchens. Today, large amaranth crops are grown in India and Nepal, Mexico, Guatemala, Peru, Kenya, India, and Thailand.

While more than 60 species of *Amaranthus* are grown worldwide, most are weedy, and only a few are suitable for cultivation. The amaranth crop yields both grain and a nutritious, gaily colored vegetable green, similar to chard. Amaranth greens are an excellent protein source, although, like turnip greens, they must be boiled to remove nitrates and oxalic acid.

Because amaranth is such a hardy plant, it is easy to grow in home gardens. However, be aware that it is related to pigweed, which farmers hate. To keep amaranth from taking over, confine your plants with deeply set barriers, and do not interplant with other vegetables. *Amaranthus cruentus*, a grain amaranth species that produces seeds with particularly good taste and milling characteristics is indigenous to Mexico and Central America, but can now be obtained in the United States. To obtain information about the availability of amaranth seed, write to the Rodale Research Center, Kutztown, Pennsylvania, or the USDA's Western Regional Research Center, Berkeley, California. Redwood City Seed Company (P.O. Box 361, Redwood City, CA 94064) lists several varieties of amaranth in their catalog, along with corn, quinoa, teff, and several other lesser known grains. One variety, *Amaranthus hypochondriacus*, is grown for seed.

Plant seeds in the spring in flats, then set out 2 feet apart when the soil warms up. Small seedlings tend to grow slowly at first and can be smothered by weeds. Cultivate the soil carefully during the first few weeks. After that, the crop grows very rapidly, particularly under conditions of bright sunlight, high temperature, and dry soil, and requires very little attention.

Commercial production of amaranth is difficult, because the seeds are too tiny to harvest mechanically using the same machinery as other grains. In addition, the grain tends to stick to the stalks when it is wet, forcing farmers to wait until after the first killing frost, by which time the seeds have dried out. In countries where amaranth is traditionally cultivated, it is hand harvested and cleaned on high screens. This is easily accomplished at home. Make a cleaning box using two layers of screen about 6 inches apart. The top screen should be made of 1¼-inch hardware cloth, with the bottom one ⅛-inch. Place the heads in the box and remove leaves and stems. Rub seeds between your hands, removing the paper-thin covering. The seeds will drop down to the smaller screen, and any dirt or unwanted matter will sift out.

BASIC COOKED AMARANTH

½ cup amaranth   1 cup water or stock
¼ teaspoon salt

Stir amaranth and salt into cold liquid and heat to boiling in a 2-quart saucepan. Reduce the heat and cook, covered, stirring occasionally to prevent sticking, until tender, about 20 minutes. If you allow the amaranth to boil over, there will be a very sticky mess to clean up, so err on the slow side and watch it carefully. If the mixture seems a bit watery after 20 or 25 minutes, remove from heat and leave covered for 5 to 10 minutes to absorb liquid. Makes 1–2 servings.

This makes a very satisfying breakfast cereal. Stir in raisins, chopped dates or nuts and honey, molasses, or maple syrup.

AMARANTH PANCAKES

These pancakes were developed by a friend whose daughter is allergic to wheat. They are delicious topped with applesauce and cinnamon. This recipe makes 8–10 pancakes.

1 large or extra-large egg
¼ cup apple or orange juice
1 teaspoon light vegetable oil
¼ cup amaranth flour
¼ cup tapioca flour
3 tablespoons arrowroot flour

¼ teaspoon ground cinnamon
⅛ teaspoon grated nutmeg
½ teaspoon wheat-free baking
  powder
¼ teaspoon salt

Beat the egg until light and foamy. Beat in juice and oil. Add remaining ingredients to egg mixture, one at a time, beating well after each addition. Spray a frying pan or griddle with vegetable oil and heat until very hot. Pour 2–3 tablespoons batter for each pancake, and flip when brown on bottom. Spray frying surface with oil after each batch. These pancakes depend for their success on being cooked immediately after batter is made.

AMARANTH BANANA NUT BREAD

1½ cups whole wheat flour
½ cup amaranth flour or meal
1 teaspoon baking powder
½ teaspoon baking soda
½ teaspoon ground cinammon
¼ teaspoon allspice
2 eggs, beaten
¼ cup light vegetable oil

¼ cup melted butter or margarine
½ cup applesauce
¼ cup honey
1 teaspoon vanilla or almond extract
1 mashed banana
1 cup chopped walnuts or almonds

Preheat oven to 350°F. Stir together dry ingredients. Beat eggs, butter, oil, applesauce, honey, vanilla, and banana together and add to dry ingredients, stirring just until moistened. Stir in nuts. Pour batter into oiled loaf pan. Bake for 60–65 minutes, or until tester comes out clean. Cool for 5 minutes before removing from pan and cooling on rack. Slices best when cool.

AMARANTH DATE MUFFINS

1 cup amaranth flour
1 cup whole wheat pastry flour
2 teaspoons baking powder
½ teaspoon baking soda
½ teaspoon salt
¼ teaspoon ground cloves
2 eggs

3 tablespoons light vegetable oil
½ cup orange or apple juice
¼ cup honey
¼ cup sour cream or yoghurt
2 tablespoons date crystals or ¼ cup
    chopped dates

Preheat oven to 425°F. Stir together dry ingredients. In separate bowl, beat eggs. Add oil, juice, honey, sour cream, and dates. Add to dry ingredients, then spoon into muffin tins that have been sprayed with vegetable oil. Fill no more than two-thirds full. Bake for 20 to 25 minutes or until cake tester comes out clean.

VARIATION: Like poppy seeds, amaranth seeds can also be added to muffins for a crunchy texture. Pour ½ cup of boiling water over 2 tablespoons amaranth seeds. Drain after 5 minutes and add seeds to batter just before placing in muffin tins.

AMARANTH-STUFFED ARTICHOKES

4 large globe artichokes	3 medium carrots, diced
boiling water	2 tablespoons light vegetable oil
½ cup amaranth	2 cloves garlic, minced
1 cup chicken or vegetable stock	½ cup canned or fresh kernel corn
½ teaspoon salt	¼ cup chopped mint
¼ teaspoon coarsely ground black pepper	3 tablespoons chopped fresh parsley

Wash artichokes, cut off stem, and slice 1 inch off top. Peel stem, dice, and set aside. Pull outer dark leaves from artichoke bottom so it can stand upright. Using kitchen shears, trim thorny tips of leaves. In a pot large enough to hold all 4 artichokes, add boiling water to cover and simmer artichokes, covered, 30 to 40 minutes. Test for doneness by poking stem end with a fork; it should go in easily. Rinse and cool slightly. Spread artichoke open and cut around choke with a small knife. Using a spoon, scrape out center petals and fuzzy center. Rinse with hot water, then turn upside down to drain.

While artichokes steam, prepare amaranth according to Basic Cooked Amaranth recipe (page 230), using stock in place of water.

While artichokes and amaranth cook, sauté carrots in oil until tender, about 5 minutes. Stir in garlic, artichoke stems, corn, mint, and parsley. Remove from heat. When amaranth is done, stir in carrot mixture and spoon between artichoke leaves and into center cavities. Reheat in shallow baking dish before serving, if desired.

MILLET AND AMARANTH MUSHROOM RISOTTO

½ cup chopped onion
1 cup sliced mushrooms (for best
appearance and flavor use exotic
mushrooms, such as morels,
portobellos, or shiitakes)
1 tablespoon canola or other light oil
¼ cup amaranth
¼ cup millet
½ cup long-grain brown rice

3 cups chicken, beef, or vegetable
stock
½ cup dry white wine
¼ teaspoon coarsely ground black
pepper
salt to taste (optional)
¼ cup chopped fresh parsley
¼ cup grated Parmesan cheese

Using a large skillet or saucepan, sauté onion and mushrooms in oil until onions are translucent and mushrooms tender. Add grains; stir with wooden spoon or spatula until coated and lightly brown, about 2 minutes. Add stock, bring to a boil, and simmer, covered, about 30 minutes, until liquid is mostly absorbed and the grains are tender. Stir in wine and pepper, and salt if desired. Remove from heat and let stand 5 more minutes, covered. Before serving, fluff with a fork and stir in parsley and cheese.

AMARANTH PUFFS (CRACKERS)

This simple cracker recipe makes tasty and nutritious after-school snacks.

½ cup finely ground amaranth flour
½ teaspoon salt

½ cup boiling water
2 egg whites, beaten until stiff

Preheat oven to 350°F. Mix flour and salt. Pour the boiling water into the mixture and stir well. Fold in beaten egg whites and drop by teaspoonfuls on a baking sheet that has been sprayed with vegetable oil. Bake for 20–25 minutes. These crispy crackers must be thoroughly cooled before storing and will keep up to a week or two in airtight containers.

ALEGRIA

This candy, said to be invented by the Aztecs, is still sold in Mexico by street vendors.

3 tablespoons honey

3 tablespoons light molasses or dark corn syrup

3 tablespoons butter

2 cups popped amaranth (see Note)

vegetable oil or vegetable oil spray

Combine honey, molasses, and butter in a large saucepan or skillet and heat slowly to boiling. Cook over medium heat 5–7 minutes, stirring constantly, until mixture turns golden-brown and becomes thick and sticky. Add amaranth and stir with wooden spoon until completely coated with the syrup. Press firmly into a 9×13 pan that has been sprayed with vegetable oil (this can best be done with the wooden spoon, a heavy spatula, or oiled fingers). Cut into bars and allow to cool. Keeps well in airtight containers for 2 or 3 days. Hard on braces, so teenagers beware!

NOTE: To pop amaranth, place in a very hot skillet, one tablespoon at a time, stirring constantly until seeds pop (this takes only 10 to 15 seconds). Transfer to a shallow bowl as they pop, then add the next batch. It takes about 9–10 tablespoons amaranth seed to make 2 cups.

NUTS AND SEEDS

*I had a little nut tree
Nothing would it bear
But a silver nutmeg
and a golden pear*

Nuts and seeds were staples in the diets of the very earliest nomadic peoples. Long before the development of agriculture, hunters and gatherers, ancestors of the men and women who would later cut down trees and burn bushes to clear land for their crops, lived from the bounty of the land.

Nuts are often considered a snack food in America, yet they are a valuable source of vitamins, minerals, and protein, and can be used in cooking just like any other vegetable. Seeds, since they contain the nourishment for the embryo of the parent plant, are very high in the essential amino acids and also in minerals.

Nuts in the shell appear in grocery stores around Thanksgiving, and most of us stock up then for the holiday season. If you live where one or more nuts are commercial crops, you may be able to buy those nuts in bulk in late summer, when most nuts are harvested. Watch roadside stands. I discovered a line of shelled raw nuts shelved with the health foods in my favorite grocery store; it includes almonds, Spanish peanuts, cashews, coconut, and sunflower seeds, and they are all very reasonably priced. Unfortunately this is a local brand, but look carefully, you may discover such a line in your area too. Natural foods stores and some ethnic food stores usually carry raw nuts, which is the most economical form in which to buy them. For cooking, leave them raw; if you want them roasted for snacks, roast them yourself.

Sunflower, pumpkin, and sesame seeds are usually available in large grocery stores, or at least in health-food outlets. Smaller seeds, such as poppy, alfalfa (used mostly for sprouting), flax, and mustard, seem to be harder to find. I buy mine from an herb and tea shop; search natural food stores and ask other customers. A year's supply of sunflower and sesame seeds doesn't take up much room, so even if you have to search hard to find them, if you stock up when you find them it won't be a constant problem. Again, it is best to buy seeds raw so that you have the choice of using them that way or roasting them as snacks.

Sunflower and pumpkin (or nearly any squash) seeds can be easily raised at home, and both have nice side benefits. My family enjoys growing the beautiful sunflower, and birds will definitely frequent your porch if it is flanked by these growing bird feeders. In order to get pumpkin seeds you have to grow pumpkins, and that means a few cheerful jack-o'-lanterns and lots of pumpkin pie.

Native Americans cultivated sunflowers before they grew any other crops; several varieties of sunflowers grew wild, particularly in the Southwest, and when replanted and watered occasionally, they gave generous bounty. Russian czars supposedly fed their soldiers two pounds of seeds a day and little else—even today sunflower seeds are the national Russian snack. In Middle Eastern countries they are often served as a regular course, just as we would serve salad or nuts and fruit.

A small packet of sunflower seeds purchased from a garden shop in early spring will produce enough plants to provide you with sunflower seeds for many months. Mammoth Russian is my favorite variety, but there are many to choose from. Do not plant a double-centered type, as its seeds are more for ornament than food. Plant the seeds along a fence or wall, or stake them to prevent wind damage. Weed regularly to avoid competition for water and nutrients, and water well. They grow with little care, though they'll produce larger heads and plumper seeds if you build up your soil with compost or fertilizer.

In the fall, break or cut the heads off, leaving several inches of stem to hang them up with, and dry them in a well-ventilated area for several weeks. Cover them with fine wire screening or let the cats loose in your drying room to keep the mice away. If you would rather leave the heads in the garden to dry, cover them with cheesecloth to prevent bird damage. The seeds are ready to harvest when you hit the back of the heads with your fingers and some of them shake loose easily. Brush the seeds out with any stiff object that works (brush, stick, curry comb), then spread them out to dry some more.

To hull, use a pair of pliers to crack the seeds lengthwise. Or put the seeds in boiling water for a few minutes and the shells will come free easily. Some people have successfully used a steel-bladed grain mill set wide open, and a 10-inch farm hammermill also works well. Remove the screens and set the mill at a low speed (350–400 revolutions per minute); pour in up to two gallons of whole seeds, slowly, speeding up the mill at the end to 1500 rpm to clear the mill and prevent it from clogging.

Hulled sunflower (and pumpkin seeds) can be stored in airtight jars in a cool place. After opening the jars, keep them in the refrigerator.

Pumpkins are one of the easiest vegetables to grow. Form hills in freshly spaded, well-drained soil, and place four to six seeds in a circle on the hill. Water well, and when the plants are two to three inches high, thin to the three strongest plants. When the plants reach six inches, stop overhead watering, as they tend to rot easily, and water the trench formed around the base of the hill. Allow pumpkins to ripen in the field; they should be ready by Halloween if you planted by the first of June. After cutting up pumpkins for jack-o'-lanterns or for cooking, remove seeds, wash thoroughly, and spread out to dry.

If you are planning to stay on your property for a reasonable length of time, a few nut trees would be a good long-term investment. An acre planted to walnuts will provide many years of harvests (for eating and for selling), and the trees themselves can be harvested in old age for their wood. Personally, I think just the idea of planting trees which in fifteen or twenty years will be fifty feet high and green is reason enough to plant walnuts, pecans, hickories, or chestnuts—the larger of the nut trees, which grow well in this country. And an acre is certainly not necessary—just one or two trees will provide a family with many more nuts than they can eat each year. If you have less room consider American hazelnuts, or filberts, which can be trimmed into five- or six-foot shrubs or left alone to become ten- to fifteen-foot trees. Almond trees also grow only fifteen or twenty feet high, and nuts can be harvested two or three years after planting. (It takes about ten years for the larger nut trees—walnuts, pecans, etc.—to begin producing nuts.) English walnuts are also somewhat smaller than the black walnut, and a particular strain, the Carpathian, produces smaller trees which produce nuts just three to four years after planting.

Choose your planting site carefully, considering the size of the variety you have chosen. Study seed catalogues for detailed information, but a good rule is to leave fifty feet in all directions around a tree. Plant two trees if you can, because cross-pollination makes for larger crops. Chinese chestnuts and hazelnuts must be grown in groups of at least two for successful reproduction. Plant in a sunny place with deep, well-drained soil. Dig your holes large enough to accept all the roots of your new tree without bending, and make sure that the roots are not exposed to sun or wind while you dig the holes; cover the roots with damp potato sacks or the like, but keep them moist. If you have a gopher problem where you live, line the hole with one-inch chicken wire, which will allow the roots to grow through as they get larger, but will protect the new shoots the first year. Trim the ends of broken roots as you would in transplanting any plant, set the tree into the hole so that the soil line will be a little higher than it was in its first planting, and lay the roots around gently, making sure that they all contact the soil. Fill the hole with damp topsoil, tamping gently with your hands to fill the spaces. Water to settle the soil, then add more soil, leaving a slight depression to catch water.

Stake your trees if strong winds are common in your area, and wrap the trunks with burlap to prevent drying out and burning during the first year.

Wire mesh fences around the bottom twelve inches of the trees will help to prevent rodent chewing.

When trees begin to bear, plan to collect nuts as soon as they are ripe (almonds, hazelnuts, and hickories need to be picked; other trees drop the nuts when they are ready). Most nuts are enclosed within a tough, fibrous hull. Hickories and walnuts will stain if the hulls are not removed immediately—your hands will stain also, so wear gloves; also, some people are sensitive to the staining agent. Black walnuts are hardest to hull, and sometimes require washing as well. Walnut hullers can be purchased from a hardware store or a department store, but you can also do it by hand or with the aid of a car (drive over them). Hazelnuts (filberts) are easier to hull if their clusters are allowed to wilt for a day or so after picking. After removing the hulls, spread the nuts thinly in a dry, well-ventilated place to cure for four to six weeks. For best quality nutmeats, crack the nuts soon after curing and store the nutmeats in airtight containers in a cold place.

NUTTY SNACKS

Nuts make excellent snacks, but I get tired of seeing them always served the same way—shelled, roasted, salted. Here are four suggestions to get you started—I'm sure you can think of many more once you begin.

- Mix a variety of freshly shelled nuts together and sauté in a little vegetable oil until brown. Cool and toss with tiny cubes of sharp cheese.
- Combine roasted, salted nuts with raisins.
- Mix equal proportions of pretzels, nuts, and two or three different types of whole grain cereals (Chex®, puffed whole corn, spoon-size shredded wheat, etc.). Make a sauce of melted butter, Worcestershire sauce, garlic salt, and celery salt; blend into cereal mixture and roast on baking sheets for ½ hour at 250°F. Stir occasionally.
- In an airtight container mix raw cashews, peanuts, almonds, and sunflower seeds. Stir in raisins, currants, and dried apricots. Keep handy for munching. Better than any commercial trail mix.

ROASTED SQUASH SEEDS

squash seeds
vegetable oil

salt to taste

Any squash seeds which are large enough to cover a small fingernail can be roasted and shelled in the same way as sunflower seeds. Dry them in the sun after removing from squash (pumpkins, etc.). Preheat oven to 250°F. Coat seeds with vegetable oil and salt to taste. Spread thinly on baking sheets and place in the oven. Stir occasionally. Roast for about 25 minutes, or until they are crisp. Store in an airtight container. Crack the shell with your teeth and eat the interior. Some folks eat the whole seed, but I compost the hulls.

Pumpkin and squash seeds can be hulled without roasting if they are fairly large, and I prefer them raw for cooking. Make sure they are thoroughly dry—sometimes placing them in a gas oven with just the pilot light on for a few hours helps—and crack with your teeth, with a small pair of pliers, or with your fingers.

CASHEW HONEY BUTTER

4½ cups lightly roasted cashews
8 tablespoons peanut or other
    vegetable oil

4 tablespoons honey
1 teaspoon salt (optional)

Pulse cashews in food processor or put through steel flour mill, which will turn them into a rather dry nut butter. Stir oil and honey into butter, beating well to combine. Add salt or not, as you prefer. This spreads best at room temperature, but should really be refrigerated if you want it to stay at its peak flavor. It will keep for several months in the refrigerator.

SAVORY SALAD

There's no way I could write a recipe for a green salad; the ingredients of any salad depend so much on what is in season, what is on sale, and what happens to be in my refrigerator. However, when you have combined fresh, crisp greens with a suitable number of vegetables, do try adding any number of the following to the bowl before tossing:

hulled sunflower seeds

cashews

sesame seeds, raw or toasted

slivered almonds

flax seeds

walnut halves

sprouted alfalfa seeds

ASPARAGUS SALAD

2 tablespoons sesame seeds

¼ teaspoon salt

2 tablespoons vegetable oil

1–1½ pounds fresh asparagus

2 tablespoons honey

6–8 ounces sugar snap peas,

3 tablespoons vinegar

strings removed and cut in half

1 teaspoon soy sauce

cold cooked rice

Sauté sesame seeds in oil until lightly browned; remove from heat, stir in honey and allow to cool. Blend in vinegar, soy sauce, and salt. Set aside.

Meanwhile, break asparagus at lower end of stalks (where the green top merges with the white bottom) and discard ends. Steam with sugar snap peas for 7–10 minutes, or until tender but not limp. Pour sauce over hot vegetables, turning stalks to cover evenly. Refrigerate.

Serve on a bed of cold cooked rice.

RAW SPINACH SALAD

1 cup olive oil

3 tablespoons vinegar

2 teaspoons salt

¾ teaspoon ground pepper

1 clove of garlic, sliced thinly

2 pounds fresh spinach, washed,
   crisped, and torn into bite-size
   pieces

½ cup freshly grated Parmesan
   cheese

1 cup coarsely chopped pecans or
   walnuts

Blend together olive oil, vinegar, salt, pepper, and garlic. Allow to sit for several hours so flavors blend properly. Toss spinach with enough dressing to coat leaves thoroughly. (Reserve remaining dressing for future salads.) Add cheese and nuts and toss lightly. Serve.

CARROT RAISIN NUT SALAD

6–8 small carrots, washed but not
   peeled

½ cup raisins

½ cup chopped pecans or walnuts

¼ cup crushed pineapple

½ teaspoon salt

¼ cup yoghurt or sour cream

Shred carrots coarsely; blend with raisins, nuts, and pineapple. Sprinkle with salt and stir well. Fold in yoghurt or sour cream. Chill thoroughly before serving.

CASHEW CHICKEN SALAD

2 cups cubed cooked chicken
1 stalk celery, diced
2 green onions, sliced
½ green bell pepper, coarsely
    chopped
2 cups cooked brown rice

¾ cup mayonnaise
1 tablespoon lemon juice
1 teaspoon powdered mustard
1 teaspoon salt
½ cup cashews, raw or roasted

Stir together chicken, celery, onions, bell pepper, and rice. Combine mayonnaise, lemon juice, and spices; blend into chicken mixture. Chill thoroughly. Stir in cashews just before serving.

CREAMY ALMOND SOUP

1 cup almonds
1 cup milk
¼ cup whole wheat bread crumbs
2 tablespoons butter
2 tablespoons whole wheat flour

4 cups chicken or vegetable stock
¼ teaspoon ground mace
1 teaspoon salt
¼ teaspoon pepper
1 cup cream

Pulse almonds in a food processor, through a nut grinder, or grate in a Mouli grater. Stir into milk and simmer gently until nuts are soft. Stir in the bread crumbs and mix well. Purée in blender, food processor, or press through a sieve, purée cone, or food mill. Melt butter; blend in flour. Add stock gradually, stirring to prevent lumps. Stir in the almond mixture; add seasonings. Simmer for 5 minutes, stirring constantly. Blend in cream and remove from heat. Makes about 6½ cups.

WALNUT CHICKEN

This can be made in a wok or a large skillet. Most of the preparation time is in the preparation of the meat, and can be done ahead. The actual cooking time is very short.

1 pound boned chicken breasts, cut into 1-inch cubes	4 tablespoons vegetable oil
3 tablespoons soy sauce	2 or 3 green onions (scallions), sliced
1 tablespoon sherry	1 garlic clove, cut in 2 pieces
½ teaspoon ground ginger or ½-inch piece fresh ginger	1 cup coarsely chopped walnuts

Marinate chicken cubes in soy sauce, sherry, and ginger mixture for from 1 hour to overnight. Heat 2 tablespoons of the oil in a wok or skillet over medium-high heat; stir-fry green onions, garlic, and walnuts for 3–4 minutes. Remove garlic pieces and transfer onions and walnuts to a small bowl or paper towel.

Add remaining 2 tablespoons oil to wok; heat, add chicken pieces and marinade. Stir-fry until chicken is tender and soy mixture coats chicken—about 5 minutes. Return walnuts and onions to pan and toss lightly. Serve over hot rice.

TOASTED SEEDS AND NOODLES

½ pound vegetable pasta	½ cup chopped almonds
¼ cup sesame seeds	½ cup wheat germ
½ cup butter or margarine	¼ cup fresh chopped parsley
½ cup sunflower seeds	¼ cup chopped onion

Cook pasta in a large pan of water. Sauté sesame seeds in butter, stirring often, until slightly brown. Remove from heat and stir in remaining ingredients. Drain noodles; toss with seed mixture. Serve immediately.

SESAME RICE

2 tablespoons cashews	4 cups hot cooked brown rice
4 tablespoons vegetable oil	1 teaspoon salt
1 cup sesame seeds	½ teaspoon cayenne pepper

Sauté cashews in oil until they are just beginning to brown; add seeds and continue frying until seeds are golden. Stir into rice, season, and serve.

CHESTNUT STUFFING

My earliest memories of chestnuts come from sitting around a fire listening to them pop as they roasted, and burning my tongue whenever one was given to me. It wasn't until I was much older that I learned that chestnuts were also put into our holiday turkey. This dressing makes about 4 cups.

3 cups shelled chestnuts (see Note) or 1 can (15.5 ounces) chestnut purée	¼ cup cream
	1 teaspoon salt
	¼ teaspoon pepper
vegetable stock to cover	½ teaspoon ground ginger
½ cup butter or margarine	½ teaspoon grated nutmeg
1 cup dry bread crumbs	¼ teaspoon paprika

If using fresh chestnuts, boil them in stock until tender (about 30 minutes); rinse in cold water and remove skins. Put through a food mill, purée cone, or sieve. To purée add butter, bread crumbs, cream, and seasonings and stir.

NOTE: You will need a sharp knife to remove shells. Make an x-shaped cut on the flat side, then work the blade around the nut from there.

ZUNI SUNFLOWER BREAD

This moist bread comes to us from the Zuni Indians, who use sunflower seeds as a valuable protein source in their diet. For this recipe the sunflower seeds can be ground in a food processor or flour mill, resulting in a moist, soft meal.

¼ cup butter or margarine, softened
¼ cup honey
2 eggs
1 cup whole wheat flour
1 teaspoon salt

1 teaspoon baking powder
1½ cups ground sunflower seeds
1 cup milk
½ cup whole sunflower seeds

Preheat oven to 325°F. Cream together butter and honey; beat in eggs. In separate bowl, stir together flour, salt, and baking powder, breaking up any lumps. Stir in ground sunflower seeds and add to first mixture alternately with milk. Beat well. Fold in whole sunflower seeds; turn into well-greased loaf pan. Bake for 1 hour. Cool for 10 minutes before removing from pan, and cool thoroughly before slicing.

PUMPKIN WHEAT MUFFINS

I first had these at a friend's house, made from pumpkin seeds fresh from her garden. To shell pumpkin and other squash seeds, see page 239.

2 cups whole wheat flour
2½ teaspoons baking powder
1 teaspoon salt
¼ cup shelled pumpkin seeds

1 egg, beaten
¾ cup milk
⅓ cup vegetable oil
⅓ cup molasses

Preheat oven to 400°F. Stir together flour, baking powder, and salt, pressing out any lumps. Add pumpkin seeds. Beat together egg and milk; blend in oil and molasses and stir into dry ingredients just until blended. Pour batter into muffin tins, filling each about ⅔ full. Bake for 20–25 minutes. Makes 1 dozen.

POPPY SEED CAKE

This cake calls for ground poppy seeds. In Eastern Europe, where poppy seeds are a common ingredient, shopkeepers will grind the seeds as a convenience to the shoppers, or people grind them at home in a household nut grinder. If you do not have a nut and seed grinder, you can grind poppy seeds in your blender, coffee grinder, or in a ridged mortar and pestle (*suribachi* and *surikogi*) used for sesame seeds and available in most gourmet food stores. I have had this cake made with whole poppy seeds, and thought it was very good that way also; the seeds tend to settle and make a layer at the bottom, but it still tastes delicious.

5 tablespoons butter	1 cup poppy seeds, ground
¾ cup plus 1 tablespoon sugar	grated rind of 1 lemon
4 eggs, separated	

Preheat oven to 300°F. Beat butter until it is creamy; add ¾ cup sugar and egg yolks and beat well. Stir in poppy seeds and lemon rind. Beat egg whites very stiff; beat in 1 tablespoon sugar, then very gently fold into butter mixture. Bake in a greased and floured springform pan 40–45 minutes.

AUSTRIAN NUT CAKE

This cake has appeared at holidays and special events in our life for many years, thanks to our friend Nina. It took me a long time to believe that there was no flour in it—but having made it myself, I finally accepted it. In Europe this cake is often topped with a coffee cream.

2¼ cups cracked walnut meats	6 large eggs, separated
1¾ cups sugar	

Preheat oven to 350°F. Grind nuts to a fine, dry meal. Mix sugar with egg yolks and beat until foamy; combine with ground nuts. Beat egg whites until very stiff; fold into first mixture. Pour into well-greased springform pan. Bake for 45 minutes. (Do not open oven while baking, or it will fall.) Let cake sit about 10 minutes before removing from pan.

CHINESE GLAZED CHESTNUTS

1 pound chestnuts   ¾ cup honey
2 cups sugar

Soak chestnuts overnight. Drain and shell. Remove skins with the help of a sharp knife; set aside to dry. Cook sugar and honey over a low heat for 1 hour. Add chestnuts and simmer 2 more hours. Separate and let cool. Store in a tightly closed container.

WHIPPED FRUIT CUPS

This is one of our favorite hot night coolers.

4 cups assorted fresh fruit in season,   ¼ cup honey
   cut into bite-size pieces   1 teaspoon vanilla extract
   (strawberries, bananas, oranges,   1 cup sour cream or yoghurt
   berries, peaches, melons, etc.)   1 cup hulled sunflower seeds

Chill fruit thoroughly. Beat honey and vanilla with sour cream until light; fold into fruit mixture. Gently stir in sunflower seeds. Heap into small serving dishes; if you are not serving right away, chill until ready to eat.

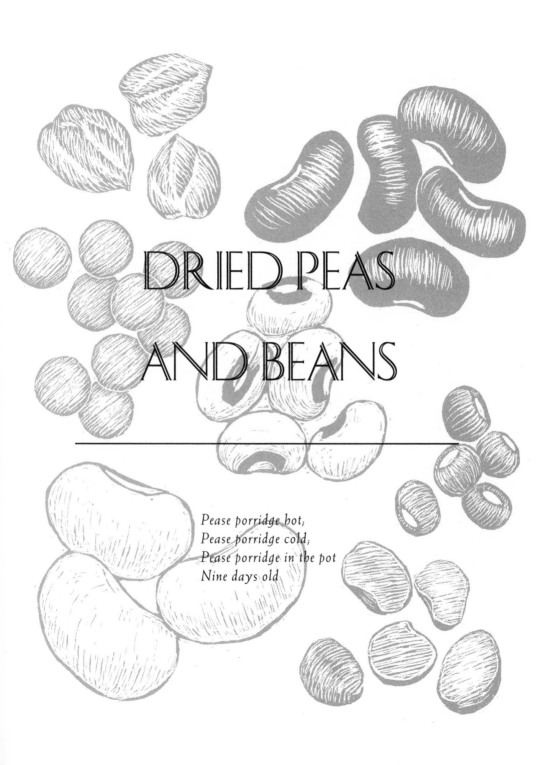

DRIED PEAS
AND BEANS

Pease porridge hot;
Pease porridge cold;
Pease porridge in the pot
Nine days old

Dried peas and beans are not whole grains, but people who eat a lot of grains also seem to use legumes in many meals. Even people who are primarily meat eaters can use these high-protein vegetables as meal-stretchers to make meat go further, as easily stored staples, or just for variety.

Beans, peas, peanuts, and lentils are all fruits of leguminous plants, and they are all attached to their parent plants in the same way—within pods which hang from the stems. They are also known as *pulses*, which interestingly enough comes from the same root word as *poultice*. Poultices were once a standard home remedy for infections and wounds, and were made by tying a mixture of oatmeal or cooked beans or peas directly to the injury with cloth strips.

Pulses have been eaten for thousands of years in many parts of the world. Archaeologists have found the remains of lentils in excavations in the Near East; they were also referred to in ancient Sumerian cuneiform texts and were one of the crops cultivated by farmers in the Tigris–Euphrates Valley nearly four thousand years ago. The red pottage of lentils for which Esau sold his birthright (Genesis 25:30–34) was probably made from the red Egyptian lentil. Today parched lentils are sold in Middle Eastern countries as an ideal food to carry on long journeys. Puréed lentils or split peas, called *dal*, form a part of most meals in India and are a major source of protein in the predominantly vegetarian diet there. Chickpeas, known also as garbanzo beans, have been a staple in South America for centuries, and were taken to Spain by early explorers, where they were incorporated into dietary patterns that persist to this day. Cowpeas (black-eyed peas) and peanuts have always been very important parts of the African diet, and were brought to North America by slaves.

The upper-class Greeks and Romans had a rather ambivalent approach to beans. Some believed them to contain the souls of the departed, while others thought they caused defective vision. Even so, many patricians enjoyed baked beans cooked with bits of chicken, sausage, leeks, and fennel. Medieval bakers frequently laced their bread with ground peas or beans to stretch the number of loaves that could be made from their limited supply of good flour. Pease porridge, known from the nursery rhyme, was a thick soup of dried peas which simmered over the fire for weeks at a time.

Peas, beans, and peanuts are easy to grow in many parts of the country, and seeds can be purchased from many sources. Search the pages of gardening magazines for the names of seed outlets, and send for catalogues. Peas are cool-season crops, and must be planted very early in the spring, but peanuts and beans prefer warmer weather, some requiring a soil temperature of 70°F. before they will germinate.

Dried whole peas are cooked and eaten in many countries, but in the U.S.A. they are mostly used with the outer skins removed, in the form of split peas. They cook faster with the skin gone, and truthfully, except for roughage, the skins serve little purpose. However, when traveling in the North of England we became fans of the mushy peas we often ate with pork pies or fish and chips, and when we returned we searched high and low for whole dried peas to try to duplicate this dish. We finally found them at our trusty feed store, where they were sold as pigeon food. If you can find them, buy some—they make delicious additions to soups and stews, or the mainstay of a dish of mushy peas.

You can also plant whole dried peas and harvest your own the following summer. If you cannot find dried peas in feed stores or grocery stores (they sometimes show up in the bean section), inquire of seed companies. There are many different varieties of peas, but most of them are garden peas, which shrivel up when fully mature, and are not suitable for drying. What you need are called field peas, so look for that type. Plant right after the last frost (gardening books always say that, but I've never figured out how you're supposed to know which is the last one), or at least after the last expected frost (they can germinate at any temperature over 40°F.), and provide poles or strings for the plants to climb on. Plant one inch deep, two to three inches apart, in rows two feet apart. Allow the peas to dry on the vine thoroughly before harvesting, then shell and dry them further in shallow trays before storing in airtight containers.

There are over twenty-five varieties of beans that are suitable for drying. All require warm weather; some (like limas and soybeans) have extremely long, warm growing periods and are best suited for growing in the southern parts of the country. Legumes in general need very little fertilizer; in fact, they are good for the soil and are often planted by commercial farmers specifically to be plowed back into the soil at the end of the growing season as green manure. Most beans come in bush varieties which can be planted three to four inches apart in rows two feet apart, but if you choose pole beans—a good idea if your horizontal space is limited—make sure you have at least six feet of vertical support (rough poles, trellis, or fence) for them to climb on. Plant two or three seeds at the base of each pole and place poles two to three feet apart, or plant seeds six inches apart along a fence. Never cultivate or harvest peas or beans when the plants are wet, as they are subject to diseases and fungi which might easily spread. Pick dry beans when the pods are fully mature and yellow, but before they break open, or you'll lose the seeds to mice and birds.

Dry on shallow trays for three or four weeks before putting into containers to store.

Most of the garbanzos and lentils we see in the U.S.A. come from South America and the Middle East, respectively, but my local agricultural extension agent feels sure that they could be grown anywhere that limas and soybeans will grow—in other words, where it is warm. If you cannot locate seeds (I couldn't), plant the dried beans you buy in the store and treat them just like other warm season legumes.

Peanuts are sadly neglected as a food staple in this country. They are usually roasted and eaten as snacks, or fed to monkeys in zoos, but they can also serve as an important part of the basic diet. These legumes originated in South America, and were taken to West Africa from Brazil by Portuguese sailors. The native Africans who were shipped to the American colonies as slaves brought peanuts with them, and they were then introduced to the American South, where they are still eaten more than in any other part of the States.

For cooking purposes, raw peanuts are preferable to roasted. They can be purchased raw in the shell in some grocery stores, or shelled in health-food sections of large grocery stores, natural food stores, and Chinese specialty shops. If you often cook with nuts, peanuts are an economical crop to grow. For a few dollars you can buy enough seed to provide your family with a year of peanut butter, snacks, and vegetable protein. They can be grown anywhere where the summer is long and warm, needing about 120 warm days to mature properly, and are a fascinating crop to grow because of the strange way they set seed. There are two kinds of peanuts, Spanish and Virginia. Their growing requirements are slightly different. Contact your seed company for further information.

Shell your peanut seeds if they come in the hull, but don't remove or injure the brown skins around each kernel. Sow one seed every six inches in rows, no closer than two feet apart. Water well right up until the first frost, or until the plants have begun to turn yellow. When the plants are six inches high, mound compost around the base of the stems—this provides an easy surface for the "pegs" to enter. A dusting of lime or other calcium-containing agent to the soil at this time will assist the plant in developing good shells. About eight to twelve weeks after planting, stems called pegs will have grown downward from the principal plant stem and entered the soil to begin forming peanuts. After the plants turn yellow, pull up the entire plant and there should be from 30 to 40 peanuts clinging to each one. Dry the entire plant thoroughly in a warm ventilated place for two or three weeks, then strip nuts from the plants and store in airtight containers.

General Instructions for Cooking Dry Beans

This is the method I have adopted as the one which uses the least fuel to prepare.

Pour required amount of beans into a large bowl or saucepan. Pick over carefully, removing any sticks or rocks which might have come to you from the field. Rinse in clean cold water, removing any beans which float. Drain. Now, figuring 3 to 4 cups of water for each cup of beans, bring beans to a boil in a large heavy saucepan. Cover tightly and remove from heat. I usually do this the night before cooking the beans, but even just a few hours before you begin cooking them will shorten the overall cooking time.

When you need the beans, drain, add fresh water, and simmer, covered, until tender (about 1½–2 hours for most dishes, perhaps longer for soup). Add seasonings and any other ingredients in the last ½ hour of cooking. If beans wind up too dry, add liquid; if they are cooked and you have too much liquid, drain slightly.

Some old recipes for cooking whole dried beans and peas suggest that you add baking soda, which breaks down the starches and reduces cooking time. It also destroys some of the vitamins in the legumes, so I do not recommend it. If you forgot to soak your beans, they will still cook, but they may take an extra hour or so of simmering. Watch for drying out during this time, and add water as needed.

Bean Sprouts

Mung beans are the basis for the well-known Asian bean sprouts. Within a bean is all the nutrition required by the growing plant to develop into a seedling, and sprouting it releases that collection of vitamins and minerals into a form which is edible raw. Mung beans can be purchased specifically for sprouting, but you can also sprout whole peas, soybeans, lentils, and other small legumes. Be sure that the beans are intended for sprouting or cooking, not for planting, as otherwise they may have been treated with an insecticide or fungicide.

Soak 1 or 2 tablespoons of beans overnight in a wide-mouth canning jar. Drain the water (a square of cheesecloth fastened with a canning ring works well, or you can buy special screened tops from health-food stores). Place the jar in a dark place. Once or twice a day, rinse the seeds by pouring water into the jar, swishing it around, and pouring it off.

Harvest the seeds when they look good to you, or try tasting them. Mung beans and lentils take 3 to 5 days; peas and soybeans a little longer. Experiment.

Sprouted beans can be stir-fried with other vegetables, or eaten raw in salads and sandwiches.

HUMMOUS SPREAD

Hummous, a staple in Lebanon and other Mediterranean countries, is a dip made from garbanzos (chickpeas) and sesame seed oil. This version of hummous makes a quick after-school snack for hungry children.

2 cups cooked or canned garbanzo beans (chickpeas)
2 tablespoons sesame seed or other vegetable oil

1 tablespoon lemon juice
½ teaspoon salt
1 tablespoon raw sesame seeds

Mash garbanzos well with a wooden spoon or heavy fork; stir in oil until the consistency is spreadable (you may need slightly less or more oil depending on the moisture content of the chickpeas). Add lemon juice, salt, and sesame seeds and blend thoroughly. This can be stored in a jar in the refrigerator for several days and used as a spread on bread.

VARIATION: Add ⅔ cup tahini (sesame seed paste), 2 cloves garlic, crushed, and ¼ teaspoon cayenne.

BESANI ROTI

This spicy bread is made like flour tortillas and is a tasty accompaniment to Mexican food, even though the original recipe came from India.

½ cup lentil or garbanzo (chickpea) flour
¾ cup whole wheat flour
1 teaspoon chile powder
¼ teaspoon ground coriander
1 teaspoon salt
1 medium onion, finely chopped
2 tablespoons oil or butter

Stir together flours and spices; stir in onion and enough water to make a soft dough. Knead until smooth. Divide into 12 small balls. Roll out like thin pancakes; fry in oil until slightly brown. Turn and fry on other side.

LENTIL SALAD

2 cups cooked and drained lentils
3 tablespoons vinegar
2 tablespoons olive oil
1 teaspoon salt
1 medium onion, finely chopped
1 stalk celery, finely chopped
½ cup cooked (or canned) garbanzos (chickpeas)

Marinate lentils in vinegar, oil, and salt mixture overnight. Combine with other ingredients and chill thoroughly. Serve over cold cooked rice or on a bed of finely chopped salad greens.

LAMB AND LENTIL STEW

1 cup dried lentils, washed
water
1 cup cooked lamb, cubed
2 stalks celery, chopped
1 medium onion, chopped

2 carrots, chopped
1 tablespoon salt
1 teaspoon freshly ground pepper
½ teaspoon ground cumin

Place washed lentils in pot, cover with water, and bring to a boil. Set aside to soak for 1–3 hours.

Add sufficient water to make about 1½ quarts, then add meat. Cover and simmer for 20–30 minutes, until lentils are just slightly tender. Add vegetables and seasonings and simmer until quite tender.

LENTIL RICE SOUP

1½ cups lentils
6 cups stock or water
2 teaspoons salt
¼ teaspoon ground cumin

¼ teaspoon pepper
½ cup long-grain brown rice
1 medium onion, chopped
3 tablespoons butter

Rinse lentils and place in a large soup kettle with stock, seasonings, and rice. Bring to a boil and simmer, covered, for about 45 minutes, or until tender. Sauté onion in butter and stir into soup just before serving.

THREE-BEAN SALAD

I'm no longer even sure what the original three beans were in the classic American marinated salad—the version I saw most often in my youth was string beans, kidney beans, and garbanzos. We generally put together whatever three beans happen to be sitting around cooked, and sometimes throw in one or two extra.

1 cup each of cooked, drained soybeans, garbanzos (chickpeas), limas, kidney beans, navy beans, or other small legumes

For each cup of beans, add the following:

3 tablespoons vegetable oil
1 tablespoon vinegar
¼ teaspoon salt
¼ teaspoon pepper

¼ teaspoon tarragon (or ½ teaspoon fresh tarragon)
¼ teaspoon dry mustard
¼ teaspoon sugar

Stir ingredients together thoroughly, cover tightly, and refrigerate for at least 24 hours. Drain and serve on a bed of chopped lettuce.

PEANUT BUTTER

Once you've tasted fresh peanut butter made from lightly roasted peanuts, I suspect you will have difficulty ever going back to the fatty, hydrogenated version they sell in most supermarkets. You can make it in a food processor, steel-bladed flour mill, or in a high-powered blender. Roast raw peanuts (leave the skins on for richer flavor) for 20 to 25 minutes at 325° on baking sheets, stirring frequently, then let cool. Run the peanuts through your food processor, cleaning it thoroughly when you are done. If you like a moister butter than you get, stir in a little vegetable oil. If you prefer salted butter, add salt to taste. There you are. If you won't finish eating what you've made within a couple of weeks, keep it in the refrigerator.

HONEY-PEANUT MILK

This is a high-protein energy booster on a hot day. It can also be made in a blender.

⅓ cup peanut butter   2 cups milk
⅓ cup liquid honey

Cream peanut butter and honey with a wooden spoon or whisk. Add milk gradually, stirring at first and then beating with a whisk or a rotary beater until foamy. Serve chilled (whisk once more just before serving).

PEANUT BREAD

1 cup peanut flour (see Note)   1 egg, beaten
3 cups whole wheat flour   3 tablespoons honey
1 teaspoon baking powder   milk to moisten
1 teaspoon salt

Stir together flours, baking powder, and salt, pressing out any lumps. Add egg and honey, then moisten with enough milk to make a soft moist dough. Place in a small pudding mold or bowl with a cloth tied around the rim, and steam in a large, tightly covered kettle of water (water should come halfway up the side of the mold) for about 1 hour, or until set.

NOTE: To make peanut flour, you need either a food processor, nut and seed grinder, or a Mouli grater (see Kitchen Equipment).

CREAM OF PEANUT SOUP

I first tasted this soup in restored Williamsburg, Virginia, where it was served to us in lovely tureens by women dressed as eighteenth-century serving maids. Accustomed to considering peanuts a snack food, I first thought the soup an oddity. When I later realized that peanuts, being legumes, have the nutritional values and taste of beans, the soup seemed more practical than whimsical.

2 stalks celery, chopped
1 small onion, chopped
2 tablespoons butter or vegetable oil
1 tablespoon flour (peanut or whole wheat)

8 cups chicken stock
½ pound peanut butter
1 pint heavy cream

Sauté celery and onion in butter or oil until quite tender. Add flour and cook, stirring constantly, until evenly blended. Add stock and bring to a boil. Stir in peanut butter. Cook slowly until celery and onion can be smashed easily against the side of the pan. Stir in cream and serve.

CHINESE FISH CAKES

¾ pound fish fillets
¾ pound raw shrimp, shelled and deveined
3 slices bacon
1 cup ground peanuts (see Note)
2 tablespoons cornstarch

1 tablespoon soy sauce
1 teaspoon salt
1 egg white
1 tablespoon vegetable oil
1 cup high-temperature oil for cooking

Grind fish, shrimp, and bacon in a food grinder with a medium blade. Mix with peanuts, cornstarch, soy sauce, salt, egg white, and oil and blend thoroughly. Form tablespoon-sized patties and fry in hot oil until crisp and brown. Makes about 2 dozen patties.

NOTE: Peanuts should be pulsed gently in a food processor, ground in a nut and seed grater or a Mouli grater, or buzzed for a second or two at high speed in a blender to obtain the dry, shredded consistency needed for this recipe.

PEANUTS AND SQUASH

4 medium summer squash
(zucchini, crookneck, etc.)
1 cup lightly roasted shelled peanuts

2 tablespoons butter
1 teaspoon salt
2 tablespoons water

Slice or cube squash. Chop peanuts or grind them coarsely. Melt butter; stir-fry squash and peanuts for 2–3 minutes. Add salt and water; close pan tightly and steam for 10 minutes.

GROUND NUTS AND GREEN BEANS

Peanuts are called ground nuts by many African people—a name which refers to the ground we walk on rather than the chopped-up state in which peanuts are sometimes used. Peanuts do grow in the ground, but they are not strictly nuts, being rather a member of the leguminous plant family. I came across various versions of this recipe in both African and southern U.S. cookbooks. (Since the peanut was introduced to America by Africans who were transported here as slaves, that shouldn't be too surprising. In fact, the southern slang for peanuts, goober peas, comes from the African word *nguba*.) Although peanuts may have traveled west on slave ships, they were not unknown in the New World before that. Peanut seeds have been found in ancient Peruvian tombs, and Indians in Virginia were raising this protein-rich food when the colonists arrived there.

1 onion, chopped

1 tablespoon vegetable oil

1 pound fresh green beans

1 16-ounce can stewed tomatoes

1 cup raw (unroasted) peanuts

1 teaspoon curry powder

1 teaspoon salt

¼ teaspoon pepper

Sauté onion in oil. Snap beans and add to onion; stir-fry for 10 minutes. Add tomatoes, peanuts, and seasonings. Cook for additional 15–20 minutes, until tender and well blended. Serve over rice or barley.

MUSHY PEAS

1 cup whole dried peas

3 cups salt to taste

Cover dried peas with water. Bring to a boil and remove from heat. Let soak, covered, overnight.

The next day, bring back to a boil and simmer, uncovered, very slowly, until peas are tender and most of liquid is absorbed. Cover and remove from heat. Let sit for 2–3 hours before reheating and serving. If peas are not mushy and soft, stir vigorously with a wooden spoon. Salt to taste.

In the north of England, mushy peas are served as a side dish with fish-and-chips or with hot pork pies.

PEASE PORRIDGE

Pease porridge was a popular accompaniment to boiled salt meat, which was the commonest flesh food of the Middle Ages, and was often cooked tied in a linen cloth within a cauldron of soup, suspended over a fire by a pot hook. In the colonies, the porridge was usually a cooked pea mush which had been sieved and flavored with spices, then returned to the pot to simmer continually, to be dipped into and added to from time to time. The old rhyme, as one writer commented, suggests that the dish had keeping qualities which endeared it more to the housewife than to her family. The following recipe comes from a cookbook called *The Family Dictionary*, published in 1705.

Take 2 gallons of peas and boil them in a little water til they are very thick and soft enough to strain. Then strain them. Take some knuckles of veal and a leg of mutton; prick it well with a knife to let out the gravy, and boil it in as much water as will cover it. When all the goodness is boiled out of the meat strain it and put it into the pulp of the peas, and boil them together very well.

Put in a good store of sparemint, and a little thime, and some bacon if you please. When it is boiled enough, have some rashers of bacon ready fried to lay round the top of the dish, and put in a great deal of butter and serve it to the table.

BLACK-EYED CHICKEN

Black-eyed peas, known also as cowpeas and black-eyed beans, are another gift to the American South from Africa. These legumes are a staple in many parts of Africa where they are ground into flour, into coarse meal, and cooked fresh or from the dried bean—the way we find them in the macaroni and beans section of our grocery stores.

2½- to 3-pound chicken	1 teaspoon thyme
½ cup whole wheat flour	½ teaspoon marjoram
1 tablespoon salt	1 teaspoon salt
1 teaspoon pepper	½ cup chicken stock or white wine
3 tablespoons vegetable oil	3 cups cooked, drained, black-eyed
1 small onion, chopped	peas
1½ pounds fresh mushrooms, sliced	1 tomato, chopped
2 cloves garlic, finely chopped	

Cut up chicken into serving-size pieces. Dredge in flour seasoned with salt and pepper. Heat oil; brown chicken on all sides. Remove but keep hot. Add onion, mushrooms, and garlic to skillet and cook until tender, stirring occasionally. Stir in seasonings, wine, and black-eyed peas. Return chicken pieces to pan, cover with tomato and close pan tightly. Simmer for 25–30 minutes, or until chicken is quite tender. Add more liquid if necessary. Serve from pan.

HOPPIN' JOHN

This black-eyed pea and rice meal is traditionally served on New Year's Eve in the South. A part of the Black heritage in the U.S.A., it is now one of the collection of dishes known as soul food.

1 cup dried black-eyed peas, soaked
  overnight
1 cup brown rice
4 cups water or stock
¼ pound bacon, chopped (or 3
  tablespoons bacon bits)

1 medium onion, finely chopped
1 clove garlic, finely chopped
1 tablespoon vegetable oil
salt, pepper, parsley, and basil to taste

Combine black-eyed peas and rice in saucepan with water; bring to a boil, reduce heat, and simmer, covered, for ½ hour. Meanwhile, sauté bacon, onion, and garlic together in vegetable oil. Add to peas and rice (fat too), and simmer for another hour, or until beans are tender. Remove from heat and add salt, pepper, parsley, and basil to taste.

BLACK BEANS AND RICE

1 cup dried black beans, soaked
  overnight
2 cups water
1 onion, thinly sliced

1 clove garlic, finely chopped
1 tablespoon chopped fresh parsley
butter for frying
salt and pepper to taste

Cook beans in water for 1½ hours, or until tender. Sauté onion, garlic, and parsley in a little butter until tender. Add drained beans and cook until blended. Season to taste. Serve over cooked brown rice.

SCOTTISH POTTAGE

2 cups kidney beans	1 stalk celery, chopped
water	6 cups water or stock
2 tablespoons butter	4 large tomatoes, sliced
1 cooked beet, peeled and sliced	salt and pepper to taste
1 small onion, chopped	

Cover beans with water, bring to boil, and remove from heat. Soak overnight. Drain, reserving liquid. Melt butter in soup pot, adding beans, beet, onion, and celery and sauté for 5 minutes.

Add reserved liquid and stock or water, and the tomatoes. Cover and simmer gently for 2–3 hours. Season to taste.

For a creamier soup, peel the tomatoes (see page 172) and rub soup through a purée cone, or purée in a food processor or blender before serving.

PAPPADUMS (PAPADS)

While teaching in the north of England, I developed a fondness for Indian food. This staple bread of India, Pakistan, and Bangladesh can be purchased in ethnic grocery stores. However, if you live outside an urban area, you might want to make them yourselves. You can find the spices in Indian markets or in ethnic grocery stores. See Sources section for other suppliers. When I serve them to my children, they call them "tortillas"—although they are much more crisp than their corn-flour cousins. This recipe was developed by Malvi Doshi.

2 pounds urad dal flour, split black bean flour	1 teaspoon papadio khar
⅛ cup split lima bean flour (optional)	2 tablespoons black peppercorns, cracked
2½ cups water	½ teaspoon asafoetida (hing)
2 teaspoons salt	oil for brushing dough

Sift both flours together. Bring water to a boil, add salt and khar. Boil for 2 minutes. Remove and let cool. Add black pepper to flour and mix well.

Gradually add 2 cups of the water to the flour mixture and prepare a very stiff dough. Dough should be flaky and dry; if too dry, add a little more water and mix well. Do not make dough smooth. Now starts the tricky part!

MALVI'S ADVICE: HOW TO FINISH PREPARATION

A heavy pestle is required. In Indian cooking we have iron or long wooden ones. For this job you have to live on the ground floor or have your own house, so that when you beat the dough, others will not be disturbed. Also needed is someplace to dry papads directly under the sun. Beat dough until smooth and soft.

Knead dough by stretching, putting it together, pressing and stretching. Knead for 5 minutes. This again is laborious and tricky, but it also is fun, and will make dough light.

Make a roll about 2½ feet long, 1½ inches thick, from the dough. Brush a little oil on roll.

Cut roll into about ½-inch-thick slices. For this you also will need a strong thread. Dental floss would be ideal. In India we use the thread for flying kites. This dough cannot be divided like wheat flour dough since it is such a sticky dough. Cutting dough with a knife might work but it still would be quite difficult. When Indian women make papads at home, they squat on the floor, tie one end of the string to their left toe, holding dough roll in the left hand. With the right hand holding the thread they go very quickly around the roll cutting it into about fifty parts. You can reverse procedure if left-handed!

Apply a little oil to flat balls and keep covered.

Again, rolling papads is not easy. They must be very thin and about 6 or 7 inches in diameter. You will need a wooden board and thin rolling pin. Never use flour when rolling papads but apply a little oil to board and rolling pin. Use a little more oil to roll dough into very thin papads.

Roll all papads and dry directly under sun. Dry both sides. In India we spread a cotton sari or bedsheet on the ground, spreading papads over it, rolling five or six at a time and spreading them on the sari. When dry, wipe excess oil off papads.

Store papads in a large, round cookie tin with tight cover. They are kept flat in a pile.

Papads can be either roasted or deep-fried. While frying papads, I sometimes fold into triangles. They take less space, are easy to serve, and look very attractive. Keep heat low when frying. Papads should not become brown. In roasting papads, use a pair of tongs to turn. They should not get brown spots.

NOTE: Malvi continued: We also have papads with green chiles and green garlic. Papads like this keep their freshness for about three or four months. Papads also come with red hot chili powder, garlic or cumin seeds. These papads keep for months. Papads with green chiles and green garlic, however, are a real treat. Since I have lived outside India, I have not made papads for over two decades. When I was small, however, we used to make them every year in large quantities. Everything is still before my eyes.

We invited neighbors and friends to help roll papads. One person is assigned the job of spreading and drying papads and the job this way is done within a few hours. All the women come with their rolling stand, mostly made of iron for papads, and rolling pins. Because of her age, my mother no longer makes them at home, but it is quite easy for her to order them from Surat, since Bombay is only five hours by train from Surat. Papads can be bought here, but the varieties mentioned are not available outside India.

HOT DOG BEAN SOUP

This is one of my children's favorite lunch soups.

1 cup navy beans, soaked overnight in 8 cups water	1 tablespoon butter
1 large onion, finely chopped	1 tablespoon flour
2–3 carrots, diced	½ cup water or milk
2 stalks celery, diced	2–4 chicken franks, sliced
water	salt to taste

Boil beans, onion, carrots, and celery in water over low heat until all are tender, at least 2 hours. Remove ½ cup beans from pan and squash them into a creamy texture with a wooden spoon. Melt butter in small pan. Stir in flour, then add squashed beans and about ½ cup water or milk, stirring until smooth. Cook for 2 minutes, stirring constantly, then add to soup and simmer 15 minutes. Stir in sliced franks, heat through, and serve. Salt to taste.

PATRICIAN BAKED BEANS

2 cups dried navy beans, soaked
   overnight
6 cups water
½ pound Italian sausage
2 leeks, chopped

1 8-ounce can tomato sauce
¼ cup dark molasses
1 tablespoon dry mustard
1 teaspoon salt

Preheat oven to 250°F. Rinse beans and bring to a boil in 6 cups water. Lower heat and simmer, covered, while assembling remaining ingredients. Chop sausage into small pieces, and fry until browned. Stir together partially cooked beans, sausage, leeks, and seasonings and turn into a large ovenproof baking dish with about ½ of the bean water. Bake, covered, for 6–8 hours, adding more bean water if necessary. Remove cover and bake for another hour.

BOSTON BAKED BEANS

There's simply no way a can of baked beans can reproduce the texture of homemade baked beans fresh from the pot. Make these on a cold day when the heat of the oven and the fragrance of the beans will cheer everyone in the house. Serve with Steamed Boston Brown Bread (see page 50).

4 cups fresh dry navy beans, white
   beans, or other small beans
boiling water
2 quarts cold water
1 tablespoon salt

3 tablespoons brown sugar (optional)
½ teaspoon powdered mustard or 1
   teaspoon Dijon mustard
⅓ cup dark molasses
1 cup boiling water

Rinse and cover fresh dry beans with boiling water. Soak overnight. Drain and cover with 2 quarts fresh water. Heat to boiling and simmer until tender, about 1½ to 2 hours. Drain again. Preheat oven to 250°F. Stir together remaining ingredients; pour over beans, adding enough additional boiling water to cover. Bake in a covered pot for 6 to 8 hours, adding water as needed. Uncover for last half hour of baking.

RED-HOT CHILE CON CARNE

This chile recipe is the culmination of several oh-so-lovely years spent tasting bowls of chile and going home to try to duplicate the results. The chile aficionados I've met insist that a real bowl of chile must meet two or three specific criteria: real beef (not ground chuck), real pinto beans (not navies or some other miscellaneous bean), and no tomatoes. I suppose you could eliminate the beef in this recipe and come out with something acceptable to the vegetarian, but to real chile fans it would seem like an apple pie made without apples.

3 pounds boneless beef (I use chuck roast cut into 1-inch cubes)	2 tablespoons whole wheat flour
	1 tablespoon oregano
3 tablespoons vegetable oil	1 quart beef stock
4 cloves garlic, chopped	1 teaspoon salt
6–8 tablespoons chile powder	1 teaspoon pepper
2 tablespoons ground cumin	2 cups cooked pinto beans

Brown beef lightly in oil, stirring frequently so that it colors evenly. Stir in garlic and sauté for 2–3 minutes. Lower heat. Stir together chile powder, cumin, flour, and oregano and blend into meat, stirring until meat is evenly coated. Add half the beef stock, and the salt and pepper, and bring to a boil, stirring frequently. Lower heat and simmer, covered, over very low heat, for 1½ hours. Check once in a while for sticking, and stir. Add rest of broth and pinto beans; cook another hour, or until meat is very tender.

If you have the discipline and good planning, refrigerate this dish overnight before serving. Like lasagne, it gets better the next day. Heat in a double boiler to prevent burning.

FALAFEL

In India and Africa beans are often ground into flour and used to thicken soups or coat food before frying, as well as to make breads and pastries. In order to prepare your own *besan* (the Indian word for this flour), take several cups of garbanzos (chickpeas), black-eyed peas, dried peas, or lentils and brown them in an ungreased pan in the oven (about 350°F.), stirring often, for about 5 minutes. Cool, then grind fine in a flour mill. For best results in most recipes, sift out the larger particles and regrind them.

1¼ cups bean flour	1 teaspoon salt
1 egg, beaten	water or stock
1 medium onion, coarsely chopped	vegetable oil for frying
½ teaspoon chile powder	

Combine ingredients in a bowl, adding a few tablespoons water or stock if necessary to make a moist enough dough to make into 1½- to 2-inch balls. Dust balls in bean flour, then fry in 1 inch of oil (at about 375°F.) until well browned. Drain before serving.

FABINI'S RED BEANS AND RICE

The mother of a friend of Bob Fabini used to make spicy red beans over rice, and Bob liked them so much that he asked me to see if I could come up with the recipe. I doubt that this is the one his friend's mother used, but he's happy with the result, so here it is.

2 cups red beans, soaked overnight and cooked in 6 cups water until tender (about 1½ hours)	¼ cup sugar
	1 teaspoon salt
	1 tablespoon cornstarch
4 slices of bacon	½ cup vinegar
1 large onion	¾ cup water
2 cloves garlic, finely chopped	

Fry bacon until crisp. Remove bacon. Sauté onion and garlic in pan drippings or oil; crumble bacon into pan and set aside. In a saucepan stir together sugar, salt, and cornstarch. Add vinegar and water and bring slowly to a boil, stirring constantly until thick and translucent. Add bacon mixture. Stir in beans, returning to a boil and stir for a few moments. Serve over hot cooked rice.

TOFU OR BEAN CURD

From *The Book of Tofu*, by William Shurtleff and Akiko Aoyagi. Published by Autumn Press.

If you find that fresh tofu is not available at a nearby store, try preparing your own at home using whole soybeans. It is a bit messy to make, but no more so than baking bread, and very satisfying.

The following recipe, which makes 22 to 26 ounces and is based on the traditional Japanese farmhouse method, is easy to follow and virtually foolproof. The tofu will be ready 50 to 60 minutes after you start. One pound of soybeans yields about 3½ to 4 pounds of tofu at a cost of about one-third to one-fourth that of commercial tofu. Solidified and served at its peak of freshness, homemade tofu contains a fullness of flavor and subtle sweetness seldom found in even the finest store-bought varieties. To make homemade tofu, you will need the following common kitchen tools.

Utensils:

An electric blender, food processor, food or grain mill, or meat grinder

A "cooking pot" with a capacity of 1½ to 2 gallons, or a basin of comparable size

A 2-quart saucepan

A wooden spatula, rice paddle, or wooden spoon with a long handle

A shallow ladle or dipper about 1-inch deep and 3 or 4 inches in diameter, or a large spoon

A rubber spatula

A sturdy 1-quart jar or a potato masher

A 1-cup measuring cup

A set of measuring spoons

A large, round-bottomed colander ("settling container") preferably square or rectangular

A shallow fine-mesh strainer or bamboo colander (*zaru*)

A coarsely woven cotton dishcloth, 2-feet square, or a "pressing sack"

A 2-foot square of cheesecloth, or a light cotton dishtowel of comparable dimension.

Two special pieces of equipment, both easy to assemble, will make the work even easier:

1. Make a "pressing sack" of the coarsely woven cotton dishtowel mentioned above, or use a piece of sturdy cotton cloth with about the same coarseness of weave as cheesecloth. Fold the towel or cloth end to end and sew up the sides to form a sack about 15 inches wide and 15 inches deep. Or use a small flour sack with a fairly coarse weave.

2. The flat-bottomed colander listed above is for use as a "settling container," which gives its shape to the finished tofu. If a 1-quart strainer or small, round-bottomed colander is used in its place, the tofu will naturally be rounded.

You will need only the following readily available ingredients:

Soybeans

The soybeans now sold at almost all natural and health food stores, most co-op stores, and many supermarkets will make good tofu. However, to obtain the highest yield, try buying soybeans directly from a tofu shop if one exists in your area, for they have been carefully chosen by the tofu maker.

SOLIDIFIER

The solidifiers most readily available in the West are Epsom salts, lemon or lime juice, and vinegar. All make delicious tofu, although they are not used in Japanese tofu shops. Japanese-style soldifiers are available from many natural food stores, local tofu shops, Japanese food markets, chemical supply houses (check your phone directory), or your local school chemistry lab. Usable seawater can be retrieved from clean stretches of ocean. Natural *nigari* is available at some salt refineries and can be ordered from Japanese natural food distributors. We recommend the use of refined *nigari* unless the natural *nigari* is certified to have come from a clean source of sea water. While the *nigari*-type solidifiers seem to be the easiest to use and result in the best tasting tofu, Epsom salts and calcium sulfate give somewhat higher bulk yields and a softer end product by incorporating more water into the tofu. The yield of tofu solids or nutrients is about the same regardless of the type of solidifier used, except that lemon juice and vinegar give rather small yields. (Note: Calcium sulfate, a fine white powder, is sometimes mislabeled in the West and sold as *nigari*. The latter usually has a coarse, granular, or crystalline texture; natural *nigari* is beige, and refined *nigari* is white.)

The recipe below calls only for "solidifier." Your choice of solidifier depends on the type of tofu you want.

For subtly sweet, nigari tofu use: 1¼ teaspoons magnesium chloride or calcium chloride; or 1 to 1½ teaspoons granular or powdered natural *nigari*; or 1 to 1¾ teaspoons homemade liquid *nigari*; or 1¼ to 3 teaspoons commercially prepared liquid *nigari*.

For mild, soft tofu use: 1¼ teaspoons Epsom salts (magnesium sulfate) or calcium sulfate.

For subtly tart or slightly sour tofu use: 2½ tablespoons lemon or lime juice (freshly squeezed); or 2 tablespoons (apple cider) vinegar.

METHOD

1 cup soybeans, washed, soaked in 4 cups of 70° water for 10 hours, rinsed, and drained	approximately 11 cups water solidifier

Prepare in advance:

Place pressing pot in sink and set colander into pot. Moisten pressing sack lightly and line colander with sack, fitting mouth of sack around rim of colander. Or line colander with a moistened 2-foot-square dishtowel.

Moisten cheesecloth or thin cotton dishtowel and use to line bottom and sides of setting container. Place container on rim of large bowl or pan placed in sink.

Fill a 2-quart saucepan with 2 cups water and warm over low heat on a side burner.

After making the above preparations, proceed as follows:

Heat 5 cups water over high heat in cooking pot. While water is heating, combine beans and 2⅔ cups water in a blender and purée at high speed for about 3 minutes, or until very smooth. (If using a grain mill, food mill, or meat grinder, grind beans without adding water and add 2⅔ cups more water to cooking pot.)

Add soybean purée to water heating (or boiling) in cooking pot, rinsing out blender with a little water to retrieve any purée that may cling to blender's walls. Taking care that pot does not boil over, continue heating on high heat, stirring bottom of pot frequently with a wooden spatula or spoon to prevent sticking. When foam suddenly rises in pot, quickly turn off heat and pour contents of cooking pot into pressing sack. Using a rubber spatula, retrieve any soybean purée that may still cling to the sides of the cooking pot and transfer to pressing sack. Quickly rinse out cooking pot and replace on top of stove.

Twist hot pressing sack closed. Using a glass jar or potato masher, press sack against colander, expressing as much soy milk as possible. Open sack, shake contents (*okara*) into one of its corners, close and press again. Now empty *okara* onto the 2 cups warm water in saucepan on side of stove; stir well, then return moistened *okara* to pressing sack set in colander. Close sack and press well; squeeze by hand to express the last of the soy milk. Empty *okara* into the 2-quart pot and set aside.

Measure solidifier into dry 1-cup measuring cup and set aside.

Pour soy milk into cooking pot and bring to a boil over high heat, stirring frequently to prevent sticking. Reduce heat to medium and cook for 5 to 7 minutes; turn off heat.

Add 1 cup water to solidifier in measuring cup (unless using seawater) and stir until dissolved. With a to-and-fro movement, stir soy milk vigorously 5 or 6 times and, while stirring, put in ⅓ cup solidifier solution. Stir 5 or 6 times more, making sure to reach bottom and sides of pot. Bring spoon to a halt upright in soy milk and wait until all turbulence ceases; lift out spoon. Sprinkle ⅓ cup solidifier over surface of soy milk, cover pot, and wait 3 minutes while curds form. Using a measuring spoon, stir remaining ⅓ cup solidifier solution, uncover pot, and sprinkle solution over surface of soymilk.

Very slowly stir upper ½-inch-thick layer of curdling soy milk for 15 to 20 seconds, then cover pot and wait 3 minutes. (Wait 6 minutes if using Epsom salts or calcium sulfate.) Uncover and stir surface layer again for 20 to 30 seconds, or until all milky liquid curdles. (White "clouds" of delicate curds should now be floating in a clear, pale-yellow liquid, the whey. If any milky, uncurdled liquid remains suspended in whey, wait 1 minute, then stir gently until curdled. If milky liquid persists, dissolve a small amount of additional solidifier (about ¼ of the original amount) in ⅓ cup water and pour directly into uncurdled portions; stir gently until curdled.)

Place cooking pot next to settling container in sink. Gently press fine-mesh strainer into pot and allow several cups whey to collect in it. Ladle all of this whey into settling container to remoisten lining cloths. Set strainer aside.

Now ladle curds—and any remaining whey—into settling container one layer at a time. Ladle gently so as not to break curds' fragile structure. Fold edges of cloth neatly over curds, place a lid on top of cloth (a small board or flat plate will do), and set a ½-to-1½-pound weight on top of lid for 10 to 15 minutes, or until whey no longer drips from settling container.

Fill pressing pot, a large basin, or sink with cold water. Remove weight and lid from atop tofu, then place container holding tofu into basin of water. Slowly invert container, leaving cloth-wrapped tofu in water; lift out container. While it is still under water, carefully unwrap and cut tofu crosswise into halves. Allow tofu to remain under water for 3 to 5 minutes, until firm. To lift out, slip a small plate under each piece of tofu; drain briefly.

For best flavor, serve immediately. Store tofu in a cold place until ready to serve. (If not to be served for 8 or 10 hours, store under cold water.) Use the remaining 6 to 7 ounces (1 firmly packed cup) *okara*, valuable for its fiber content, in baked goods or other recipes. Refrigerate in an airtight container until used. Use the 6 to 7 cups whey in stocks and/or for washing your utensils.

"FRESH" FALAFELS

For this recipe I use canned garbanzo beans and, when in season, add fresh fava beans (broad beans). The mixture has a moister texture than the variety made with bean flour.

2 cups canned garbanzo beans (chickpeas), drained
3 tablespoons bulgur or cracked wheat, soaked in boiling water to cover for 1 hour
1 cup fresh fava beans, hulled
2 tablespoons whole wheat flour

2 cloves garlic, minced or pressed
1 teaspoon ground cumin
½ teaspoon salt
½ teaspoon chile power
⅛ teaspoon ground coriander
vegetable oil for frying

Drain garbanzo beans and bulgur; combine with fava beans and either grind through the fine blade of a meat grinder or process in an electric food processor with the steel blade until the mixture is finely ground. Place in a mixing bowl and add flour and seasonings. With wet hands, combine all ingredients and form into about 30 balls, approximately 1 inch in diameter. Fry in 1 inch of oil (about 375°F.) until well browned. Drain before serving.

NOTE: Falafels can be served with lettuce and tomato in pita bread halves, or as part of a main dish. They are traditionally served with a fresh vegetable relish or tahini, and can also be placed on a bed of rice, bulgur, or couscous.

BROWN RICE PORRIDGE WITH TOFU AND VEGETABLES

From *The Book of Tofu*, by William Shurtleff and Akiko Aoyagi. Published by Autumn Press.

Brown Rice Porridge, called *congee* in China and *okayu* in Japan, is a popular main course at breakfast in many homes and temples. This version of it, containing soybean curd (tofu), is much higher in useable protein then rice alone would be.

½ cup brown rice, soaked overnight
    in 4½ cups water
1 tablespoon sesame or other oil
½ small carrot, slivered or diced
2 onions, thinly sliced
½ cup diced celery, cabbage, or
    vegetable leftovers

12 ounces tofu
1½ tablespoon shoyu (soy sauce) or
    3½ tablespoons red miso
    (fermented soy mixture)
dash of pepper

In heavy covered pot, bring water and rice to a boil over high heat. Reduce heat to low and simmer for about 90 minutes with lid slightly ajar. About 15 minutes before porridge is ready, heat a wok or skillet and coat with the oil. Add carrot and sauté for 3 minutes. Mix in onions and celery and sauté for 5 additional minutes. Add tofu, mash well, and sauté for 3 minutes. Stir in shoyu and pepper and remove from heat. Add sautéed tofu-vegetable mixture to the finished porridge, mix well, and allow to stand for 5 to 10 minutes before serving.

SOYBEAN FESTIVAL

This makes a quick dinner—stir-fry it in a wok or a large skillet.

1 green bell pepper, slivered
1 red bell pepper, slivered
2 tablespoons oil
1 large onion, chopped

1 cup cooked soybeans
1 cup sprouted beans
salt and pepper to taste

Sauté bell peppers and onions in oil until onion is slightly brown. Add soybeans and sprouts; stir frequently and cook 2–5 more minutes. Season to taste.

RECOMMENDED READING—

KITCHEN CLASSICS AND

NEW FAVORITES

Once you begin incorporating whole grains, legumes, nuts, and seeds into your diet, you'll probably begin substituting whole grain flours into familiar recipes, and adding groats, brown rice, and beans to soups, salads, and meat dishes. Although you can probably get by quite well in this fashion, it's always helpful to have several sources of recipes when you are feeling creative. The following list contains some of the books I have found the most reliable, containing clear instructions and delicious meals to complement the recipes in *The New Book of Whole Grains*.

Marlene Anne Bumgarner
*Organic Cooking for (Not-So-
Organic) Mothers*
Chesbro Press
Morgan Hill, CA 1984

Adelle Davis
Let's Eat Right to Keep Fit
NAL Dutton
New York, 1988

Ellen Buchan Ewald
Recipes for a Small Planet
Ballantine Books
New York, 1985

Marjorie Winn Ford et al.
*The Deaf Smith Country
Cookbook*
Avery Communications
Group
New York, 1992

Jean Hewitt
*New York Times New Natural
Foods Cookbook*
Avon
New York, 1983

Mollie Katzen
The Moosewood Cookbook
Ten Speed Press
San Francisco, 1992

Pauline Mitchell
*The New American Vegetarian
Menu Cookbook*
Rodale Press
Emmaus, PA, 1984

Laurel Robertson et al.
The New Laurel's Kitchen
Ten Speed Press
San Francisco, 1996

Irma S. Rombauer and
Marion Rombauer Becker
Joy of Cooking
NAL Dutton
New York, 1989

SOURCES

Most natural food stores and health food sections of large grocery stores carry some whole grain flours, stone-ground cornmeal, grits (grain cracked into several pieces), nuts, seeds, and dried beans. Some even carry the whole grains (groats or berries) themselves. Search the yellow pages of your local telephone directory if you don't know the location of such stores, and ask people you know who use whole grains in their meals.

Some grains (notably wheat, corn, oats, millet, and sorghum or milo) can be purchased at animal feed stores. Again, consult your telephone book, or ask someone who has animals if you don't know where to go.

If your search fails to locate the products you want, or if you would like to order in bulk (perhaps several families placing their order together to save on trucking costs), try contacting one or more of the following sources.

Artesian Acres, Inc.
RR 2
Lacombe, Alberta
Canada TOC 1SO
403/782-5075

Kamut®, quinoa grains, and flour

Arrowhead Mills, Inc.
Box 866
Hereford, TX 79045
806/364-0730

A wide range of whole grains and flours. Price list available

Birkett Mills
P.O. Box 440-A
Penn Yan, NY 14527
315/536-3391

Buckweat groats and flour. Price list available

Bob's Red Mill
Natural Foods, Inc.
5209 SE International Way
Milwaukie, OR 97222
800/553-2258

Specialty grains, diastatic malt, xanthan gum, gluten-free flours

Ener-G Foods, Inc.
P.O. Box 84487
Seattle, WA 98124-8787
800/331-5222 (outside WA)
800/325-9788 (in WA)

Dietetic specialty foods (soyquik, egg replacer, gluten-free flours and bread machine mixes, methocel, xanthan gum, guar gum)

Frieda's Inc.
P.O. Box 58488
Los Angeles, CA 90058
714/826-2561

Lost Crops of the Americas (quinoa, blue and red cornmeal, chestnuts, etc.)

Giusto's Specialty Foods Inc.
241 E. Harris Avenue
South San Francisco, CA 94080
(415) 873-6566

Amaranth, quinoa, spelt, triticale, whole grain cornmeal, whole wheat, whole rye, etc. Price list available

Jaffe Bros
P.O. Box 636-Z
Valley Center, CA 92082-0636
619/749-1133

Flours, grains, dried fruits, nuts, seeds

Jowar Foods
113 Hickory Street
Hereford, TX 79045
806/364-3258

Sorghum flour, pancake mix, muffin mix, and brownie mix

King Arthur Flour
RR 2, Box 56
Norwich, VT 05055
800/827-6836

Various flours

Lundberg Family Farms
5370 Church Street
Richvale, CA 95974
916/882-4551

Organically grown brown rice

Redwood City Seed Company
P.O. Box 316
Redwood City, CA 94064
415/325-7333

Grains and legumes for planting such as amaranth, basri, beans, corn (including popcorn and several old varieties), peanuts quinoa, sunflower, teff, and various wheats (including Kamut® and durum)

Saco Buttermilk Powder
P.O. Box 5461
Madison, WI 53705
800/373-SACO

Dried buttermilk powder

J. B. Dough & Co.
200 Paw Paw Avenue
Benton Harbor, MI 49022-3400
800/528-6222

A large assortment of bread machine mixes

Universal Foods Corporation
433 East Michigan Street
P.O. Box 737
Milwaukee, WI 53201
800/445-4746

Red Star Active Dry Yeast in bulk

Walnut Acres
Penns Creek, PA 17862
800/433-3998

Organic flours, grains, cereals, dried fruits, nuts, herbs

EQUIPMENT AND ACCESSORIES

Chef's Catalog
3215 Commercial Avenue
Northbrook, IL 60062-1900
800/338-3232

Professional restaurant equipment for the home chef

Community Kitchens
P.O. Box 2311
Baton Rouge, LA 70821-2311
800/535-9901

Bread-making equipment, including knives, bread machines, bread mixes, bread pans, bread box

Cumberland General Store
Route 3
Crossville, TN 38555
800/334-4640

Grain mills, traditional kitchen equipment

DAK Industries, Inc.
8200 Remmet Avenue
Canoga Park, CA 91304
800/DAK-0800

Bread machines, accessories

Delta Rehabilitation, Inc. 411 Bryn Mawr Island Bradenton, FL 34207	Bread machines, grain mills
Lehman's Non-Electric Hardware and Appliances Lehman Corner P.O. Box 321 Kidron, OH 44636 330/857-57571	Specializes in needs of the Amish, non-electric gardening and cooking equipment
Magic Mill 1515 South 400 West Salt Lake City, UT 84115-5110 800/888-8587	Dough enhancer, gluten, yeast, mills, dehydrators
Mountain Home Basics P.O. Box 42 Clifton, CO 81520 800/572-9549	Grain mills, food processors, dehydrators
Quinoa Flour Corporation 124248 Crenshaw Boulevard Suite 220 Torrance, CA 90505 213/530-8066	Quinoa flour
The Wooden Spoon P.O. Box 931 Clinton, CT 06413 800/431-2207	Bread-making equipment and accessories
R & R Mill P.O. Box 187 48 West First North Smithfield, UT 84335	Corona hand mill, stone conversion kit, dehydrators, electric flour mills, Universal food grinders. Has catalogue

TABLES OF EQUIVALENTS

In the American kitchen, ingredients are measured in units referred to as the U.S. Customary System. According to this system nearly all items (liquid and dry ingredients alike) are measured by volume, using teaspoons, tablespoons, fluid ounces, pints, quarts, and gallons. Some ingredients, notably meat and vegetables, are measured by weight, using ounces and pounds. Because it is impossible to convert volumetric measurements into units of weight, cooks accustomed to weighing dry ingredients will need some guidelines in order to use the recipes in this book.

The following table gives approximate values in British and Metric liquid units for the most commonly used U.S. measurements. Remember that these are units of volume, not of weight. Tables of length, weight, and temperature are given in the next table, for general reference. Following the U.S.-British-Metric tables is a table giving equivalents within the U.S. system.

TABLE 1

Units of Volume

U.S.—BRITISH—METRIC   APPROXIMATE CONVERSIONS

Basis, 1¼ U.S. tsp = 1 British tsp = 6.16 ml

⅛ U.S. tsp =	scant ⅛ Brit tsp =	0.6 ml
¼ U.S. tsp =	scant ¼ Brit tsp =	1.2 ml
½ U.S. tsp =	scant ½ Brit tsp =	2.5 ml
¾ U.S. tsp =	rounded ½ Brit tsp =	3.7 ml
1 U.S. tsp =	¾ British tsp =	4.9 ml

Basis, 1¼ U.S.T = 1 British T = 18.48 ml

	1 U.S.T =	¾ Brit T =	14.8 ml
1 U.S. fl oz =	2 U.S.T =	1½ Brit T =	29.6 ml
	3 U.S.T =	2½ Brit T =	44.4 ml
	4 U.S.T. =	3¼ Brit T =	59.1 ml

Basis, 1 U.S. fluid oz = 1.040 British fluid oz = 29.574 ml

	1 U.S. fluid oz =	1 Brit fluid oz =	29.6 ml
¼ U.S. cup =	2 U.S. fluid oz =	2.1 Brit fluid oz =	59.1 ml
	3 U.S. fluid oz =	3.1 Brit fluid oz =	88.7 ml
½ U.S. cup =	4 U.S. fluid oz =	4.2 Brit fluid oz =	118.3 ml
	5 U.S. fluid oz =	5.2 Brit fluid oz =	147.9 ml
			approx. 1 Brit teacup
	6 U.S. fluid oz =	6.2 Brit fluid oz =	177.4 ml
1 U.S. cup =	8 U.S. fluid oz =	8.3 Brit fluid oz =	236.6 ml
	10 U.S. fluid oz =	10.4 Brit fluid oz =	295.7 ml
			approx. 2 Brit teacups
1 U.S. pint =	16 U.S. fluid oz =	16.6 Brit fluid oz =	473.2 ml
1 U.S. quart =	32 U.S. fluid oz =	33.3 Brit fluid oz =	946.4 ml

Basis, 1 U.S. fluid cup = 0.417 British pints = 2367.7 ml

¼ U.S. cup	=	.10 Brit pint	=	.05 Brit quart	=	59 ml
⅓ U.S. cup	=	.14 Brit pint	=	.07 Brit quart	=	79 ml
½ U.S. cup	=	.21 Brit pint	=	.10 Brit quart	=	118 ml
⅔ U.S. cup	=	.28 Brit pint	=	.14 Brit quart	=	158 ml
¾ U.S. cup	=	.31 Brit pint	=	.16 Brit quart	=	177 ml
1 U.S. cup	=	.42 Brit pint	=	.21 Brit quart	=	237 ml
2 U.S. cups	=	.83 Brit pint	=	.42 Brit quart	=	473 ml
3 U.S. cups	=	1.25 Brit pints	=	.62 Brit quart	=	710 ml
4 U.S. cups	=	1.67 Brit pints	=	.83 Brit quart	=	946 ml
5 U.S. cups	=	2.08 Brit pints	=	1.04 Brit quart	=	1183 ml

Table 1 Units of Volume

Basis, 1 U.S. fluid quart=0.833 British quart=0.946 liter

1 U.S. fluid qt	=	1.67 Brit pints	=	.83 Brit qt	=	.95 liter
1½ U.S. fluid qts	=	2.50 Brit pints	=	1.25 Brit qts	=	1.42 liters
2 U.S. fluid qts	=	3.33 Brit pints	=	1.67 Brit qts	=	1.89 liters
2½ U.S. fluid qts	=	4.17 Brit pints	=	2.08 Brit qts	=	2.37 liters
4 U.S. fluid qts	=	6.66 Brit pints	=	3.33 Brit qts	=	3.79 liters

Table II
Units of Weight, Length, and Temperature

Basis, C = $5/9$ (F-32)

Degrees Fahrenheit	Degrees Celsius (centigrade)	Gas Mark
−10	−23	
0	−18	
10	−12	
20	−7	
30	−1	
32	freezing 0	
40	4	
50	10	
60	16	
70	21	
80	27	
90	32	
100	38	
125	52	
150	66	
175	79	
200	93	
212	boiling 100	
225	107	¼
250	very cool 121	½
275	135	1
300	cool 149	2
325	moderately cool 163	3
350	moderate 177	4
375	moderately hot 191	5
400	204	6
425	hot 218	7
450	232	8
475	very hot 246	9
500	260	10
550	288	

WEIGHT

Basis, 1 oz. = 28.349 gm.,
1 lb. = 453.59 gm avoirdupois

½ ounce (oz)	14.2 grams
1 ounce	28.3 grams
2 ounces	56.7 grams
3 ounces	85.0 grams
4 ounces (¼ pound)	113.4 grams
8 ounces (½ pound)	226.8 grams
16 ounces (1 pound)	453.6 grams
2 pounds	907.2 grams
5 pounds	2268.0 grams

LENGTH

Basis, 1 inch = 2.540 cm

¼ inch	.64 centimeters
½ inch	1.27 centimeters
1 inch	2.54 centimeters
2 inches	5.08 centimeters
6 inches	15.24 centimeters
12 inches (1 foot)	30.48 centimeters
24 inches (2 feet)	60.96 centimeters
36 inches (3 feet or 1 yard)	91.44 centimeters

Table III		
United States Measurements—Equivalents		
A pinch	=	Less than ⅛ teaspoon
1 teaspoon (tsp)	=	⅓ tablespoon
1 tablespoon (T)	=	3 teaspoons
2 tablespoons	=	1 fluid ounce
1 gill	=	4 fluid ounces
8 fluid ounces	=	1 cup
1 cup	=	16 tablespoons
1 pint	=	2 cups
16 fluid ounces	=	1 pint
2 pints	=	1 quart
4 quarts	=	1 gallon
¼ lb butter	=	½ cup

If converting entire recipes seems like too formidable a task, or if you would simply prefer to prepare the recipes using the measurements as written, it would be wise to obtain a set of U.S. measuring cups and spoons. If you are unable to locate these items in your area, they may be ordered from Chesbro Press, Post Office Box 1326, Morgan Hill, CA 95038.

INDEX

Carrot
  raisin nut salad, 244
  triticale cookies, 105
Cashew
  chicken salad, 245
  honey butter, 242
Casseroles
  barley and shrimp, 116
  eggplant, 172
  kasha, 219
  mushroom, 116
  tuna festival, 152
  wild rice, 175
Chapati, 39
Cheese
  bake, with hominy, 145
  bannocks, 72
  corn muffins with, 146
  cornmeal wedges, 152
  green chile cornbread with,
    146
Chestnuts
  Chinese glazed, 250
  stuffing, 247
Chick peas. *See* Garbanzo beans
Chicken
  barley and, 114
  black-eyed peas and, 264
  kasha-stuffed, 218
  rice soup, 169–170
  salad with cashews, 245
  stuffed with rye, 89
  walnuts and, 246
Chile
  cheese cornbread, 146
  con carne, red-hot, 270
Chinese
  almond cookies, 177
  fish cakes, 261–262
  glazed chestnuts, 250
Chocolate
  cake (triticale), 103
  -chip cookies, whole wheat,
    56

sauce, 58
Coffee cake
  cornmeal, 153
  whole wheat, 55
Colchicine, 97
Colonial corn puddings,
  137–139
Congee, 190, 277
Converted rice, 160–161
Cookies
  Bizcochos, 53
  Bolivian almond, 211
  brandy snaps, 57
  Chinese almond, 177
  granola, 56
  Lebkuchen (honey cakes),
    90
  oatmeal, 76–78
  oat wafers, 74
  peanut butter, 104
  pfeffernusse, 90–91
  rice flour, 177
  rye-honey refrigerator,
    89
  sorghum peanut, 201
  triticale carrot, 105
  whole wheat chocolate
    chip, 56
  Yorkshire parkin, 74
Corn, 126–155
  atole, 136
  breads, 50–51, 139–142,
    146–148
  gruel, 128
  hominy cheese bake, 145
  hominy enchiladas, 144
  kenke, 155
  mamaliga, 154
  muffins, 144, 146
  pancakes, 141, 147
  piki, 135
  polenta, 154
  pones, 140
  popcorn, 133–134

puddings, 137–139
  scrapple, 143
  tamales and tamale pie,
    149–150
  tortillas, 136–137
  tuna festival, 152
  whiskey, 109
  Zuni succotash, 134
  See also Cornmeal
Cornish pasty, 34, 119
Cornmeal, 132–133
  bread, 147
  cheese wedges, 152
  coffee cake, 153
  mush, 137, 138, 154–155
  onion loaf, 151
  wafers, 151
  See also Corn
Couscous, 183–184
Cowpeas. *See* Black-eyed peas
Cracked
  grain soup, 153
  millet, 183–184
  rye, 81, 88
  wheat, 28–33
Crackers
  amaranth, 234
  quinoa, 209
  rice, 164
Creamed
  almond soup, 245
  peanut soup, 261
  rye, 83
Crisps
  apple oat crumble, 76
  peach rye, 93

Dal, 252
Dark rye, 81
Date muffins, amaranth, 232
Degerminated cornmeal,
  132–133
Dent corn, 129
Domath, 167